THE
FRONT-LOADING
PROBLEM *in*
PRESIDENTIAL
NOMINATIONS

THE
FRONT-LOADING
PROBLEM *in*
PRESIDENTIAL
NOMINATIONS

William G. Mayer
Andrew E. Busch

BROOKINGS INSTITUTION PRESS
Washington, D.C.

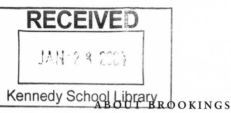
ABOUT BROOKINGS

The Brookings Institution is a private nonprofit organization devoted to research, education, and publication on important issues of domestic and foreign policy. Its principal purpose is to bring knowledge to bear on current and emerging policy problems. The Institution maintains a position of neutrality on issues of public policy. Interpretations or conclusions in Brookings publications should be understood to be solely those of the authors.

Copyright © 2004
THE BROOKINGS INSTITUTION
1775 Massachusetts Avenue, N.W., Washington, D.C. 20036
www.brookings.edu

Library of Congress Cataloging-in-Publication data

Mayer, William G., 1956–
  The front-loading problem in presidential nominations / William G. Mayer, Andrew E. Busch.
    p.   cm.
Includes bibliographical references and index.
  ISBN 0-8157-5520-1 (cloth : alk. paper)
  ISBN 0-8157-5519-8 (pbk. : alk. paper)
  1. Primaries—United States. 2. Caucus. 3. Presidents—United States—Nomination. I. Busch, Andrew. II. Title.
  JK207.M39 2003
  324.273'154—dc22   2003019912

9 8 7 6 5 4 3 2 1
The paper used in this publication meets minimum requirements of the American National Standard for Information Sciences—Permanence of Paper for Printed Library Materials: ANSI Z39.48-1992.

Typeset in Sabon

Composition by Stephen D. McDougal
Mechanicsville, Maryland

Printed by R. R. Donnelley
Harrisonburg, Virginia

To our wives,
Melinda Busch and Amy Logan

Contents

Acknowledgments

All research, we were both taught in graduate school, is a communal effort, in the sense that it builds upon and responds to issues, concepts, and questions developed by previous work in the field. But this book is a communal product in a somewhat stronger sense. Front-loading is a complicated phenomenon that is caused by or has ramifications for a wide range of significant forces in contemporary American politics. In our attempt to do justice to that complexity, we received important assistance from a large number of people who provided us with data or helped us understand the nuances of the presidential nomination process.

We wish to express our particular thanks and appreciation to Lois Timms Ferrara, God's gift to the public opinion community, and the Roper Center for Public Opinion Research, for making available to us the national survey data analyzed in chapters 3 and 4; David Goodfriend of the Associated Press, for providing us with a considerable number of unpublished AP delegate count stories; Rhodes Cook, former reporter extraordinaire with *Congressional Quarterly,* now the editor of an invaluable newsletter, for helping us understand the history and development of front-loading and for providing us with the preference vote from the 1984 Illinois Democratic primary broken down by congressional district; Anthony Corrado of Colby College, for answering innumerable questions about the complexities of campaign finance laws and reporting forms; Richard Noyes, then of the Center for Media and Public Affairs, for sending us a detailed printout of media coverage by state during the 1988 and 1992 nomination races; and Michael Tolley of Northeastern University and Emmet T.

Flood of Williams and Connolly, for comments on the constitutional analysis presented in chapter 6.

Our thanks also to Christopher Bosso of Northeastern University and Barbara Norrander of the University of Arizona, for careful and perceptive readings of the entire manuscript; Richard Boylan and Philip McNamara of the Democratic National Committee, for answering a number of detailed questions about that party's delegate selection rules and for sending us copies of past party rules and rules commission reports; Steven Kania of the Federal Election Commission, for his help in reconstructing the month-by-month receipts of the Carter and Jackson campaigns in 1976; Clyde Wilcox of Georgetown University, for making available to us a number of then-unpublished reports about the survey of campaign contributors he helped conduct; Emmett Buell of Denison University, for a long series of exchanges about various aspects of the presidential nomination process and for providing us with copies of several valuable monographs on the subject; and Eun Kyung Kim of the Associated Press, who explained the procedure she used to compile the AP delegate counts for the 2000 nomination races.

From the moment we first thought of writing this book, we had hoped that it would be published by Brookings Institution Press. For making that ambition a reality, we are particularly grateful to Christopher Kelaher, the acquisitions editor at Brookings, for all his support and encouragement. Thanks also to Janet Walker and Katherine Kimball for shepherding the book through the production process.

Finally, this book is a communal effort in one particularly strong sense: that we were enabled to write it only because of the extraordinary love and support we received from our families. For their patience, and for helping us remember what is genuinely important in life (it ain't frontloading), we thank our children: Natalie and Thomas Mayer and Katherine and Daniel Busch. During the final editing of our manuscript, the Busch family welcomed its newest member, Elizabeth. We hope that years from now she will read this acknowledgment and have some sense of the joy she brought to her new family—and perhaps of the small part played by one of her father's collaborators in cutting through the Ukrainian red tape. Above all, we thank our wives, Amy Logan and Melinda Busch, for their support and encouragement, but much more for their love and friendship.

THE
FRONT-LOADING
PROBLEM *in*
PRESIDENTIAL
NOMINATIONS

CHAPTER ONE

Introduction

Of all the major institutions and processes in contemporary American government, few have been as consistently controversial as the presidential nomination process. The basic rules governing delegate selection and convention decisionmaking were completely rewritten in the early 1970s, and from the moment the "reforms" first took effect, they faced a firestorm of criticism. The new rules were attacked from almost every conceivable angle: for producing candidates who were ideological extremists or not very experienced or just plain mediocre; for weakening the parties and empowering the news media; for making nomination campaigns longer and more expensive; for producing convention delegates who were unrepresentative of the party rank and file; for conferring disproportionate power on Iowa and New Hampshire; for emphasizing campaigning over governing; for almost entirely excluding party leaders and top elected officials from the decisionmaking process; for undermining the support that a president could expect to receive from members of his own party within Congress and the executive branch; and for accentuating potential sources of party division and thus making it more difficult for the parties to present a united front in the general election.[1]

Three decades later, most of these criticisms have receded from the front burner of American politics. In some cases, the problem was perhaps not as serious as it initially appeared to be. The charge that the system favored candidates who were ideological extremists, for example, seemed quite credible in the late 1970s, when the Democrats had just recently nominated George McGovern and the Republicans had almost denied their nomination to Gerald Ford, a conservative incumbent president, on the grounds that he was not conservative enough.[2] By 2003, however, this criticism would probably strike most observers as preposterous. Whatever else may be said of a system that, over the past four election cycles, has nominated Michael Dukakis, Bill Clinton, and Al Gore on the Democratic side and George Bush, Bob Dole, and George W. Bush on the Republican, it can hardly be accused of fielding candidates who are extreme ideologues.

In other cases, the parties recognized the problem and took corrective action. There is little doubt, for example, that the new rules did lead to a sharp decline in the number of Democratic governors, senators, and representatives who served as national convention delegates. In 1982, however, the Democrats "reformed the reforms" by adding a rule that conferred automatic delegate status on a substantial number of party leaders and elected officials. And, sad to say, in a fair number of instances—such as the extraordinary length of the nomination campaign, the disproportionate power of Iowa and New Hampshire, and the troubling role of the news media—we have lived with the problem so long and found it so difficult to change that we have simply grown inured to it.

The subject of this book is a relative latecomer to the list of faults and derelictions, but by the final years of the twentieth century, it had emerged as perhaps the single most criticized feature of the entire process. Front-loading—the concentration of primaries and caucuses at the beginning of the delegate selection season—is what might be called a "second-order" effect of the new nomination rules. It did not become a major problem until the new system had been in operation for two or three election cycles and its basic tendencies and incentives had started to become apparent. Unfortunately, this also means that front-loading has probably not yet run its course. Whereas most other features of the contemporary nomination process have now reached a point of stability, there are strong reasons to think that front-loading will only get worse.

The rules of the presidential nomination process are, as a general matter, a pretty arcane subject, of some concern to the party officials who must write them and the campaign managers who must live under them but not especially interesting to anyone else. By the mid-1990s, however, a large number of political commentators and observers had taken notice of front-loading and, with a singular degree of unanimity, deplored its effects on the presidential selection process. In 1996 the system that resulted from front-loading was described as "madness," "insane," "war~~~ and virtually mindless," "absurdly accelerated," "self-defeating," "debilitating," a "high-speed demolition derby," and a "parody of participatory democracy" in which "candidates have rushed through the country like passengers late for a connection."[3] In 2000 various commentators called the nomination process "a sound-bite-saturated sprint," a "stampede," a "disaster for democracy," "absurd," a "mosh pit," "terrible," "dangerously irrational," a "mutant game of hopscotch," a "freight train," and a "crazy-quilt system" that produced a "lemming-like rush."[4]

The writings of political pundits and newspaper editorial boards are not always the most reliable basis for constructing public policy. In this case, however, the criticism is on target. Front-loading has had a variety of undesirable effects on the presidential nomination process. It deprives many early primary voters of deliberate choice and late primary voters of any meaningful choice at all. It degrades campaign quality, gives an unreasonable advantage to front-runners, and substantially reduces the field of viable candidates before a single vote is cast. In short, it makes the presidential nomination process less rational, less flexible, and more chaotic. At a time of domestic challenge and international peril, these are risks the country can ill afford to take.

By 2000 both the Democrats and Republicans were concerned enough about the problem that each party established a commission whose principal assignment was to see whether something could be done to halt or reverse the front-loading trend. Nothing concrete came of these efforts, however. As the 2004 nomination race gets under way, the front-loading problem is still with us, fundamentally unchanged from the last time around.

The purpose of this book is to provide a comprehensive examination of the front-loading issue: what it is, why it developed, what consequences it has for the nomination process as a whole, and what, if anything, can be done about it.

CHAPTER TWO

The Rise of Front-Loading

Front-loading is the name that has been given to an important recent trend in the presidential nomination process, in which more and more states schedule their primaries and caucuses near the beginning of the delegate selection season.[1] The result is a nomination calendar in which a large proportion of the delegates are selected within a few weeks after the process formally commences, as opposed to having the primaries and caucuses spread out evenly or having them concentrated near the end of the process.

To appreciate the nature and significance of this development, it is useful to begin by taking a look at how the system worked before the basic ground rules of the nomination process were completely rewritten in the early 1970s. In the 1950s and 1960s (and, in fact, for several decades before that), the calendar of presidential primaries started up rather slowly. The Democratic primary calendar of 1960, shown in table 2-1, is typical of the way the system worked during this period.[2] The first presidential primary held that year took place, as it still does today, in New Hampshire on March 8. There were no other primaries held during the remainder of March. Then, in each of the first three weeks in April, a single primary was held. Not until week 8 (that is to say, seven weeks after New Hampshire) did two primaries take place on the same day. Of the 648 delegates to the 1960 Democratic National Convention who were selected or bound by primary, only about a third had been selected by the end of the eighth week of primaries. At the other end of the spectrum, the 1960

Table 2-1   *Calendar of Democratic Presidential Primaries, 1960*[a]
Number of delegates, except as indicated

Week	State holding primary and date	Number of delegates selected	Cumulative number of delegates selected	Cumulative percentage of delegates selected
1 (March 6–12)	New Hampshire:			
	March 8	10	10	2
2 (March 13–19)	None	0	10	2
3 (March 20–26)	None	0	10	2
4 (March 27–April 2)	None	0	10	2
5 (April 3–9)	Wisconsin: April 5	30	40	6
6 (April 10–16)	Illinois: April 12	50	90	14
7 (April 17–23)	New Jersey: April 19	40	130	20
8 (April 24–30)	Massachusetts:			
	April 26	40		
	Pennsylvania:			
	April 26	60	230	35
9 (May 1–7)	Alabama: May 3	29		
	District of Columbia:			
	May 3	9		
	Indiana: May 3	33		
	Ohio: May 3	63	364	56
10 (May 8–14)	Nebraska: May 10	15		
	West Virginia:			
	May 10	24	403	62
11 (May 15–21)	Maryland: May 17	23		
	Oregon: May 20	17	443	68
12 (May 22–28)	Florida: May 24	29	472	73
13 (May 29–June 4)	None	0	472	73
14 (June 5–11)	California: June 7	80		
	New York: June 7	86		
	South Dakota: June 7	10	648	100

a. Table includes all primaries used to select or bind delegates, regardless of whether or not they included a presidential preference vote. In Illinois, New York, and Pennsylvania, some delegates were chosen by primary, others at a state convention; only the delegates chosen by primary are included in this table.

version of Super Tuesday, when California and New York both held their primaries and about a quarter of the primary delegates were selected, did not take place until week 14, at the very end of the primary season.

Tables 2-2 and 2-3 present two summary indicators of the extent of front-loading in the delegate selection process for every presidential election year between 1952 and 2000: the number of primaries held during each week of the primary season and the cumulative percentage of delegates that had been selected by the end of each week. (For a more de-

Table 2-2   *Two Summary Measures of Front-Loading in the Democratic Primaries, 1952–2000*
Units as indicated

Week	1952	1956	1960	1964	1968	1972	1976	1980	1984	1988	1992	1996	2000
Number of primaries held during each week of the primary season													
1	1	1	1	1	1	1	1	1	1	1	1	2	1
2	1	1	0	0	0	1	1	1	0	1	1	0	0
3	0	0	0	0	0	1	1	3	5	0	4	9	0
4	2	1	0	0	1	0	1	1	1	16	8	7	0
5	1	1	1	1	0	1	1	2	1	1	2	3	0
6	1	1	1	1	0	0	0	3	1	0	1	1	14
7	2	2	1	1	1	0	2	0	1	1	0	0	6
8	1	2	2	2	1	2	0	0	0	1	3	0	1
9	4	4	4	4	4	6	0	1	0	0	0	0	0
10	2	2	2	3	2	2	2	0	3	1	0	1	2
11	0	0	2	1	0	2	4	4	4	1	1	0	0
12	0	1	1	1	2	2	2	2	2	3	3	3	0
13	2	4	0	3	3	0	2	1	0	2	2	2	0
14	0		3		1	4	6	3	0	1	1	1	3
15	1				1	0	3	8	5	0	2	1	2
16					1	3				0	6	4	1
17										4			2
18													0
19													5
Cumulative percentage of delegates selected by the end of each week during the primary season													
1	1	1	2	1	2	1	1	1	1	1	1	1	1
2	6	6	2	1	2	5	5	6	1	1	1	1	1
3	6	6	2	1	2	14	9	14	18	1	9	26	1
4	13	10	2	1	8	14	17	22	27	42	31	46	1
5	22	18	6	6	8	17	19	36	29	49	41	60	1
6	27	24	14	11	8	17	19	43	41	49	43	74	47
7	53	39	20	18	15	17	35	43	49	51	43	74	65
8	60	44	35	33	22	30	35	43	49	54	56	74	71
9	80	64	56	53	43	50	35	51	49	54	56	74	71
10	86	68	62	61	49	53	47	51	56	63	56	81	79
11	86	68	68	66	49	62	55	61	74	70	62	81	79
12	86	72	73	71	58	65	57	64	77	79	68	87	79
13	99	100	73	100	84	65	66	66	77	81	70	89	79
14	99		100		89	86	73	70	77	83	72	91	86
15	100				100	86	76	100	100	83	75	92	88
16						100	100			83	100	100	89
17										100			92
18													92
19													100

Table 2-3   *Two Summary Measures of Front-Loading in the Republican Primaries, 1952–2000*
Units as indicated

Number of primaries held during each week of the primary season

Week	1952	1956	1960	1964	1968	1972	1976	1980	1984	1988	1992	1996	2000
1	1	1	1	1	1	1	1	1	1	1	1	2	1
2	1	1	0	0	0	1	1	2	0	1	1	4	1
3	0	0	0	0	0	1	1	3	5	1	4	9	1
4	2	1	0	0	1	0	1	1	1	15	8	7	2
5	1	1	1	1	0	1	1	2	1	1	2	4	2
6	1	1	1	1	0	0	0	3	2	0	1	3	13
7	2	2	1	1	1	0	2	0	1	1	0	0	6
8	1	1	2	2	1	2	0	0	0	1	4	0	1
9	1	4	3	3	3	5	0	1	0	0	0	0	0
10	2	2	2	3	2	2	2	1	4	1	0	1	2
11	0	0	1	1	0	2	4	4	4	1	1	0	0
12	0	1	1	1	2	2	2	2	2	3	3	3	0
13	2	4	0	3	3	0	2	2	1	2	2	2	0
14			3		1	4	6	3	0	1	2	1	3
15					1	0	2	8	5	1	3	2	2
16						1	3		1	0	5	3	1
17										3	1		3
18										1			0
19													4

Cumulative percentage of delegates selected by the end of each week during the primary season

Week	1952	1956	1960	1964	1968	1972	1976	1980	1984	1988	1992	1996	2000
1	3	2	2	2	1	2	1	1	2	1	1	2	1
2	8	7	2	2	1	7	4	6	2	3	2	9	2
3	8	7	2	2	1	14	9	14	18	5	12	28	4
4	17	11	2	2	7	14	15	20	24	49	36	51	9
5	26	19	8	7	7	17	19	30	26	54	44	65	13
6	33	25	16	15	7	17	19	37	37	54	46	77	49
7	61	40	23	22	16	17	30	37	43	56	46	77	68
8	68	41	40	36	22	28	30	37	43	59	56	77	72
9	78	61	56	53	38	50	30	42	43	59	56	77	72
10	84	67	63	61	44	55	42	48	58	65	56	81	78
11	84	67	66	64	44	64	52	57	72	70	60	81	78
12	84	71	71	70	53	68	55	61	75	78	66	88	78
13	100	100	71	100	77	68	64	68	77	80	67	89	78
14			100		86	90	75	72	77	82	71	91	84
15					100	90	78	100	99	83	75	93	86
16						100	100		100	83	99	100	87
17										99	100		92
18										100			92
19													100

tailed explanation about how—and how not—to measure front-loading, see appendix A.) As these figures show, between 1952 and 1968 the system was actually quite "back-loaded." The primary season began slowly, with a small number of primaries in March and, usually, a few weeks in which there were no primaries at all. Most presidential primaries took place during a span of about seven weeks stretching from late April to early June (weeks 8 to 14). Nor is there any indication that this regime was starting to break down under the antipartisan stresses of the mid-1960s: to the contrary, the delegate selection process actually became somewhat less front-loaded between 1952 and 1968.

Early Rumblings: Front-Loading from 1972 to 1984

And then, on August 27, 1968, on the second day of the Democratic National Convention, the Democrats narrowly approved a confusing, vaguely worded resolution that, as ultimately interpreted, endowed a commission set up by another resolution with a quite broad mandate to rewrite the party's delegate selection rules. By 1972 that commission had succeeded in almost completely transforming the basic ground rules of the presidential selection process. Byron Shafer, who wrote an award-winning history of that commission, has called it "the greatest systematic change in presidential nominating procedures in all of American history."[3] One of the few aspects of the nomination process that the Democrats' commission did not attempt to refashion was campaign finance. Two years later, however, Congress filled that void, passing legislation in 1974 that radically altered the ways in which presidential campaigns could raise and spend money. The U.S. Supreme Court would later call this act "by far the most comprehensive reform legislation ever passed by Congress concerning the election of the President, Vice-President, and members of Congress."[4]

What effect did the new rules have on the scheduling of presidential primaries? The answer, initially, was not much. Table 2-4 shows the calendar of Democratic primaries that took place in 1976. A few more primaries were held during the first few weeks of the delegate selection season than in previous presidential election years, but the much more significant change was an increase in the total number of primaries—from seventeen in 1968 to twenty-three in 1972 and then to twenty-nine in 1976.[5] When allowance is made for this latter trend, the clustering or pacing of the primaries—which is what front-loading measures—does not look dramatically different from what it had been sixteen years earlier. In

Table 2-4   *Calendar of Democratic Presidential Primaries, 1976*[a]
Number of delegates, except as indicated

Week	State holding primary and date	Number of delegates selected	Cumulative number of delegates selected	Cumulative percentage of delegates selected
1 (February 22–28)	New Hampshire: February 24	17	17	1
2 (February 29– March 6)	Massachusetts: March 2	104	121	5
3 (March 7–13)	Florida: March 9	81	202	9
4 (March 14–20)	Illinois: March 16	169	371	17
5 (March 21–27)	North Carolina: March 23	61	432	19
6 (March 28–April 3)	None	0	432	19
7 (April 4–10)	New York: April 6	274		
	Wisconsin: April 6	68	774	35
8 (April 11–17)	None	0	774	35
9 (April 18–24)	None	0	774	35
10 (April 25–May 1)	Pennsylvania: April 27	178		
	Texas: May 1	98	1,050	47
11 (May 2–8)	Alabama: May 4	35		
	District of Columbia: May 4	17		
	Georgia: May 4	50		
	Indiana: May 4	75	1,227	55
12 (May 9–15)	Nebraska: May 11	23		
	West Virginia: May 11	33	1,283	57
13 (May 16–22)	Maryland: May 18	53		
	Michigan: May 18	133	1,469	66
14 (May 23–29)	Arkansas: May 25	24		
	Idaho: May 25	16		
	Kentucky: May 25	46		
	Nevada: May 25	11		
	Oregon: May 25	34		
	Tennessee: May 25	46	1,646	73
15 (May 30–June 5)	Montana: June 1	17		
	Rhode Island: June 1	22		
	South Dakota: June 1	17	1,702	76
16 (June 6–12)	California: June 8	280		
	New Jersey: June 8	108		
	Ohio: June 8	152	2,242	100

a. Table includes all primaries used to select or bind delegates, regardless of whether or not they included a presidential preference vote. In Texas and Arkansas, some delegates were chosen by primary, others by caucus; only the delegates chosen by primary are included in this table.

1976 the primary season calendar still started up rather gradually, with most of the primaries—and most of the multiple-primary dates—taking place in late April, May, and early June. Moreover, Super Tuesday (in 1976 it was known as Super-Bowl Tuesday) occurred at the end of the primary season.

Yet there were some signs in 1972 and 1976 of where the system was heading—signs that appear not so much in the overall shape of the delegate selection calendar as in the reasons that lay behind some of the scheduling decisions of the individual states. In particular, it was during the first half of the 1970s that widespread complaints were first heard about the disproportionate role New Hampshire played in the presidential nomination process. Though most states were apparently content to fume and fret, several states made a more active effort to compete with the Granite State.

The first such challenge came from Florida.[6] In June 1971 the Florida legislature passed a bill moving that state's presidential primary to the second Tuesday in March, the date on which New Hampshire had been holding its primary for the past four decades. The sponsors of the bill, according to the *New York Times*, "said it was designed to promote a sunshine primary to compete with New Hampshire's chilly one."[7] But New Hampshire would have none of it: before the Florida bill was even signed into law, New Hampshire legislative leaders from both parties were declaring that they would move their primary up a week. The result was that the 1972 New Hampshire primary took place on March 7 (that is, the first Tuesday in March), with the Florida primary following on March 14.[8]

In the 1976 election cycle, New Hampshire faced a second challenge, as political leaders in a number of neighboring states sought to establish a New England regional primary on the first Tuesday in March, the same day on which New Hampshire was now scheduled to hold its primary. As it turned out, the drive for a New England regional primary never amounted to much. In late May 1975 elected officials from Massachusetts, Maine, Rhode Island, and Vermont met in Boston and pledged to urge their state legislatures to pass bills that would establish presidential primaries in all four states on the same early March date. But only Massachusetts actually came through as promised. Rhode Island held its primary on June 1, Maine continued to select its delegates by caucus, and Vermont established only an advisory "beauty contest" primary that played no actual role in selecting delegates. That scarcely mollified New Hampshire, however: before any of its neighbors could act, the Granite State legislature passed a law mandating that the New Hampshire primary be held one week before that of any other state.[9] The upshot was that in 1976, the New Hampshire primary was held on the last Tuesday in February, followed by Massachusetts (and Vermont) on March 2 and Florida on March 9.

In the first two election cycles of the new era, however, the number of states involved in this early March maneuvering was not large. Most states that had held presidential primaries before 1972 stuck with the dates they had previously used. Even more revealing is the behavior of those states that switched from caucuses to primaries during this period. Of the thirteen states that established new primaries in either 1972 or 1976, every one of them scheduled its primary in May or June.[10] Not one, in other words, apparently saw any great advantage in having an early primary. The same point emerges from a look at contemporary press coverage. In stories about the presidential nomination process as a whole, the dominant themes were the increased number of primaries and how long and expensive the process had become, not how the primaries were scheduled.[11]

It was not until the 1980 and 1984 election cycles that front-loading started to attract some attention. One indication of this can be found in the agendas of the "party reform" commissions that the Democrats were creating on a regular basis throughout this period to reexamine their party rules and delegate selection procedures. The commission set up after the 1976 election (generally known as the Winograd Commission, after its chairman, Michigan state party chair Morley Winograd) considered a number of major issues in the course of its deliberations—but by all reports, front-loading was not one of them.[12] By contrast, when the Hunt Commission was created in mid-1981, the phenomenon of front-loading was said to be "one of the major topics of discussion" within the commission.[13]

Yet in comparison with the way the delegate selection calendar would look just a few years later, front-loading in the early 1980s was still at an early stage of development. The 1980 primary calendar began (as always) in New Hampshire, followed a week later by Massachusetts and a non-binding contest in Vermont. But now week 3 featured a small bloc of southern primaries: Alabama, Florida, and Georgia for the Democrats, these three states plus South Carolina for the Republicans.[14] Of these states, only Florida had previously held a primary in March. Between 1977 and 1979 the other states had moved their primaries to March to enhance their own influence in the presidential selection process or to give a boost to the campaign of a particular candidate.

The latter motivation seems to have been particularly important in Georgia. In the 1980 Democratic contest, the campaign of Jimmy Carter worried that the early nomination calendar was highly favorable to the candidacy of Edward Kennedy, since almost all of the major delegate selection events in February and early March took place in Kennedy's home region of New England. (In addition to the New Hampshire primary on February 26, these included the Maine caucuses on February 10 and the Massachusetts and Vermont primaries on March 4.) Hence in mid-1979 the Carter campaign persuaded sympathetic officials in Georgia to schedule its primary one week after that in Massachusetts, in case the Carter forces needed a shot of momentum after a string of early losses.[15]

Even taking account of this first major attempt at a southern regional primary, front-loading increased rather modestly in 1980. Of the twenty-seven states that held primaries in both 1976 and 1980, just three (Alabama, Georgia, and Tennessee) moved to substantially earlier dates in the nomination calendar, while two (North Carolina and West Virginia) actually moved to later dates. The other twenty-two states held essentially the same position in 1980 that they had had in 1976.[16] Perhaps the most notable difference between 1976 and 1980 was in the scheduling decisions of states that switched from caucuses to primaries. Of the six states that were holding newly minted primaries in 1980, one (South Carolina) moved to an early March date and three held their primaries in the last week of March or the first week of April, while only two set up shop in May or June.

Much the same verdict can be rendered about the 1984 nomination calendar: a bit more front-loading than in the previous election cycle but a lot more continuity than change. Before the first delegates had even been selected that year, a mythology had developed that the campaign of Walter Mondale had tried to stack the deck in its own favor by creating a significantly more front-loaded calendar. As one observer noted, "Seeking to wrap up the nomination early, Mondale forces also encouraged early scheduling [of primaries and caucuses]. 'We're all for front-loading and are encouraging it whenever we can,' acknowledged one Mondale operative in mid-1983."[17] Jack Germond and Jules Witcover reached a similar conclusion in their book about the 1984 election: "To no one's surprise, the new rules encouraged states to move their caucuses and primaries to earlier dates in the hope of having some influence on the result. And it was this 'frontloading' more than anything else that both Mondale and Big Labor depended upon to produce an early decision and to minimize the internal damage to the party from the contest for the nomination."[18]

A close examination of the 1984 calendar, however, indicates that it was not noticeably more front-loaded than the calendar the Democrats had used four years earlier. Perhaps the most notable feature of the 1984 calendar was the timing of what the press called "Super Tuesday." The term had once been used to describe a cluster of primaries at the very end of the primary season, but in 1984 most commentators applied it to a group of five primaries and four caucuses held on the second Tuesday in March, just two weeks after New Hampshire.[19] But of the five states that held primaries on Super Tuesday, only one—Rhode Island, with just twenty-two delegates—was a new addition to the early-season calendar. The Alabama, Florida, and Georgia primaries had all been held on the same date in 1980 (the second Tuesday in March), while Massachusetts had actually been moved back a week.

Similarly, in the four weeks following Super Tuesday, three big states held their primaries: Illinois, New York, and Pennsylvania. Mondale won all three, establishing a comfortable lead in the delegate count that he never surrendered. Here again, however, there was little new about the 1984 lineup. Illinois had been holding its presidential primary in the third week of March since 1972; New York actually voted a week later in 1984 than it had in 1980. Only Pennsylvania's primary had been moved up, and then by just two weeks. In short, if the Mondale campaign did try to encourage front-loading, the effort was not conspicuously successful.[20]

Front-Loading Takes Off: 1988–2000

To summarize the story so far, during the first four elections held under the new nomination rules, front-loading increased, but at a fairly modest pace. Then, in 1988, it took a huge leap forward.

What finally kicked front-loading into high gear was a carefully orchestrated effort to organize a southern regional primary. Southern political leaders had been making proposals of this sort since the early 1970s, but it was not until the mid-1980s that the movement caught fire. Its prime mover was the Southern Legislative Conference (SLC), a group that included representatives from sixteen southern and border-South states. In 1982 the SLC adopted a resolution calling on its member states to establish a southern regional primary, but it was not until September 1985 that it created a Regional Primary–Caucus Task Force to spearhead the effort. Charles Hadley and Harold Stanley have described what followed:

> With the national Democratic Party closely monitoring the progress of the southern primary, the Southern Legislative Conference systematically shepherded the 8 March 1988 primary date ... through the legislatures of the member states. Task force members prefiled the necessary legislation and guided it through both houses to their governors for signature. In each instance, the Southern Legislative Conference issued press releases with appropriate quotations from state legislators, heralded the primary's enactment by yet another member state, and summed up the progress to date. In short, the southern regional primary was kept in the public eye so as to maintain momentum.[21]

While southern Republicans were generally supportive of the regional primary initiative, the most prominent and enthusiastic proponents were Democrats, and some of their motives had an openly partisan cast. While regional primary supporters often spoke about the need to reduce the "disproportionate impact" of Iowa and New Hampshire (variants of this phrase show up over and over again in their public statements), they were especially concerned about the effect this had on the ideological complexion of the Democratic Party. The existing nomination calendar, many southern Democrats argued, gave too much weight to liberal voices and interests within the party and thus made it more difficult to nominate the kind of moderate-to-conservative candidate who could run a credible general election campaign in the South. Exhibit A in this indictment (and a major explanation for why the regional primary movement finally gained traction in 1985) was the fate of the Mondale-Ferraro ticket in 1984. Much as one might have expected, a ticket featuring two northern liberals had not played well in the South. Mondale's best showing in the South was in Tennessee—and Reagan still beat him there by 16 percentage points.

Whatever the motives, the result was a primary-season calendar that looked dramatically different from the one the parties had used in 1960 or 1976. After two small-state primaries in the first three weeks, the 1988 presidential candidates were suddenly required to run an all-but-national campaign. On March 8 the Democrats held sixteen primaries and four caucuses; the Republicans had fifteen primaries and one caucus. The primaries alone accounted for 26 percent of the delegates attending the Democratic convention and 31 percent of all Republican delegates.

It is a matter of widespread agreement that the southern Super Tuesday of 1988 did not accomplish most of the major goals set by those who created it. As several careful studies have shown, it did not lead the presidential candidates to downplay Iowa and New Hampshire—or to spend more time or money campaigning in the South.[22] The news media paid no more attention to the South than they had four years earlier; and although voter turnout rates did increase over 1984, most of this increase came in Republican primaries and in states that had switched from caucuses to primaries.[23] Above all, the Democrats still nominated a northern candidate who was easily portrayed as a liberal—and who failed to carry a single southern state in the 1988 general election.

The upshot was that in 1992 the southern regional primary was partially disassembled—and front-loading took a small step backward. Of the sixteen states that had held primaries on Super Tuesday in 1988, four moved to substantially later dates in the 1992 calendar; two others abandoned their primaries entirely and returned to the caucus systems they had employed before 1988. The ten remaining states divided their primaries across two different weeks in early March. The calendar that resulted had a slightly more relaxed pace than the one that had been used in 1988, though it was more front-loaded than the 1984 calendar. There were four primaries in week 3, eight more in week 4. With two large midwestern states holding their primaries in the week after that, more than 40 percent of the primary-state delegates had been selected by the end of just the fifth week of primaries.

In any event, the retreat turned out to be temporary. By early in the 1996 election cycle, it was clear that front-loading would soar to unprecedented heights. Whereas the 1988 calendar had been reshaped by the drive to establish a southern regional primary, in 1996 states from all over the country passed legislation to move up their primaries. A New England regional primary—now including every New England state except New Hampshire—was set for March 5. Four large midwestern states (Illinois, Michigan, Ohio, and Wisconsin) all scheduled their primaries for March 19.

Far and away the most publicized change was the scheduling of the California primary. In every presidential election year since 1948, California had selected its national convention delegates on the first Tuesday in June. By the late 1970s, however, many California political leaders were beginning to complain that, as a result of its late position in the schedule, the Golden State primary had turned into a large-scale irrelevancy: voters saw little of the candidates (except when they wanted to raise money), and the results had almost no impact on the outcome of either party's nomination race. After hemming and hawing for a number of years, in September 1993 California finally took the plunge and moved its primary to the fourth Tuesday in March.[24] California's decision set off further reverberations. In an effort to create a West Coast regional primary, Nevada and Washington quickly decided to move their primaries to the same date as California's. More significantly, New York, which had been holding its primary in early April, worried that coming after California would greatly diminish its role in the presidential nomination process. Hence in mid-1994 the Empire State moved its primary to the first week in March.

It is no exaggeration to say that the 1996 Republican primary calendar, which is shown in table 2-5, was only a few steps short of a national primary.[25] After two primaries in the first week and four more in the second week, the Republican candidates suddenly faced an onslaught: nine primaries in week 3, seven in week 4, four in week 5, and then three more, including California's, in week 6. All told, within just five weeks of the polls' closing in New Hampshire, the Republicans held twenty-nine primaries, which together selected 77 percent of the primary-state delegates (61 percent of all delegates) sent to the Republican convention. These twenty-nine primaries, moreover, included six of the seven largest delegations attending the Republican convention. The only real big-state primary that remained after March 26 was Pennsylvania's (on April 23).

In the early stages of the 2000 election cycle, it appeared that front-loading would get significantly worse. Although California had held its 1996 primary on the last Tuesday in March—relatively early, by previous standards—it still found that both parties' nomination races were effectively over by that time. So in 1998 California took the logical next step, moving its primary to the first Tuesday in March, the earliest date permitted under Democratic Party rules. It was joined by ten other states, including New York, Ohio, and every New England state except New Hampshire, in an event variously dubbed "Titanic Tuesday" and the "Bicoastal Blowout." Three other primaries were scheduled for later that week, and six southern and border-South states, including both Texas and Florida, would go to the polls on the second Tuesday in March.

Yet one last-minute decision had the effect of significantly opening up the beginning of the 2000 delegate selection calendar and making it, by our measures, actually somewhat less front-loaded than the calendars of 1988, 1992, and 1996.[26] When California moved its primary to March 7,

Table 2-5   *Calendar of Republican Presidential Primaries, 1996*[a]
Number of delegates, except as indicated

Week	State holding primary and date	Number of delegates selected	Cumulative number of delegates selected	Cumulative percentage of delegates selected
1 (February 18–24)	New Hampshire: February 20	16		
	Delaware: February 24	12	28	2
2 (February 25–March 2)	Arizona: February 27	39		
	North Dakota: February 27	18		
	South Dakota: February 27	18		
	South Carolina: March 2	37	140	9
3 (March 3–9)	Colorado: March 5	27		
	Connecticut: March 5	27		
	Georgia: March 5	42		
	Maine: March 5	15		
	Maryland: March 5	32		
	Massachusetts: March 5	37		
	Rhode Island: March 5	16		
	Vermont: March 5	12		
	New York: March 7	93	441	28
4 (March 10–16)	Florida: March 12	98		
	Louisiana: March 12	9		
	Mississippi: March 12	33		
	Oklahoma: March 12	38		
	Oregon: March 12	23		
	Tennessee: March 12	38		
	Texas: March 12	123	803	51
5 (March 17–23)	Illinois: March 19	59		
	Michigan: March 19	57		
	Ohio: March 19	67		
	Wisconsin: March 19	36	1,022	65
6 (March 24–30)	California: March 26	165		
	Nevada: March 26	14		
	Washington: March 26	18	1,219	77
7 (March 31–April 6)	None	0	1,219	77
8 (April 7–13)	None	0	1,219	77
9 (April 14–20)	None	0	1,219	77

(continues)

Table 2-5   *Calendar of Republican Presidential Primaries, 1996*[a]
(Continued)
Number of delegates, except as indicated

Week	State holding primary and date	Number of delegates selected	Cumulative number of delegates selected	Cumulative percentage of delegates selected
10 (April 21–27)	Pennsylvania:			
	April 23	66	1,285	81
11 (April 28–May 4)	None	0	1,285	81
12 (May 5–11)	District of Columbia:			
	May 7	14		
	Indiana: May 7	30		
	North Carolina:			
	May 7	58	1,387	88
13 (May 12–18)	Nebraska: May 14	9		
	West Virginia:			
	May 14	18	1,414	89
14 (May 19–25)	Arkansas: May 21	20	1,434	91
15 (May 26–June 1)	Idaho: May 28	18		
	Kentucky: May 28	26	1,478	93
16 (June 2–8)	Alabama: June 4	40		
	New Jersey: June 4	48		
	New Mexico: June 4	18	1,584	100

a. Table includes all primaries used to select or bind delegates, regardless of whether or not they included a presidential preference vote. In Idaho, Illinois, Indiana, Louisiana, Nebraska, New York, Pennsylvania, and Washington, some delegates were chosen by primary, others by caucus; only the delegates chosen by primary are included in this table.

most observers assumed that the New Hampshire primary would take place in the final week or two of February. (In 1996, for example, it had been held on February 20.) But after a bit of preliminary maneuvering, New Hampshire finally announced, in late September 1999, that it would hold its first-in-the-nation primary on February 1, 2000. Though its significance was not immediately appreciated, New Hampshire's decision imparted a quite different dynamic to the beginning of the 2000 delegate selection season. Instead of a situation in which, as the *New York Times* put it, "candidates coming out of the New Hampshire race in February will *immediately* be forced into a massive, bicoastal campaign," now, suddenly, five weeks separated the New Hampshire primary and the California–New York extravaganza.[27]

The parties filled these five weeks in different ways. Because Democratic Party rules forbade any states except Iowa and New Hampshire to hold a delegate selection event before the first Tuesday in March, the five-week gap remained just that: not a single Democratic primary or caucus took place during this period.[28] Republican national rules were more permissive, so a handful of states jumped into the void, ultimately creating a calendar that had at least some pretensions to a gradual beginning.[29] In the end, only one Republican primary was held in each of the two weeks immediately after New Hampshire's and two in each of the following two weeks. And most of these primaries took place in small or medium-sized states.

Caucuses

To this point, our discussion of the rise of front-loading has dealt entirely with the scheduling of presidential primaries. We have limited the analysis in this way for several reasons. First, we have been attempting to take a long-term view of the problem, by comparing more recent nomination races with those held in the 1950s and 1960s. Unfortunately, it is impossible to get usable data on the timing of the first-stage "caucuses" held in nonprimary states before the Democratic rules reforms of the early 1970s. In most cases, these initial meetings (they were rarely called caucuses at the time) were held at the discretion of local party officials, who generally held them on different dates in different areas, sometimes without any public notice. In other states, participation in delegate selection activities was limited to party functionaries who had been elected in party primaries held two years earlier.[30] In short, if one wants to establish a meaningful measure of front-loading over time, the only alternative is to limit the analysis to presidential primaries.

Second, unlike presidential primaries, which occur on a single, definite date, caucuses are multistage affairs, in which meaningful delegate selection decisions are made over a period of several months.[31] The fabled Iowa precinct caucuses, for example, simply elect delegates to county conventions who, in turn, elect delegates to district and state conventions, and it is only at these last two sets of meetings that national convention delegates are actually chosen. What needs to be stressed is that in the vast majority of states (including Iowa), the delegates to the district and state conventions are not bound by the preference votes recorded at the precinct caucuses or county conventions. Since the district and state conventions are held several weeks or months after the precinct caucuses, and since the shape of the race has sometimes changed quite substantially in the intervening time period, the final delegation sent to the national conventions can—and generally does—bear little resemblance to the results of the precinct caucuses.[32] In this sense, the caucus system offers an important measure of flexibility that is generally lacking in a presidential primary. More to the immediate point, it is generally not possible to identify a single date on which the national convention delegates in a caucus state were selected—any more than one can identify the precise day on which Rome was built.

Nevertheless, to fill out the portrait we have been developing here, table 2-6 provides data on the scheduling of Democratic caucuses from 1976 to 2000.[33] As these data show, the Democratic caucus calendar has become more compressed at both ends. In 1976 the Democratic caucuses were spread out rather evenly over a period extending from mid-January to mid-May. By 1996 almost all Democratic caucuses took place in the month of March.

The sharp decline in the number of caucuses held in January and February is directly attributable to a new rule the Democrats adopted in 1978. In 1972 and 1976 national rules had required that "all steps in the delegate selection process . . . take place within the calendar year of the Democratic National Convention."[34] The Winograd Commission considerably tightened this "window," requiring that all first-stage delegate selection events (that is, primaries and caucuses) take place between the second Tuesday in March and the second Tuesday in June.[35] Though the party granted exemptions to a small number of states (most notably, Iowa and New Hampshire), the promulgation of this rule had a decisive effect on the caucus schedule, as table 2-6 shows. The number of states holding a Democratic caucus in January or February declined from seven in 1976 to three in 1980 and then to just one in 1984.

At the same time, states holding caucuses apparently began to learn the same lesson that primary states had learned about the value of going early. By 1992 states had essentially stopped holding caucuses in June, May, or the second half of April.[36]

One final point about how the primary and caucus schedules fit together is worth noting. In 1976 and 1980 the caucus schedule began five weeks earlier than the primary schedule. The Iowa caucuses were held about January 20, with the New Hampshire primary coming on the final Tuesday in February. This, of course, further stretched out the beginning of the presidential selection process. If the Iowa caucuses produced an unexpected outcome, candidates and reporters—and voters—all had five weeks to adjust before the next major showdown occurred.[37] Beginning in

Table 2-6   *Calendar of First-Round Democratic Caucuses, 1976–2000*
Number of Caucuses

Time period	1976	1980	1984	1988	1992	1996	2000
January 16–31	2	1	0	0	0	0	1
February 1–15	3	1	0	1	1	1	0
February 16–29	2	1	1	2	1	0	0
March 1–15	3	8	8	8	12	11	9
March 16–31	0	1	10	3	1	4	3
April 1–15	2	1	2	1	2	1	1
April 16–30	5	5	3	4	0	0	0
May 1–15	4	2	2	0	0	1	1
May 16–31	1	1	1	0	0	0	0
June 1–15	1	0	0	0	0	0	0

1984, however, the national Democratic Party forced Iowa to move its caucuses to late February, just eight days before the New Hampshire primary. Thus not only have the primary and caucus schedules become individually more front-loaded, but the total calendar has, in a sense, become even more front-loaded than the sum of its parts.

The Outlook for 2004

As we write this book, in early 2003, it is impossible to say with any assurance just what the nomination calendar for the 2004 election cycle will look like. Many of the more important scheduling decisions will not be made until the middle or even the end of 2003. But one important decision, taken by the Rules and Bylaws Committee of the Democratic National Committee in November 2001 strongly suggests that the 2004 calendar, in both parties, will be significantly more front-loaded than the one used in 2000.[38]

In 2000, as noted earlier in this chapter, there was an important disjunction between the delegate selection windows established in each party's national rules. Democratic rules specified that, except for Iowa and New Hampshire, no state could hold a caucus or primary before the first Tuesday in March. Republican rules prohibited states from holding a caucus or primary before the first Monday in February. The result was that, between February 1 and March 7, there were six Republican primaries and two Republican caucuses but not a single binding Democratic event of any kind. In the opinion of many Democrats, this "ceded the spotlight to the Republicans for an entire month" and thus put their party at a "competitive disadvantage."[39] To negate this disadvantage, in formulating their delegate selection rules for the 2004 election the Democrats moved the start of their window up a month to match that of the Republicans.

At a minimum, this decision will almost certainly increase the level of front-loading in the Democratic calendar. In 2000 the six states that held Republican primaries between February 1 and March 7 either held no Democratic primary or held a purely advisory one (that is, one that played no role in delegate selection). In 2004 any states in this position will very likely hold binding Democratic primaries at the same time as the Republican ones.[40] More important, a lot of states were discouraged from holding their primaries in February because of the prohibition in the Democratic rules. The state of California, in particular, was determined in 2000 to vote at the earliest feasible date, before either party's race was settled. Yet had they tried scheduling their primary on February 8, the week after New Hampshire, they would have been faced with the prospect of either holding a second statewide primary for Democrats one month later or forcing state Democrats to select their delegates through a separate caucus procedure. As a result, California set its 2000 primary for March 7, the earliest date allowable under both parties' rules. Ten other states, including New York, made the same calculation. It is difficult to believe that in 2004 some of these states will not try to move their primaries up a few weeks. James Roosevelt, the cochair of the Democratic rules committee, has offered an especially gloomy prognosis: "My speculation is that more and more states will move to the earliest date the parties allow. We are moving toward a de facto national primary."[41]

Conclusion

Whether one looks at primaries or at caucuses, the inescapable conclusion is that the presidential nomination process has become a great deal more front-loaded over the past three decades. The delegate selection calendar, which once started up rather slowly, now begins with a bang. Most delegates are selected within about six weeks after the New Hampshire primary. There is, moreover, no reason to believe that front-loading has run its course. To the contrary, there are strong reasons to think that it will get worse in 2004.

CHAPTER THREE

Explaining
Front-Loading

Why has the shape of the delegate selection calendar changed so dramatically over the past three decades? Why did so many states try to move their primaries and caucuses to earlier dates in the nomination season? As the history and analysis presented in chapter 2 has shown, the single proximate cause that lies behind most recent state scheduling decisions is a phenomenon best described as New Hampshire envy. In simple terms, New Hampshire envy is the perception that New Hampshire, because it holds the first primary in the nation, derives a substantial array of political and economic benefits from that position and plays a highly significant role in determining who ultimately wins the major-party presidential nominations, despite the fact that it is a small state and is, in important ways, not particularly representative of the country as a whole. As more and more states became aware of all the advantages accruing to New Hampshire—and after 1976, to Iowa as well—they, too, naturally came to believe that it would be to their benefit either to vote on the same day as New Hampshire or, if that were not possible, at least to schedule their primary or caucus somewhere near the start of the delegate selection calendar.

When one examines the details of individual state scheduling decisions, several different variants of New Hampshire envy become apparent. Some states moved to the front of the pack out of a desire to enhance their political and economic position. Others were primarily interested in giving a boost to the fortunes of one particular candidate. Still others wanted to make it more likely that one party or the other would nominate a particular type of candidate, one who shared the values and ideology of their state or region. What unites all these motives is the simple perception that earlier is better: that whatever goals a state seeks to achieve through the presidential nomination process, the odds of attaining those goals are much greater if it holds an early primary or caucus than if it selects its delegates in the middle or at the end of the process.

The Joys of Being First

The benefits that New Hampshire and Iowa derive from their privileged position in the presidential selection process have been amply documented in a score of good studies. Those benefits fall into five principal categories: press coverage, attention from the candidates, influence on the nomination race, economic benefits, and various types of special policy concessions.

Press Coverage

From the moment that political scientists first began to apply content analysis to media coverage of the presidential nomination process, one of their first and most consistent findings has been the extent to which that coverage is dominated by New Hampshire and Iowa. In one of the best studies of this kind, Michael Robinson and Margaret Sheehan counted up the number of stories devoted to a particular primary or caucus that were run on the *CBS Evening News* and the United Press International (UPI) wire service between January 1 and June 6, 1980. As shown in table 3-1, in both outlets Iowa and New Hampshire each received about 14 percent of the total coverage, well ahead of every other state, including such big primary states as Illinois, Pennsylvania, California, and New York.[1]

Yet these figures may actually understate the dominance of these early events, since the Robinson and Sheehan analysis did not begin until January 1, by which time much of the campaigning in Iowa and New Hampshire—and much of the press coverage about that campaigning—had already taken place. In an earlier study, Robinson examined newspaper and television coverage of the 1976 nomination races between November 24, 1975, and February 27, 1976. During this period, New Hampshire alone accounted for 42 percent of all the print campaign news and 60 percent of all the campaign coverage on television.[2] In the year before the 1988 Iowa caucuses, according to yet another study, Iowa and New Hampshire to-

Table 3-1 *Media Coverage of the 1980 Presidential Primaries and Caucuses, by State*
Units as indicated

State	Coverage in news seconds	Percentage of total	Seconds per delegate[a]
CBS Evening News			
Iowa	2,940	14	33.8
New Hampshire	2,815	14	68.7
Illinois	2,000	10	7.1
Pennsylvania	1,950	9	7.3
New York	1,515	7	3.7
Massachusetts	1,450	7	9.5
California	1,205	6	2.5
Wisconsin	1,165	6	10.7
Ohio	915	4	3.8
Maine	795	4	18.5

State	Coverage in column inches	Percentage of total	Inches per delegate[a]
United Press International			
New Hampshire	774	15	18.9
Iowa	679	13	7.8
Pennsylvania	366	7	1.4
Illinois	349	7	1.2
Michigan	342	7	1.5
New York	307	6	0.8
Wisconsin	271	5	2.5
California	183	4	0.4
South Carolina	172	3	2.8
Massachusetts	160	3	1.0

Source: Michael J. Robinson and Margaret A. Sheehan, *Over the Wire and On TV: CBS and UPI in Campaign '80* (New York: Russell Sage Foundation, 1983), pp. 176–77.

a. Based on the total number of delegates each state sent to both the Democratic and Republican national conventions.

gether received 77 percent of all the network news coverage that was devoted to a specific state contest.[3]

Attention from the Candidates

Whether as cause or as effect of this coverage, New Hampshire and Iowa also receive a lot more attention from the candidates than do other states. The best way of quantifying how much campaigning occurs in each state is to follow the money. Since 1974 federal law has required all candidates who accept matching funds (and almost all do)[4] to report how much they spend in each state. Table 3-2 shows the total amount of money spent by

Table 3-2   *Total Campaign Spending by All Major-Party Presidential Candidates in the 1988 Nomination Races, by State*
Dollars

State	Spending by all major-party candidates	Spending per delegate
Iowa	7,901,939	80,632
New Hampshire	5,366,001	119,244
Texas	4,346,422	13,498
New York	3,759,048	8,783
Illinois	3,729,528	12,772
Massachusetts	3,728,137	21,802
Florida	3,448,310	14,611
Michigan	2,922,400	12,228
South Carolina	1,997,509	22,195
North Carolina	1,946,225	13,062

Source: Federal Election Commission, *FEC Reports on Financial Activity 1987–1988: Final Report, Presidential Pre-Nomination Campaigns* (Washington, 1989), pp. 12–17.

all candidates, Republican and Democratic, in the 1988 nomination races, for the ten states that attracted the most spending. Once again, Iowa and New Hampshire outdistanced all competitors, particularly in terms of the average amount of spending for each national convention delegate (see the final column in this table).

Another way of measuring how much attention the candidates paid to each state is to count up the number of days they actually spent campaigning there. As a practical matter, however, it is considerably more difficult to get reliable data on the candidates' personal campaign schedules than on their financial allocations.[5] But such data as do exist suggest the same pattern as the figures on spending: that Iowa and New Hampshire see a lot more of the candidates than they would if they did not hold the first caucus and the first primary in the nation. In the 1988 election cycle, for example, the seven major Democratic candidates spent 546 days campaigning in Iowa, 288 days in New Hampshire, and 441 days in all fourteen of the southern and border-South states that voted on Super Tuesday (that is, about 32 days per state). The figures on the Republican side are similar: the GOP's six major presidential contenders devoted 300 days to Iowa, 367 days to New Hampshire, and just 396 days to the entire South (28 days per state).[6]

Influence on the Nomination Race

Not surprisingly, all this press coverage has an effect on public opinion. At a time when almost all delegates are selected by ordinary voters participating in primaries and caucuses, the results in New Hampshire and Iowa can dramatically reshape the standings in a contested nomination race. Candidates who win or do "better than expected" in these two states generally see a large increase in their support across the country; candidates who lose frequently see their stock tumble.

This effect can also be measured with a fair amount of precision. For at least a year before the first delegates are selected, pollsters routinely ask national samples of party identifiers which candidate they would like to see their party nominate in the upcoming presidential election. For every contested nomination race from 1984 to 2000, table 3-3 shows the results of three such polls: the last poll before the Iowa caucuses, one conducted between the Iowa caucuses and the New Hampshire primary, and the first poll after New Hampshire.[7] Clearly, what happens in Iowa and New Hampshire reverberates through the rest of the country. In four of the eight races shown here, one candidate gained at least 15 percentage points in the national polls as a result of his performance in one or both of these states.

Economic Benefits

Holding the first caucus and the first primary also brings a host of economic benefits to Iowa and New Hampshire. In addition to all the candidate campaign spending mentioned above, there is the far larger amount of money spent by reporters and media organizations, plus a great deal of free publicity for the states' resorts, tourist attractions, and industries. A recent report by the Library and Archives of New Hampshire's Political Tradition estimates the total economic impact of the 2000 primary on that state's economy to have been $264 million.[8]

Special Policy Concessions

Finally, though this effect is difficult to quantify, it seems clear that both Iowa and New Hampshire receive a diverse array of what might be called "special policy concessions" as a result of their privileged positions in the presidential nomination process. As candidates spend time in these two states and talk to their voters and political leaders, they are made especially sensitive to each state's problems and concerns; and while some of these problems affect the country as a whole, others are more local and specific in character. In 1988, for example, candidates campaigning in Iowa were regularly treated to extended discussions of the plight of the

Table 3-3   *Effect of Iowa and New Hampshire on the Presidential
Nomination Preferences of National Party Identifiers, 1984–2000*
Percent

Race	Last poll before Iowa	Poll between Iowa and New Hampshire	First poll after New Hampshire	Total change
1984 Democrats				
Mondale	43	57	31	–12
Glenn	16	7	7	–9
Jackson	12	8	7	–5
Hart	1	7	38	+37
1988 Democrats				
Hart	17	9	7	–10
Dukakis	13	16	22	+9
Jackson	13	12	14	+1
Gephardt	9	20	13	+4
1988 Republicans				
Bush	43	38	39	–4
Dole	24	32	30	+6
Robertson	6	10	7	+1
Kemp	4	5	5	+1
1992 Democrats				
Clinton	42	n.a.ᵃ	41	–1
Brown	16	n.a.ᵃ	7	–9
Kerrey	10	n.a.ᵃ	6	–4
Tsongas	9	n.a.ᵃ	31	+22
1992 Republicans				
Bush	84	n.a.ᵃ	78	–6
Buchanan	11	n.a.ᵃ	20	+9
Duke	4	n.a.ᵃ	*	–4

(continues)

family farm, an issue that was then highly salient in certain areas of the Midwest but was not a high priority in the rest of the country.[9] Not surprisingly, by the end of the Iowa campaign, most of the presidential candidates, particularly in the Democratic Party, had publicly committed themselves to quite generous farm support programs.

In a similar vein, when incumbent presidents face contested races for renomination, they generally shower Iowa and New Hampshire with all sorts of discretionary funds and favorable bureaucratic decisions.[10] In 1992, for example, when President George Bush was attempting to fend off a challenge in New Hampshire from the conservative commentator Pat Buchanan, the *New York Times* reported one month before the primary,

Race	Last poll before Iowa	Poll between Iowa and New Hampshire	First poll after New Hampshire	Total change
1996 Republicans				
Dole	47	n.a.ᵃ	41	−6
Forbes	16	n.a.ᵃ	8	−8
Buchanan	7	n.a.ᵃ	27	+20
Alexander	3	n.a.ᵃ	14	+11
2000 Democrats				
Gore	60	67	65	+5
Bradley	27	21	24	−3
2000 Republicans				
Bush	63	65	56	−7
McCain	19	15	34	+15
Forbes	6	7	2	−4

Source: Results for 1984 are taken from CBS–*New York Times* surveys of January 14–21, February 21–25, and March 5–8, 1984, and are based on the responses of likely Democratic primary voters. Results for 1988 are taken from Gordon S. Black surveys of January 21–28, February 10–13, and February 23–28, 1988, and are based on the responses of registered voters who identified with the Democratic and Republican Parties, respectively. Results for 1992 are taken from Gallup surveys of January 31–February 2 and February 19–20, 1992, and are based on the responses of registered voters who identified with the Democratic and Republican Parties, respectively. Results for 1996 are taken from Gallup surveys of January 26–29 and February 23–25, 1996, and are based on the responses of registered voters who identified with the Republican Party. Results for 2000 are taken from Gallup surveys of January 17–19, January 25–26, and February 4–6, 2000, and are based on the responses of registered voters who identified with the Democratic and Republican Parties, respectively.

*Candidate was supported by less than one-half of one percent of the survey respondents.

a. In 1992 and 1996 no national poll with a nomination preference question was asked between the Iowa caucuses and the New Hampshire primary.

"In rapid succession last month, Federal and state officials announced three Federal initiatives that would create 400 jobs and pump more than $274 million in financial aid and loan guarantees into New Hampshire."[11] In January 1976 Gerald Ford assured a group of New Hampshire newspaper editors visiting the White House that, though he was striving to make the Defense Department more efficient, he had "no plan whatsoever" to close the Portsmouth Naval Shipyard in New Hampshire.[12] In 1980 *Newsweek* reported another compelling lesson in early-state presidential politicking:

> One obstacle in [Edward Kennedy's] pursuit is Carter's lock on the vast resources of the presidency—not just the call of patriotism but the power of the Federal purse. "He's got $87 billion a year to give out," says a House Democratic elder, and this President, like most, has been giving where and when it counts. . . . Mayor Maurice Arel of Nashua [New Hampshire] was leaning to Teddy until Carter phoned his best wishes for a local housing project then trammeled in red tape.

> The mayor switched to Carter, the red tape quickly unwound and $500,000 headed north to Nashua. . . . New Hampshire's further bounty includes a $34 million highway bypass, a much-admired if little-used commuter train to Boston and some small-business relief money for ski resorts hurting from a mostly snowless winter.[13]

The 1980 Carter campaign made such aggressive use of the executive branch in early primary and caucus states that a group of Kennedy supporters actually filed suit against a number of top administration officials for improper use of government funds.[14]

Early Is Also Good

There is little doubt, then, that Iowa and New Hampshire derive an impressive set of advantages from being the first caucus and the first primary. But what about states that are not first but merely early? If a state knows that it will not be first in line, does it matter if it votes or caucuses in, say, mid-March rather than mid-May? Some of the same data that have just been used to establish the privileged position of Iowa and New Hampshire can also be used to investigate the advantages that accrue (or do not accrue) in more typical cases.

Since 1974 all presidential candidates who receive federal matching funds have been required to report the total amount of money they spend during the nomination contest in each of the fifty states and the District of Columbia. For each contested nomination race from 1980 to 1988, we use these data as the dependent variables for a series of regression equations.[15] Each equation includes five independent variables. For our purposes, the most important of these variables is the date on which the state held its primary or caucuses, measured as the total number of days that had passed since the first delegate selection event in which the general public was allowed to participate (meaning, in most cases, the Iowa caucuses). The other four variables are

—the number of national convention delegates the state had,

—the type of delegate selection system the state used (primary or caucus),

—separate dummy variables for Iowa and New Hampshire, to allow for the possibility that the alleged advantages of holding an early primary or caucus go entirely or disproportionately to these two states. (For further details on the specification of these equations, see appendix B.)

The results are shown in table 3-4. In general, candidate spending varies by state in quite predictable ways. Candidates spend more money in states in which lots of delegates may be acquired than in states with comparatively small delegations. Primaries attract more spending than do caucuses; Iowa and New Hampshire both derive huge monetary advantages from being at the head of the calendar. Most significant for our purposes, the date coefficient is large and statistically significant in every equation. Even with the singular effects of Iowa and New Hampshire taken out of the picture, moving up the date of a primary or caucus pays off at a rate between $4,000 and $12,000 a day. In the 1984 Democratic contest, to take a case in the middle of this range, a state that moved its primary up by one month (thirty days) could expect that total candidate spending in that state would increase by about $180,000. A state that moved from early June to mid-March could expect about $500,000 in additional spending. To put these figures in perspective, the median spending per state in 1984 was just $237,000.[16]

Campaign spending declines over the course of the delegate selection season for two distinct reasons. First, many candidates withdraw from the race shortly after Iowa and New Hampshire and thus do not spend any money on later primaries and caucuses. Second, those candidates who do stay in the race generally run out of money or reach the federal campaign spending limits and therefore cannot spend as much in later states as they might like.[17]

To document the latter effect, we ran a second series of regression equations (detailed results are not reported here), this time using as the dependent variable the state-by-state spending totals for those candidates who waged an active campaign until the very end of the primary and caucus season. In the three election cycles analyzed in table 3-4, there were seven such candidates: Carter and Kennedy in 1980, Mondale, Gary Hart, and Jesse Jackson in 1984, and Dukakis and Jackson in 1988.[18] The coefficient for the "date of primary or caucus" variable was negative and statistically significant for all of the conventional candidates (that is, Carter, Kennedy, Hart, Mondale, and Dukakis). In this respect (as in many others), Jackson marched to a different drummer: in 1984 his spending per state was unaffected by the date on which a state's primary or caucus took place, and in 1988 it actually seems to have increased over the course of the nomination season. Not all candidates, then, are forced to curtail their spending as the delegate selection season drags on. But at least in these three election cycles, that dynamic did

Table 3-4   *Effect of Primary or Caucus Date on Total Campaign Spending per State, 1980–1988*[a]

Variable	Coefficient	Standard error
1980 Democratic race		
Date of primary or caucus	–4,500	968***
Number of delegates	3,987	461***
Primary states	214,702	69,288**
Iowa	535,504	216,555**
New Hampshire	575,920	216,700**
Constant	236,380	83,754
Summary statistics		
R^2 = .76		
Adjusted R^2 = .73		
N = 51		
Median spending per state = $88,368		
1980 Republican race		
Date of primary or caucus	–11,708	2,491***
Number of delegates	9,612	2,624***
Primary states	723,711	230,588**
Iowa	782,178	571,046
New Hampshire	177,389	553,745
Constant	615,023	254,334
Summary statistics		
R^2 = .58		
Adjusted R^2 = .52		
N = 42		
Median spending per state = $202,998		
1984 Democratic race		
Date of primary or caucus	–6,042	1,725***
Number of delegates	7,086	692***
Primary states	409,988	107,451***
Iowa	2,351,957	328,545***
New Hampshire	1,669,365	342,083***
Constant	80,517	99,215
Summary statistics		
R^2 = .85		
Adjusted R^2 = .83		
N = 51		
Median spending per state = $236,751		

(continues)

apply to all of the candidates who had a realistic chance of winning their party's nomination—and who spent the most money.

Data are also available that show the amount of television coverage each state received during the nomination races of 1980, 1988, and 1992. For 1980 coverage is measured as the total number of seconds devoted to

Variable	Coefficient	Standard error
1988 Democratic race		
Date of primary or caucus	–4.075	1,746*
Number of delegates	7,369	777***
Primary states	51,216	118,691
Iowa	3,635,698	380,475***
New Hampshire	2,716,117	380,450***
Constant	52,113	117,393
Summary statistics		
$R^2 = .85$		
Adjusted $R^2 = .83$		
$N = 51$		
Median spending per state = $234,454		
1988 Republican race		
Date of primary or caucus	–10,070	2,363***
Number of delegates	7,739	2,503**
Primary states	386,500	204,030*
Iowa	3,035,571	546,028***
New Hampshire	1,490,390	538,735**
Constant	497,130	191,978
Summary statistics		
$R^2 = .66$		
Adjusted $R^2 = .62$		
$N = 45$		
Median spending per state = $407,704		

* $p < .05$; ** $p < .01$; *** $p < .001$.

a. The dependent variable in all equations is the total amount of money spent in each state by all candidates for that party's presidential nomination who filed state spending reports with the Federal Election Commission.

each state on the *CBS Evening News;* for 1988 and 1992 the measure is the total number of stories on any of the three major networks that mentioned each state's primary or caucus. It is worth noting that these variables indicate how much coverage each state received for both parties combined: the measures do not distinguish between coverage of the Democratic nomination race and that associated with the Republican contest.

To account for the state-by-state variation in television coverage, we ran two different equations for each dependent variable. (For further details on these equations, see appendix B.) The first set of equations employs the same five independent variables used in table 3-4 to explain candidate spending patterns. As shown in table 3-5, the date on which a state held its primary or caucus had a significant effect on television coverage in 1980 and 1992 but not in 1988. In the 1980 campaign, during which the median state received just 65 seconds worth of coverage on the *CBS Evening News,* moving up a state's primary or caucus date by just

Table 3-5 *Effect of Primary or Caucus Date on Media Coverage per State, Various Years*[a]

Variable	Without controlling for the number of other primaries on the same day		Controlling for the number of other primaries on the same day	
	Coefficient	Standard error	Coefficient	Standard error
1980				
Date of caucus or primary	−5.31	1.80**	−4.39	1.85*
Total number of delegates	10.32	1.57***	10.32	1.54***
States where both parties used a primary	387.84	157.31**	422.75	155.51**
States where just one party used a primary	136.15	207.99	101.64	204.71
Iowa	2,492.54	388.94***	2,487.92	380.67***
New Hampshire	2,344.09	377.61***	2,305.81	370.35***
Number of other contests on the same day	—	—	−34.23	21.48
Constant	107.13	178.61	110.87	174.82
Summary statistics				
R^2 =	.82		.84	
Adjusted R^2 =	.79		.80	
N =	42		42	
Median coverage per state (seconds) =		65		
1988				
Date of caucus or primary	−0.05	0.08	−0.37	0.06***
Total number of delegates	0.38	0.07***	0.37	0.04***
States where both parties used a primary	−2.68	6.07	14.51	4.28***
States where just one party used a primary	5.16	10.20	10.44	6.27
Iowa	269.55	16.33***	250.19	10.27***
New Hampshire	204.63	16.08***	170.39	10.71***
Number of other contests on the same day	—	—	−1.84	0.23***
Constant	2.27	5.79	22.99	4.38
Summary statistics				
R^2 =	.93		.97	
Adjusted R^2 =	.92		.97	
N =	45		45	
Median number of stories per state =		5		

(continues)

Variable	Without controlling for the number of other primaries on the same day		Controlling for the number of other primaries on the same day	
	Coefficient	Standard error	Coefficient	Standard error
1992				
Date of caucus or primary	−0.25	0.06***	−0.35	0.06***
Total number of delegates	0.31	0.05***	0.34	0.04***
States where both parties used a primary	7.86	7.15	14.59	6.08*
States where just one party used a primary	0.54	8.98	4.27	7.43
Iowa	−2.42	14.18	−11.59	11.84
New Hampshire	188.36	13.26***	173.57	11.42***
Number of other contests on the same day	—	—	−2.28	0.53***
Constant	10.03	6.67	19.07	5.87
Summary statistics				
R^2 =	.89		.93	
Adjusted R^2 =	.87		.91	
N =	43		43	
Median number of stories per state =		5		

*p < .05; **p < .01; ***p < .001.

a. The dependent variable in 1980 is the number of seconds devoted to each state on the *CBS Evening News*. In 1988 and 1992 it is the number of stories mentioning that state on all three major networks.

one month increased its expected television coverage by about 159 seconds (that is, at the rate of about 5 seconds a day).

Why doesn't this relationship hold for the 1988 nomination season? There is actually a simple answer to this question: in 1988 too many primaries and caucuses were scheduled on one day. Given the severe time limits each television network faces in allocating the half hour of its evening news program, as the number of primaries held on the same day increases, the total amount of campaign coverage will generally not increase on anything like a proportionate basis. Thus when nineteen primaries and caucuses take place on a single day, as happened on March 8, 1988, they necessarily compete with one another for media attention.

To take account of this competition, we estimated a second set of equations, using the same five independent variables employed earlier plus one other: the total number of other states that held a primary or caucus on the same day. These results are also shown in table 3-5. In all three equations (1980, 1988, and 1992), this last variable has a significant effect on television coverage: as the total number of primaries and caucuses held on a given day increases, each individual event, not unexpectedly, receives less coverage. More important for our analysis, after controlling for the effects of this variable the 1988 anomaly disappears: the date on which a state holds its primary or caucus now has a significant effect on the amount of coverage it receives in all three cases.[19]

Taken together, the two sets of equations presented in table 3-5 suggest several important points about the effects of front-loading on media coverage. On the one hand, the results point to one major limitation on the benefits a state can expect to receive by moving its primary or caucus to the head of the nomination calendar. States holding early delegate selection events will, in general, receive more press coverage; but as more and more states do the same thing, they inevitably compete with one another for a relatively inelastic newshole. Obviously, the best situation for a state is to have an early date all to itself. (Besides Iowa and New Hampshire, the best example of this is the South Carolina Republican primary.) But the number of states that can do this is inherently limited.

Yet the bottom line is that moving to the front of the calendar generally does pay off.[20] To assess the benefits of front-loading from the perspective of an individual state, the more relevant results are probably those from the first set of equations. To a state legislature or state party that is thinking about rescheduling its primary or caucus, it is of no consolation to know that moving to an early date will increase coverage, after controlling for the number of other states that vote on the same day. States want to know whether early dates bring increased coverage, period, without qualifications. For two of the three elections considered here, the answer is yes.

The Impact of the New Rules

Thus far we have shown that front-loading occurs because states believe—correctly—that holding their primaries and caucuses near the start of the delegate selection season provides them with important benefits, such as increased attention from the candidates and increased press coverage. Yet this conclusion is plainly not a complete explanation of the front-loading phenomenon. In particular, New Hampshire envy, by itself, fails to explain why front-loading occurred when it did. New Hampshire, after all, has been holding the first primary in the nation since at least 1952.[21] Moreover, as a number of studies have shown, the New Hampshire results were having a noticeable impact on presidential politics throughout the 1950s and 1960s.[22] Yet as demonstrated in the previous chapter, front-loading did not begin to emerge as a major trend until the early 1980s. What was it, then, that finally set front-loading in motion?

The answer, we believe, was the wholesale restructuring of the rules of presidential politics that took place in the early and middle 1970s.[23] The new rules changed the presidential nomination process in a variety of ways, but three such changes deserve special attention here: the increased proportion of committed delegates, the early withdrawal of most candidates, and the regularity with which nomination races get settled well before the opening of the national convention. Together, these factors helped upset the equilibrium that had held the old nomination calendar in balance, eliminating most of the incentives that had once existed for holding late primaries and caucuses and dramatically increasing the importance of going early.

The Increase in Committed Delegates

The presidential nomination process that existed between 1912 and 1968 is often called "the mixed system," for though it included some elements that allowed for public participation and the expression of mass preferences, other features were clearly designed to preserve the power of state and local party leaders and insulate the delegate selection process from ordinary voters and short-term activists. As a result, the number of delegates that a candidate could win by contesting the presidential primaries was quite limited, even if the candidate campaigned actively in the primary states and won most of the primaries he entered. Only about a third of the states held primaries at this time; and even in those states, the rules were often set up with the deliberate intention of making it more difficult for the voters to translate their candidate preferences into national convention delegates. In several states, for example, candidates for national convention delegate were simply not allowed to indicate on the primary ballot which presidential candidate they favored. The situation in caucus-convention states was, if anything, even more forbidding. Delegates from these states were generally selected through a process closely run by state and local party organizations, often without formal rules of procedure or public notice of important meetings and thus highly resistant to the efforts of candidate organizations or issue activists.[24]

The new rules changed this situation in at least three ways. First, there was a huge increase in the number of states holding presidential primaries, from seventeen in 1968 to twenty-three in 1972 and then to twenty-nine in 1976. Second, with few exceptions, primaries were now designed to translate voter preferences directly into convention delegates. Democratic national rules, for example, specifically forbade states to hold primaries in which the presidential preference of all delegate candidates was not identified right on the ballot. Third, even in caucus states, the new rules generally required state parties to adopt formal, written rules, to publicize all meetings in advance, and to allow almost every interested voter the right to participate in the first stage of the caucus process.[25]

Taken together, these changes have had a decisive impact on how delegates are selected and the kinds of commitments they are required to make. In an attempt to quantify that change, we make use here of another major data source on presidential nominating politics. In every contested nomination race since 1952, at least one major media organization has maintained, throughout the nomination season, a regular, ongoing count of the number of delegates that had been selected and which candidate, if any, they were committed to. (For further information about these delegate counts, see appendix C.) In table 3-6, we use these delegate counts to show the number and percentage of delegates who were still uncommitted at two crucial points in the nomination race: at the end of the primary season and on the weekend just before the start of the national convention.

As these data demonstrate, in the 1950s and 1960s a quite large proportion of all convention delegates were selected in a way that did not commit them, in advance, to vote for one of the major national candidates. On the one hand, a large number of delegates during these years were classified as uncommitted. At the same time, another sizable bloc of delegates were committed but to favorite-son candidates: candidates who received most or all of their delegates from their own home states and had almost no support in any other state.[26] In a number of cases, these favorite-son candidates perhaps genuinely did entertain some hope that, if the convention deadlocked for the first few ballots, the party might eventually turn to one of them as a compromise candidate. In most cases, however, favorite-son candidacies were simply a way of holding delegates in abeyance until the favorite son or the state party leaders (or both) decided that it was an opportune time to support one of the front-runners.[27] A better measure, then, of the number of truly uncommitted delegates at the conventions of the 1950s and 1960s would probably include both the uncommitted and favorite-son categories. By this measure, at the end of the primary season between a third and a half of all delegates were still

Table 3-6 Uncommitted and Favorite-Son Delegates in Contested Nomination Races, 1952–2000

| | At the end of the primary season | | | | | | Just before the start of the national convention | | | | | |
| | Uncommitted | | Favorite son | | Total | | Uncommitted | | Favorite son | | Total | |
Race	Number	%	Number	%	Number	%	Number	%	Number	%	Number	%
1952 Democratic	402	33	217	18	619	51	380	31	203	17	583	47
1952 Republican	212	18	118	10	330	28	118	10	118	10	236	20
1956 Democratic	370	33	192	17	562	51	382	28	262	19	644	47
1960 Democratic	379	28	248	18	627	47	356	23	197	13	553	36
1964 Republican	253	24	114	11	367	35	201	15	59	5	260	20
1968 Democratic	n.a.	n.a.	n.a.	n.a.	n.a.	n.a.	636	24	388	15	1,024	39
1968 Republican	n.a.	n.a.	n.a.	n.a.	n.a.	n.a.	42	3	162	12	204	15
1972 Democratic	488	16	58	2	546	18	416	14	30	1	446	15
1976 Democratic	481	17	94	3	575	20	411	14	0	0	411	14
1976 Republican	159	8	0	0	159	8	101	4	0	0	101	4
1980 Democratic	95	3	0	0	95	3	111	3	0	0	111	3
1980 Republican	150	8	0	0	150	8	113	6	0	0	113	6
1984 Democratic	214	6	36	1	250	7	191	5	36	1	227	6
1988 Democratic	478	11	0	0	478	11	n.a.	n.a.	n.a.	n.a.	n.a.	n.a.
1988 Republican	207	11	0	0	207	11	n.a.	n.a.	n.a.	n.a.	n.a.	n.a.
1992 Democratic	498	12	0	0	498	12	343	8	0	0	343	8
1992 Republican	26	1	0	0	26	1	n.a.	n.a.	n.a.	n.a.	n.a.	n.a.
1996 Republican	129	7	0	0	129	7	n.a.	n.a.	n.a.	n.a.	n.a.	n.a.
2000 Democratic	136	3	0	0	136	3	n.a.	n.a.	n.a.	n.a.	n.a.	n.a.
2000 Republican	51	2	0	0	51	2	n.a.	n.a.	n.a.	n.a.	n.a.	n.a.

Source: Computed from delegate counts maintained by major media organizations, especially the Associated Press. For further details, see appendix C.

uncommitted. Indeed, even on the very eve of the convention, about 32 percent of all delegates, on average, had yet to commit their votes to one of the major national contenders.

As table 3-6 also shows, however, this situation changed quite dramatically in the postreform period.[28] Simply put, few delegates today get selected on an uncommitted basis. In the ten contested nomination races after 1976, only about 6 percent of all delegates, on average, were classified as uncommitted when the primary season came to an end. As for favorite sons, they have almost completely disappeared from the world of presidential politics.

The Rise of Early Withdrawals

The new rules regime that went into effect in the mid-1970s has had two apparently contradictory effects on the length of the presidential selection process. On the one hand, the process has become longer. In the 1950s and 1960s even the earliest and most energetic entrants into the presidential race did not announce their candidacies until the last few months of the year preceding the election or the first few weeks of the election year. Since 1976, by contrast, candidates who seriously hope to win their party's presidential nomination have usually been compelled to declare their intentions in the late winter or early spring of the year before the election and thus devote almost two full years to the campaign.[29]

Yet once the formal delegate selection season begins, the new rules have had exactly the opposite effect, forcing candidates to withdraw from the race soon after the first caucuses and primaries, before most of the actual delegates have been chosen. To demonstrate this point, tables 3-7 and 3-8 show the withdrawal date of every unsuccessful major-party presidential candidate from 1952 to 2000. As with the data examined earlier on the prevalence of uncommitted delegates, there is a clear and sharp contrast between the way the system worked in the 1950s and 1960s and the way it has operated in more recent decades. In the prereform period, candidates who got into the race generally stayed in the race—at least until the end of the primary season, usually all the way up to the actual convention balloting. Beginning in 1976, however, one starts to see the emergence of a quite different pattern. Candidates who had done poorly in one or two early contests—in particular, the Iowa caucuses and the New Hampshire primary—were withdrawing from the field just days after the race had formally commenced. In 1984, for example, eight major

Table 3-7   *Withdrawal Dates for Major Democratic Presidential Candidates, 1952–2000*[a]

Year	Candidate	Withdrawal date	Number of days after the first primary[b]
1952	Alben Barkley	July 21	132[c]
	Averell Harriman	July 25	136[c]
	Estes Kefauver	None	137
	Richard Russell	None	137
	Robert Kerr	None	137[c]
1956	Estes Kefauver	July 31	140
	Averell Harriman	None	156[c]
1960	Hubert Humphrey	May 10	63
	Lyndon Johnson	None	127[c]
	Stuart Symington	None	127[c]
1964	George Wallace	July 19	131
1968	Lyndon Johnson	March 31	19
	Eugene McCarthy	None	169
	George McGovern	None	169[c]
1972	John Lindsay	April 4	28
	Edmund Muskie	April 27	51
	Henry Jackson	May 2	56
	Hubert Humphrey	July 11	126
	Eugene McCarthy	July 12	127
	George Wallace	None	127
	Terry Sanford	None	127
	Shirley Chisholm	None	127
1976	Birch Bayh	March 4	9
	Milton Shapp	March 12	17
	Sargent Shriver	March 16	21
	Fred Harris	April 8	44
	Henry Jackson	May 1	67
	George Wallace	June 9	106
	Morris Udall	June 14	111
	Frank Church	June 14	111[c]
	Jerry Brown	None	141[c]
1980	Jerry Brown	April 1	35
	Edward Kennedy	August 11	167
1984	Alan Cranston	February 29	1
	Reubin Askew	March 1	2
	Ernest Hollings	March 1	2
	George McGovern	March 14	15
	John Glenn	March 16	17
	Gary Hart	None	141
	Jesse Jackson	None	141
1988	Bruce Babbitt	February 18	2
	Gary Hart	March 11	24
	Richard Gephardt	March 28	41
	Paul Simon	April 7	51
	Al Gore	April 22	65
	Jesse Jackson	None	155

(continues)

Table 3-7   *Withdrawal Dates for Major Democratic Presidential Candidates, 1952–2000ª (Continued)*

Year	Candidate	Withdrawal date	Number of days after the first primaryᵇ
1992	Bob Kerrey	March 5	16
	Tom Harkin	March 9	20
	Paul Tsongas	March 19	30
	Jerry Brown	None	148
2000	Bill Bradley	March 9	37

a. Table does not include candidates who dropped out before the start of the delegate selection season.

b. For candidates who did not withdraw, figure is the number of days between the first primary and the party's final presidential roll call vote.

c. Candidate announced his candidacy after the first primary had already taken place.

candidates sought the Democratic presidential nomination. By the middle of March, less than three weeks after the New Hampshire primary, five of the eight were already out of the race. In 1988 every one of George Bush's Republican opponents except Pat Robertson had dropped out by the end of March. In 1992 three of the five Democratic contenders had withdrawn by the end of the third week in March.

What is it about the new rules that pushes candidates toward an early withdrawal? In some cases, presidential aspirants exit the race because it has become clear that their candidacies are just not catching on with the voters and that they have, therefore, no realistic chance of winning the nomination. Yet this explanation, though much beloved by political pundits, plainly fails to fit the circumstances of a considerable number of candidates.

Many candidates, for example, were clearly forced to withdraw before having had a chance to run in the kinds of primaries and caucuses in which their strength should have been most evident. In 1984 Senator Ernest Hollings of South Carolina and former governor Reubin Askew of Florida both based their candidacies, in part, on the belief that they would run well in the South. Yet both candidates ultimately withdrew from the race on March 1, before a single southern primary or caucus had taken place.

Moreover, early withdrawal is not just a fate suffered by candidates who fare poorly in the early contests; it also befalls many candidates who show considerable strength in the early going. In 1988, for example, Richard Gephardt came in first in the hotly contested Iowa caucuses, placed second in the New Hampshire primary (given its location, first place had long been conceded to Michael Dukakis), and won the South Dakota pri-

Table 3-8   *Withdrawal Dates for Major Republican Presidential Candidates, 1952–2000*[a]

Year	Candidate	Withdrawal date	Number of days from the first primary date[b]
1952	Robert Taft	None	122
	Earl Warren	None	122
	Harold Stassen	None	122
1964	Nelson Rockefeller	June 15	97
	Margaret C. Smith	None	127
	William Scranton	None	127[c]
1968	Ronald Reagan	None	149[c]
	Nelson Rockefeller	None	149[c]
1976	Ronald Reagan	None	177
1980	Howard Baker	March 5	8
	John Connally	March 9	12
	Robert Dole	March 15	18
	Philip Crane	April 17	51
	John Anderson	April 24[d]	58
	George Bush	May 26	90
1988	Alexander Haig	February 12	–4[e]
	Pierre DuPont	February 18	2
	Jack Kemp	March 10	23
	Robert Dole	March 29	42
	Pat Robertson	April 6	50
1992	Patrick Buchanan	August 17	181
1996	Phil Gramm	February 14	–6[e]
	Lamar Alexander	March 6	15
	Richard Lugar	March 6	15
	Steve Forbes	March 14	23
	Patrick Buchanan	None	176
2000	Orrin Hatch	January 26	–6[e]
	Gary Bauer	February 4	3
	Steve Forbes	February 10	9
	John McCain	March 9	37
	Alan Keyes	July 25	175

a. Table does not include candidates who dropped out before the start of the delegate selection season.

b. For candidates who did not withdraw, figure is the number of days between the first primary and the party's final presidential roll call vote.

c. Candidate announced his candidacy after the first primary had already taken place.

d. Date shown is the day on which Anderson announced that he was running for president as an independent candidate.

e. Candidate withdrew before the New Hampshire primary.

mary a week later. That record notwithstanding, the Gephardt campaign limped into Super Tuesday and was forced to shut down entirely in late March, just a month and a half after the start of the delegate selection season. Similarly, in 1992, Paul Tsongas won the New Hampshire primary on February 18, the Maryland primary and the Utah and Washington caucuses on March 3, the Arizona caucuses on March 7, and the Massachusetts and Rhode Island primaries and the Delaware caucuses on March 10 and finished second in a large number of other primaries and caucuses. Yet just nine days after his last set of victories—and a bare thirty days after New Hampshire—Tsongas withdrew from the race entirely.

In fact, it is money, more than votes, that has been the precipitating cause of these early withdrawals.[30] When Congress decided to overhaul the campaign finance laws in 1974, it created a system that made it extremely difficult for many candidates to fund a lengthy, competitive campaign. Until 1974 even the most progressive, populist-style presidential candidates raised much of their money from large contributions. In 1972, for example, George McGovern received at least $50,000 from each of forty-one different contributors, including twelve who gave $100,000 or more.[31] By limiting individual contributions to $1,000, the 1974 law forced every candidate to work a lot harder to raise an adequate war chest.

The effect was especially severe, however, for candidates who struggled in the early stages of a nomination race, for it was precisely candidates in this position who were least likely to be able to raise money from a large number of contributors—and who were thus most in need of large loans or contributions from a few fervent supporters. With this sort of assistance no longer possible, candidates who lost early were almost always confronted with a set of highly disagreeable choices. They could continue to campaign in the hopes of doing better, but in most cases, they had almost no money available to wage the kind of active and vigorous campaign that would have made a better showing likely. They could borrow money, but the 1974 campaign finance law also made borrowing difficult, and if the candidates' fortunes did not revive, the law made it all but impossible for them to pay off large campaign debts. The only other option was to withdraw—an option that most candidates quickly, if reluctantly, realized they had to take.

Against this background, it should come as no surprise that financial difficulties play a large, frequently determinative role in most candidates' withdrawal decisions. Here, for example, is one reporter's account of Senator Henry Jackson's decision to drop out of the 1976 Democratic race:

> On Friday morning, Jackson met with his political lieutenants once more to review the prospects. The will to continue was there, but not the resources. To the end, Jackson nurtured the hope that the

Supreme Court would free the federal matching funds due him once Congress and President Ford could agree on new campaign finance legislation, but the Court refused. . . . Finally, reluctantly, Jackson decided to get out. . . . "It was money," Jackson told me later. "There wasn't any question but that money was the overwhelming direct causal connection."[32]

In 1984 former Florida governor Reubin Askew withdrew from the Democratic nomination race two days after the New Hampshire primary—and with the Florida, Alabama, and Georgia primaries just twelve days away. Why withdraw at such an apparently inopportune moment? A top aide to Askew has provided this explanation:

> We believed that we could go on and head south and win the Florida primary despite [Askew's poor showings in Iowa and New Hampshire], in part because of the loophole primary. But it would have cost us half a million dollars to do so. We could have borrowed that money, but that would have begun running up a deficit. Some of the other candidates are still in debt and very much so. Governor Askew has a debt now of $61,000. His decision was based on avoiding a deficit.[33]

The *New York Times*'s account of Paul Tsongas's exit from the 1992 nomination race sounded many of the same themes: "Mr. Tsongas announced his departure at a news conference in Boston, where he said his campaign did not have enough money to continue. . . . [Said Tsongas,] 'The hard fact is that the nomination process requires resources, and last evening it was clear that we did not have the resources necessary to fight the media war in New York. We simply did not have the resources.'"[34]

Campaign finance connects with front-loading in a number of ways and may be an important part of any effort to remedy the problem (see chapters 4 and 5). For the moment, however, the explanation of these early withdrawals is less important than the brute fact that they occur. In terms of the incentives for front-loading, it matters a great deal *when* candidates drop out. Under the rules that existed up through 1968, a state that held its primary in May or June could generally count on being able to choose from among the full field of declared candidates: almost every candidate who entered the New Hampshire primary in March would still be active two or three months later. In the contemporary era, by contrast, voters in later primaries have a much more restricted set of options available to them. Many of the candidates they might want to vote for—or at least would like having the opportunity to consider—have long since exited the race.

Clinching the Nomination

With more and more delegates being selected on a committed basis, and with fewer candidates still in the race to divide up these delegates, a third change was almost inevitable: one of the presidential candidates would clinch the nomination well before the convention opened. In table 3-9 we again use the media delegate counts to document the extent of this transformation. Under the old rules, the leading candidate at the end of the primaries had generally accumulated only about 40–70 percent of the number of delegates needed to win the nomination (that is, about 20–35 percent of the total number of delegates). Even on the eve of the convention, the eventual winner had usually not yet won enough commitments to put him over the top. Indeed, of all the candidates from the prereform era shown in table 3-9, only Barry Goldwater in 1964 had achieved a delegate majority before the convention was gaveled to order. Candidates like Adlai Stevenson in 1956, John Kennedy in 1960, and Hubert Humphrey in 1968 were well ahead of the competition, and most news outlets clearly saw each of them as a strong favorite to win his party's nomination. Nevertheless, the conventions were still an arena in which significant bargaining and decisionmaking took place and the final pieces in the winning coalition were put together. In 1952, indeed, both national conventions ultimately rejected the preconvention front-runner (Estes Kefauver in the Democratic Party, Robert Taft in the Republican) and nominated someone else in his stead.

Contemporary nomination contests clearly respond to a different dynamic. In every contested nomination race after 1976, one candidate has secured a majority of the delegates by the final day of the primary season. Though the convention still serves a number of functions—putting together the platform, reuniting the party, selling the candidate to a national television audience—it does not play any real role in choosing the party standard-bearer.[35]

A Different World

There is, of course, nothing particularly new or revelatory about the notion that national conventions no longer play anything more than a sym-

Table 3-9   *Number of Delegates Won by the Leading Presidential Candidate in Contested Nomination Races, 1952–2000*

Race	Number of delegates needed for nomination	At the end of the primary season		Just before the start of the national convention	
		Number won by leading candidate	Percentage of total	Number won by leading candidate	Percentage of total
1952 Democratic	616	251	20	257	21
1952 Republican	604	462	38	530	44
1956 Democratic	687	266	19	509	37
1960 Democratic	761	363	24	546	36
1964 Republican	655	438	33	731	56
1968 Democratic	1,313	n.a.	n.a.	1,087	41
1968 Republican	667	n.a.	n.a.	652	49
1972 Democratic	1,509	1,342	44	1,490	49
1976 Democratic	1,505	1,125	37	1,607	53
1976 Republican	1,130	961	43	1,120	49
1980 Democratic	1,666	1,949	59	1,986	60
1980 Republican	998	1,465	73	1,692	85
1984 Democratic	1,967	1,974	50	2,062	52
1988 Democratic	2,081	2,264	54	n.a.	n.a.
1988 Republican	1,139	1,669	73	n.a.	n.a.
1992 Democratic	2,145	2,512	59	2,848	66
1992 Republican	1,106	1,846	84	n.a.	n.a.
1996 Republican	996	1,477	74	n.a.	n.a.
2000 Democratic	2,170	3,804	88	n.a.	n.a.
2000 Republican	1,034	1,760	85	n.a.	n.a.

Source: Computed from delegate counts maintained by major media organizations, especially the Associated Press. For further details, see appendix C.

bolic role in nominating presidential candidates. But what has not been generally noted—and what we wish to stress here—is the way that the changes just described have altered the incentive structure for state legislators and state party leaders who are trying to decide when to schedule their primary or caucus.

In the prereform system, a state that hoped to "get something" out of the presidential nomination process—whether that something was patronage, attention from the campaigns and the media, a concession in the national platform, or the nomination of a particular candidate—could seek these benefits in a variety of ways. Although New Hampshire achieved its status as the first-in-the-nation primary largely by accident, by the 1960s, at the very latest, the Granite State's political leaders had clearly come to appreciate that there were important benefits to this position.[36] Yet if New Hampshire relished its ability to help define the field, many other states were content to hold what might be called "showdown primaries": primaries that served as a major test of strength between two or more of the leading candidates. Which particular states would be the sites of these critical contests varied from election to election, depending on who the candidates were and which states they chose to target. But given the much smaller number of states that had presidential primaries during this period, the odds that any one state would hold a contest of national significance were considerably greater than they would be today. Among the states that sometimes served as the site of an important presidential primary were California, Oregon, Wisconsin, West Virginia, Indiana, Florida, and Nebraska.

For most states, however, the expected benefits of a contested nomination race came from the bargaining and maneuvering that came after the primaries. When the last state primary results had been duly recorded, even the most formidable front-runner still needed at least two hundred more delegates to lock down the nomination (and this at a time when conventions were significantly smaller than they are today). With only a handful of delegates still to be selected at late-running state conventions, the presidential candidates knew there was only one real way to add to their delegate totals: they would have to court, cajole, persuade, and bargain with those states having large numbers of delegates who were either uncommitted or pledged to favorite sons. This bargaining period, which usually lasted for a month or more, was in many cases the most intense part of the entire nomination campaign.

To a classic party "boss" like the late Mayor Richard J. Daley of Chicago, then, it scarcely mattered when the Illinois primary was held. March, May, or June, the important thing was that, when the primary was over, the state had a large—and largely uncommitted—delegation that could be used to bargain with the candidates and other top party leaders. In both 1960 and 1968 Daley did not actually announce his support for a particular candidate until the national convention was in progress.

But the new nomination rules effectively eliminated this kind of postprimary bargaining. For what gave life to the entire process, by all accounts, was precisely that it was a matter of bargaining: that each side had something the other wanted, that presidential candidates were willing to offer access or other special benefits to those states and state party leaders who provided them with the delegates they needed to secure the nomination. The general rule, as Nelson Polsby stated it in 1960, was that "in order to achieve access, delegates must support the eventual winner *before he achieves a majority.*"[37] If one of the candidates routinely achieved a majority by the end of the primaries, there was nothing left to bargain over.[38]

A Vicious Cycle

Up to this point, we have examined how changes in the basic dynamics of the presidential nomination process led to the front-loading of the delegate selection calendar. But the relationship also worked in the opposite direction: as the calendar became more front-loaded, many of the trends that had first given rise to front-loading were accelerated and intensified.

This sort of "feedback loop" appears most clearly if one examines the date on which the winning candidate in each contested nomination race finally won enough delegates to clinch his party's nomination. In the first three postreform election cycles (1976–1984), this critical threshold generally was not crossed until the very end of the primary season (see table 3-10). Jimmy Carter in 1980 and Walter Mondale in 1984 both crossed the line on the final day of primaries; Ronald Reagan mathematically secured his party's 1980 nomination ten days before the last set of primaries. Gerald Ford, according to most media counts, did not achieve a delegate majority in 1976 until the first night of the Republican convention.

Over the past four election cycles, however, most nomination races have not even lasted until the end of the primaries. In 1988 George Bush mathematically clinched his party's nomination on April 26—and even that development was distinctly anticlimactic, since all of his major opponents had actually withdrawn a month earlier. On the Democratic side, Michael Dukakis, like Carter and Mondale before him, sewed up his party's nomination on the final day of primaries. Unlike Carter and Mondale, however, Dukakis had so clearly established himself as the prohibitive favorite that all of his most serious competitors had long since exited the race. Dukakis's only opponent through the final month of primaries was Jesse Jackson. Of the five contested nomination races since 1988, one was over by the end of March, two were over by the middle of March, one dragged on into early May; only Bill Clinton in 1992 had to wait until the final week of primaries before he, too, finally secured a delegate majority.

The problem, of course, is that the earlier nomination races get settled, the more the incentives for front-loading increase. In 1984 a state that

Table 3-10 *Dates on Which Presidential Candidates in Contested Races Clinched Their Party's Nomination, 1976–2000*

Party and year	Date on which candidate clinched his party's nomination[a]	Opening day of the national convention
Republican Party		
1976	August 16	August 16
1980	May 24	July 14
1988	April 26	August 15
1992	May 5	August 17
1996	March 26	August 12
2000	March 14	July 31
Democratic Party		
1976	June 24	July 12
1980	June 3	August 11
1984	June 6	July 16
1988	June 7	July 18
1992	June 2	July 13
2000	March 14	August 14

Source: 1976 Democratic date is based on unpublished data from the Associated Press. All other dates are based on contemporary reports in the *New York Times* and *Congressional Quarterly Weekly Report*.

a. Date shown is the day on which the eventual nominee won enough pledged delegates to guarantee a first-ballot convention victory.

wanted to have at least some effective input into the selection of the major-party presidential candidates could still schedule its primary in April or early May. By 1996, however, any primary held in April or May was almost certain to be irrelevant. A vicious cycle had been set in motion.

As of 2003, we have no reason to think that this cycle has run its course. To the contrary, there is every reason to think that, absent some sort of remedial action, front-loading will only get worse. In 2000 even the states that held their primaries on March 14 (a group that included Texas and Florida) found that by the time they voted, both McCain and Bradley had withdrawn from the race. If the same thing happens in 2004, it is hard not to believe that many of these states will try to move their primaries up to coincide with those of New York and California.

An Elite Conspiracy?

Front-loading, then, in our view, is a classic example of what is often called the tragedy of the commons. A set of autonomous actors (in this case, states) pursue a course of action that is designed to make them individually better off—but the aggregate effect of these individual decisions makes everybody worse off (or, at least, everybody except Iowa and New Hampshire).

There are, it should be noted, some observers of the presidential nomination process who are not entirely convinced by this explanation. A number of progressive Democrats, in particular, have occasionally voiced the suspicion that front-loading has a somewhat darker and more conspiratorial origin: that it was deliberately contrived by party elites who wanted to stack the deck against outsider and insurgent candidates and thus make sure that someone like George McGovern or Jimmy Carter would never again win the Democratic Party's presidential nomination. In late 1998, for example, Democratic senator Paul Wellstone criticized the 2000 nomination calendar by declaring, "This is transparent. It's nothing less than an effort to wire the whole thing."[39] A recent study of the presidential nomination process by four political scientists at the University of California at Los Angeles makes the same argument, calling front-loading "a device intended to disadvantage outsiders. . . . The first move toward front-loading was part of a conscious strategy by Democratic Party leaders to regain control of the nomination process."[40] Having studied the history of front-loading in some detail, however, we are able to find remarkably little evidence to substantiate this theory.

Of all the various rules and regulations the Democratic Party has seen fit to adopt over the past three decades, the only ones that would appear to have an obvious and direct connection to the shape of the delegate selection calendar are those concerned with the timing of primaries and caucuses.[41] This section of the national party rules has its origin, not unexpectedly, in the controversies of 1968. In many states, the antiadministration forces complained, delegates were selected by party committees or state conventions whose members had been chosen in 1966 or 1967— before the issues of the 1968 campaign had been defined, before McCarthy and Kennedy had even decided to get into the race. Hence the McGovern-Fraser guidelines included a requirement that no state start its delegate selection procedures until the "calendar year" of the election.[42] Beginning in 1980, this "window," as it was called, was tightened somewhat: all primaries and caucuses now had to take place between the second Tuesday in March and the second Tuesday in June, though a number of states— in particular, Iowa and New Hampshire—were eventually exempted from the rule. Between 1992 and 2000, the Democratic Party's window extended from the *first* Tuesday in March to the second Tuesday in June.

The imposition of a delegate selection window, in short, was originally seen as a reform: it was clearly designed to limit the power and discretion of the regular party organizations and make the delegate selection process more accessible to candidate enthusiasts and issue activists. Whatever the motivation, in any event, there is little evidence that the various Democratic window rules have had much effect on front-loading. To begin with, though primaries are clearly the dominant selection mechanism of the contemporary era, the original timing rule was directed principally at caucus-convention states.[43] The guideline adopted in 1972 did prohibit certain kinds of slate-making procedures in a number of primary states.[44] But in terms of the dates on which primary elections took place (which is, of course, the point at issue in front-loading), none of the seventeen Democratic primaries held in 1968 was in violation of the 1972 timing rule, and just one held its primary outside of the window the Democrats would later adopt for the 2000 campaign.[45] Even in caucus states, though the adoption of the window necessarily led to a somewhat greater clustering of the first-round meetings, it does not explain the distinctive characteristic of front-loading: why caucuses and primaries were scheduled at the beginning of the window rather than at the end of it.

One decision the Democrats made during this period may offer a bit of support to the conspiracy theories. In both 1976 and 1980 the Iowa caucuses and the New Hampshire primary were held more than five weeks apart: Iowa held its precinct caucuses on the third Monday in January; New Hampshire voters did not go to the polls until the last Tuesday in February. In 1980 this meant that both events were well outside the Democratic window, but both were eventually exempted from its provisions. Both states were also granted exemptions in 1984—but this time the exemptions were considerably more limited. According to the delegate selection rules for the 1984 Democratic National Convention, Iowa was supposed to hold its caucuses just fifteen days before the start of the window, and the New Hampshire primary was to occur seven days in advance of the window.[46] The new exemptions policy thus greatly accelerated the start-up of the delegate selection season. Whereas New Hampshire voters had once had five weeks to react to the Iowa results and reassess the candidates, they were now given just eight days to do so. Once established, the same policy was applied in every subsequent election cycle: Iowa and New Hampshire have continued to be scheduled just eight days apart.[47]

Contemporary press coverage of this decision suggests that the new exemptions policy was adopted, in part, as a way of helping Edward

Kennedy and Walter Mondale, the early front-runners for the 1984 nomination.[48] But the window was tightened for other reasons as well: to shorten the nomination process and to reduce the influence of Iowa and New Hampshire.[49] Even here, in short, the evidence of an elite conspiracy is hardly overwhelming. Yet this is the strongest evidence—indeed, the only evidence—we can find that a rule with a direct impact on front-loading was altered by national party leaders with the deliberate intention of hurting outsider and insurgent candidates.

If the parties can be fairly accused of anything with regard to front-loading, it is inaction. Front-loading was widely recognized as a problem by the mid-1980s; it was one of the issues on the agenda of the Hunt Commission, the Democratic Party reform body that met during 1981 and 1982.[50] Yet it was not until 1996 that either party adopted even the most timid set of proposals to cope with it. Inaction, however, can occur for a variety of reasons, and in this case, there is nothing to indicate that it emerged out of a conscious and deliberate policy—that some large number of party leaders actually wanted front-loading to get worse.

There are several reasons why the parties failed to get after front-loading more aggressively. Perhaps the most important is that there simply are no easy or obvious solutions to the problem (see chapter 5). Many proposals seem unlikely to have much effect; others might actually make the problem worse or have other serious, negative consequences. In addition, many of the more talked-about "solutions" would prove very difficult to implement and enforce, given the severe fragmentation of authority over the presidential nomination process (see chapter 6).

Front-loading also emerged at the wrong time in the party reform cycle. From the late 1960s to the early 1980s the Democrats created party reform commissions on a regular basis, almost all of which believed they had a mandate to reexamine every facet of the party's presidential selection process. During this time, however, front-loading was still at a fairly primitive stage of development; reasonable observers could disagree about whether there really was a problem and whether it would get any worse.[51] By the late 1980s, as evidence of front-loading became impossible to deny, even the Democrats had had enough of rules reform. As one adviser to the last Democratic reform commission put it, "Democratic leaders want to deemphasize the whole business of writing rules. The general consensus is that the party has got to stop mucking around with the nominating process."[52] Having discovered that new rules generally bring unanticipated consequences, the Democrats (and the Republicans) have generally been content to put up with whatever flaws the system has rather than take a chance on making things worse.

If the national parties cannot be accused of deliberately encouraging front-loading, what about state and local parties? State parties and state party leaders have, of course, often tried to move their own primaries and caucuses forward in the calendar, but as we have argued throughout this chapter, they did this to enhance the influence and visibility of their own state or region, not because they hoped to give a particular cast to the nomination calendar as a whole.[53] California, for example, did not move to the front of the calendar to promote front-loading. It moved because it wanted to increase the significance of the California primary. Front-loading was simply the unintended by-product of this decision (and similar decisions by lots of other states).

Only in 1984 is there evidence that a number of state party leaders, acting at the behest of the Mondale campaign, pursued front-loading as a concerted policy. Yet the results of this initiative were actually quite mixed (see chapter 2). Contrary to what some have asserted, 1984 is not a key turning point in the evolution of front-loading.[54] Among states holding primaries, front-loading barely increased between 1980 and 1984. There was a somewhat greater movement to the head of the calendar among caucus states, but its long-term significance is unclear. Most of the caucus states had comparatively small numbers of delegates; and by 1988 many of them had abandoned their caucuses in favor of primaries.[55]

This difference between primary and caucus states is no accident, and it points up a further weakness in any attempt to blame front-loading on the machinations of party leaders. In most states, caucus rules and procedures are set up principally at the discretion of the state parties, whereas primaries are the creation of state legislatures, which have generally not been very responsive to the concerns of the institutional parties or their leadership. Thus even if state party leaders had wanted to promote front-loading, that alone would hardly have guaranteed action on the part of state legislatures. If state legislatures have been willing participants in the front-loading trend, they have done so for reasons of their own, not because it helped out the state parties.

Finally, such front-loading as there was in 1984 proved of questionable advantage to the Mondale campaign. Front-loading may have benefited the former vice president in certain subtle ways (see chapter 4); but in more immediate and visible terms, it almost brought his entire campaign to an early end. When Gary Hart unexpectedly won the New Hampshire primary, Mondale was suddenly faced with the real prospect of los... almost every one of the primaries and caucuses that were being held two weeks later, on Super Tuesday. Had that happened, Mondale and several of his top advisers have indicated, he probably would have dropped out of the race.[56] In the end, Mondale did recover—but he probably would have found it easier to mount a comeback if the system had been less front-loaded. Not surprisingly, then, no subsequent candidate—and no cabal of party leaders—has ever tried to follow Mondale's example.

In a sense, it would be comforting to find that front-loading had developed out of a conscious and deliberate policy, for that would imply that the problem could be readily remedied. We would only need to convince party leaders (or whoever is responsible for it) that the policy is mistaken. Finding a way to reverse front-loading, however, turns out to be considerably more difficult.

CHAPTER FOUR

The Consequences
of Front-Loading

The rules and procedures of politics, like referees in football, generally work best when they are least noticed. If either becomes a major topic of discussion in the media, it is usually a sign that somebody thinks they are not working properly.

It was, then, almost certainly not a good omen that so much was written about front-loading during the 1996 and 2000 election cycles. It is not quite true to say that no one had a good word for front-loading—but the yea-sayers were clearly few and far between. With a remarkable degree of consensus, front-loading has been attacked by commentators and participants from both parties and across the political spectrum.

Yet as is often true with issues of this type, the problems allegedly created by front-loading have not, in general, been precisely defined or extensively documented. Since many of the proposed solutions for front-loading raise significant problems of their own, it is important to be clear about exactly how front-loading has affected the process of choosing a presidential candidate and just how serious the negative consequences associated with it are.

Consequences for Voter Learning and Decisionmaking

The principal problem with front-loading is that it greatly accelerates the voters' decision process and thus makes the whole system less deliberative, less rational, less flexible, and more chaotic. It will probably strike some readers as strange to see the American presidential nomination process described as reaching a decision too quickly. This is, after all, a system in which almost every serious presidential aspirant except an incumbent president must announce his or her candidacy in the late winter or early spring of the year preceding the election. (In fact, most contenders have been laying the groundwork for their campaigns for months or even years before the official announcement is made.) Even unsuccessful presidential candidates generally spend a full year on the campaign trail. Foreign observers of American politics, particularly those from Great Britain, are alternately amazed and appalled at the extraordinary amount of time that presidents and would-be presidents devote to campaigning instead of governing.[1]

By any reasonable standard, American presidential campaigns are very long. The problem is that too much of the campaigning occurs while none of the voters are paying attention—and too little when they finally start to become interested. To get a better sense of what the voters know about presidential candidates and when and how much they learn, consider the data presented in tables 4-1 and 4-2. In national polls conducted over the past several election cycles, CBS News and the *New York Times* have periodically queried respondents about their impressions of each of the major presidential contenders by asking, "Is your opinion of _____ favorable, unfavorable, undecided, or haven't you heard enough about _____ yet to have an opinion?" The tables show the results for the 1992 Democratic (table 4-1) and 1996 Republican (table 4-2) nomination races.[2]

A number of significant conclusions emerge from these data. First, when the period of active campaigning begins—usually several months after the midterm elections—most presidential candidates are almost entirely unknown to most of the potential electorate. This statement applies not only to those obscure nonentities with little or no previous governmental experience who somehow see fit to run for president; it is also true of people with distinguished careers as governors or senators, whom informed observers universally regarded as serious and legitimate candidates for the White House. In October 1991 more than 75 percent of all registered voters openly admitted that they did not know enough about Bill Clinton, Paul Tsongas, Bob Kerrey, or Tom Harkin to provide an evaluation of them; another 10 percent said they were "undecided."[3] Jerry Brown, who had run for president in two previous elections and served as governor of the nation's largest state, was somewhat better known. Yet even in his case, 51 percent of those surveyed said they had not heard enough about him to form an opinion.

Table 4-1   *Voter Knowledge of the 1992 Democratic Presidential
Candidates during the Invisible Primary and Primary Seasons*[a]
Percent

Candidate and date of poll	Favorable	Not favorable	Undecided	Haven't heard enough
Bill Clinton				
October 15–18, 1991	7	5	8	80
January 6–8, 1992	11	6	14	69
February 19–20, 1992	24	26	30	19
February 26–March 1, 1992	20	31	30	18
March 26–29, 1992	24	41	27	8
April 20–23, 1992	26	40	28	6
Jerry Brown				
October 15–18, 1991	11	21	15	51
January 6–8, 1992	9	26	12	52
February 19–20, 1992	8	28	22	41
February 26–March 1, 1992	8	27	21	43
March 26–29, 1992	18	31	27	24
April 20–23, 1992	15	47	20	18
Paul Tsongas				
October 15–18, 1991	6	7	8	78
January 6–8, 1992	6	10	11	73
February 19–20, 1992	28	11	25	36
February 26–March 1, 1992	25	18	25	31
March 26–29, 1992	28	21	23	26
April 20–23, 1992	25	17	26	32
Bob Kerrey				
October 15–18, 1991	8	4	11	77
January 6–8, 1992	7	7	17	69
February 19–20, 1992	10	12	25	53
February 26–March 1, 1992	11	16	26	46
Tom Harkin				
October 15–18, 1991	8	5	8	78
January 6–8, 1992	5	7	14	74
February 19–20, 1992	7	15	21	57
February 26–March 1, 1992	7	20	23	50

Source: Polls conducted by CBS/*New York Times*. Data are based on registered voters.
a. Figures show responses to the question, "Is your opinion of _____ favorable, not favorable, undecided, or haven't you heard enough about _____ yet to have an opinion?"

Similarly, as of August 1995 about 80 percent of the public had heard next to nothing about Lamar Alexander and Richard Lugar; 52 percent drew a blank on Phil Gramm. Pat Buchanan, who had run for president four years earlier and received considerable exposure as a television commentator, was unknown to about a third of the public—and another 24 percent said they were undecided about him. Only in the case of Bob

Table 4-2   *Voter Knowledge of the 1996 Republican Presidential Candidates during the Invisible Primary and Primary Seasons*[a]
Percent

Candidate and date of poll	Favorable	Not favorable	Undecided	Haven't heard enough
Bob Dole				
February 22–25, 1995	40	23	22	15
August 5–9, 1995	30	24	24	21
October 22–25, 1995	26	28	25	20
December 9–11, 1995	25	29	21	24
January 18–20, 1996	24	35	22	18
February 22–24, 1996	23	42	24	10
March 10–11, 1996	25	35	23	17
Pat Buchanan				
February 22–25, 1995	10	28	28	34
August 5–9, 1995	11	28	24	36
October 22–25, 1995	12	33	22	32
December 9–11, 1995	11	40	24	24
January 18–20, 1996	11	44	23	22
February 22–24, 1996	19	48	22	10
March 10–11, 1996	12	51	18	18
Lamar Alexander				
February 22–25, 1995	4	3	8	84
August 5–9, 1995	4	4	5	85
October 22–25, 1995	5	8	10	76
December 9–11, 1995	6	10	10	74
January 18–20, 1996	5	9	13	71
February 22–24, 1996	14	18	22	45
Phil Gramm				
February 22–25, 1995	14	13	20	52
August 5–9, 1995	12	17	19	52
October 22–25, 1995	13	22	19	45
December 9–11, 1995	12	25	20	43
January 18–20, 1996	13	26	24	37
Richard Lugar				
August 5–9, 1995	5	4	10	79
October 22–25, 1995	7	6	12	74
January 18–20, 1996	5	10	15	69
Steve Forbes				
October 22–25, 1995	8	9	14	67
December 9–11, 1995	7	10	16	67
January 18–20, 1996	14	16	23	46
February 22–24, 1996	10	37	25	28
March 10–11, 1996	14	31	22	33

Source: Polls conducted by CBS/*New York Times*. Data for February–December 1995 are based on all respondents; data for January–March 1996 are based on registered voters.

a. Figures show responses to the question, "Is your opinion of _____ favorable, not favorable, undecided, or haven't you heard enough about _____ yet to have an opinion?"

Dole, Senate majority leader and two-time presidential candidate, could a majority of the American adult population actually give the candidate a rating (favorable or unfavorable).[4]

Second, the general public learns remarkably little during the invisible primary. They do learn something: in almost every case, the number of respondents who said they had not heard enough about a candidate does decline over time. But it declines very slowly. In February 1995, 84 percent of the CBS–*New York Times* sample said they had not heard much about Lamar Alexander. By January 1996, after eleven months of almost constant campaigning, 71 percent still said they had not heard enough about Alexander to form an opinion about him. The trend is similar for Gramm, Buchanan, and Lugar—and for Brown, Harkin, Kerrey, and Tsongas in 1992. In every case, public familiarity with the candidate grew at the rate of about 1 percent per month. Of the candidates shown, only Bill Clinton in 1992 (table 4-1) and Steve Forbes in 1996 (table 4-2) were able to get their names out to a somewhat larger segment of the electorate during the invisible primary.

When the caucus and primary season finally begins, the pace of voter learning dramatically accelerates. From mid-January to mid-February, every candidate listed in tables 4-1 and 4-2 succeeded in making himself known to a substantially larger segment of the potential electorate. Yet given the low levels of information from which the public starts and the highly compressed schedule of primaries that results from front-loading, this process of educating the public, it appears, never gets all that far along. Many major presidential candidates—including Tom Harkin, Bob Kerrey, and Lamar Alexander—exit the race with almost half of all registered voters still saying that they have not heard enough about them to form an opinion.[5]

How might this situation have changed if these nomination races had not come to an end so quickly? To answer this question, we need to look at data from races that did *not* end just a few weeks after New Hampshire and on candidates who, though not initially well known, stayed in the race to the bitter end. Table 4-3 shows the public's assessment of two such candidates: Gary Hart in 1984 and Michael Dukakis in 1988. What is noteworthy about these results is how much voter learning occurred after the first round of primaries and caucuses. As of early March 1984, a week after Hart's breakthrough victory in New Hampshire—when Hart was actually leading Mondale in many national polls—fully 36 percent of likely Democratic primary voters still said they had not heard enough about

Table 4-3   *Growth of Voter Familiarity with Gary Hart in 1984 and Michael Dukakis in 1988*
Percent

Candidate and date of poll	Favorable	Not favorable	Undecided	Haven't heard enough
Gary Hart[a]				
January 14–21, 1984	6	10	13	71
February 21–25, 1984	15	15	19	50
March 5–8, 1984	37	7	19	36
March 21–24, 1984	41	12	19	28
April 23–26, 1984	36	19	26	18
June 23–28, 1984	39	19	23	18
Michael Dukakis[b]				
May 5–6, 1987	12	4	13	70
October 18–22, 1987	21	9	14	56
November 20–24, 1987	14	8	23	55
January 17–21, 1988	17	6	22	54
February 17–21, 1988	34	9	18	39
March 19–22, 1988	39	12	22	25
May 9–12, 1988	48	9	23	20
July 5–8, 1988	40	6	36	15

Source: Polls conducted by CBS/*New York Times*.

a. Figures based on registered voters, except for March 21–24, which is based on likely voters in the Democratic primary.

b. Figures based on likely voters in the Democratic primary, except for July 5–8, which is based on registered voters who identify with the Democratic Party.

Hart to form an opinion about him. Not until late April did this figure fall below 20 percent. Similarly with Dukakis: in a poll conducted immediately after the New Hampshire primary, Dukakis had a clear lead over the rest of the Democratic field—yet 39 percent of likely Democratic primary voters said they did not know enough about the Massachusetts governor to express an opinion about him. In early May, when Dukakis had all but clinched his party's nomination, 20 percent still said they had not heard much about him.

To this point, our analysis of voter learning has been limited to questions that ask the voters whether they know enough about the candidates to "have an opinion" about them. But this is, to say the least, a rather low standard against which to evaluate voter knowledge. Undoubtedly, many of those who said they had a favorable or unfavorable opinion of a particular candidate did so on the basis of only the most superficial impressions, without much solid information about the candidate's policies, past record, or personal abilities. How much do the voters know about these more substantive matters—and when do they learn it?

The best available answer to these last two questions comes from an analysis of the 1984 Democratic nomination race conducted by Henry Brady and Richard Johnston, which made use of a special national survey that interviewed about seventy-five people every week throughout the election year.[6] At one level, Brady and Johnston found that, soon after Hart's victory in New Hampshire, most survey respondents were willing to provide answers when asked about Hart's positions on the issues or his rating on various personal traits, such as intelligence, compassion, and leadership. On closer inspection, however, there was considerable reason to doubt how much the public really knew about Hart. Brady and Johnston found that evaluations of Hart, when compared with those given to better-known figures such as Reagan and Mondale, were quite unstable, varying a good deal from week to week depending on the latest news reports or recent events in the campaign. Public assessments of Hart were also, in this early period, relatively undifferentiated. Unlike Reagan and Mondale, who were seen as strong on some personal traits and weak on others, most respondents tended to give Hart uniformly good or bad ratings, no matter what specific trait or ability was being asked about.

As the campaign progressed, evaluations of Hart became more solidly grounded. That is to say, the public's view of him became both more stable and more differentiated. The progress on both dimensions, however, was fairly slow. Specifically, Brady and Johnston estimated that it would have taken twenty weeks for Hart's image to become as stable as Mondale's and thirty weeks for people to develop as differentiated an image of Hart as they held about Mondale. The problem, of course, was that the entire 1984 delegate selection season lasted just sixteen weeks.

In the end, Brady and Johnston argued that one of the major weaknesses of the presidential nomination process as it existed in 1984 was that it forced primary voters to register their judgments too quickly, before they knew much about all of the major candidates.[7] But compared with more recent nomination races, the 1984 contest actually proceeded at a quite slow and leisurely pace. The battle between Hart and Mondale lasted for about three and a half months (from the middle of February to the first week in June). By contrast, the competitive phase of the 1996 Republican race took less than one month. The Iowa caucuses were held on February 12; by March 5 most news organizations were saying the race was over. In 2000 the first showdown between Bush and McCain came in New Hampshire, on February 1. On March 9, a little more than five weeks later, McCain announced his withdrawal.

In a front-loaded system, in short, voters are forced to reach a final decision about their party's next presidential nominee in a remarkably short period of time. The evidence strongly suggests that they do so on the basis of fairly shallow and superficial knowledge about many of the top candidates—and no knowledge at all about some major contenders. Equally important, front-loading makes it all but impossible for the voters to reconsider their initial judgment if new information becomes available. In 1984 many Democrats who jumped on the Hart bandwagon moved back to Mondale once they had learned more about Hart's convoluted personal history and the specific kinds of policies he favored. In 1996 any second thoughts that Republican voters entertained about Bob Dole as he fell further and further behind Bill Clinton in the polls came after Dole had already locked up the nomination.

Poor-Quality Campaigns

Besides greatly compressing the effective decisionmaking period, front-loading also affects the quality of the campaign and thus further complicates the voters' task. During the crucial weeks immediately after New Hampshire, when most primaries are being held and the races are being decided, the campaign, according to most observers, becomes increasingly superficial and nonsubstantive.

Though it may be unrealistic to expect every primary state to get the kind of sustained attention and intensive, face-to-face campaigning that occurs in Iowa and New Hampshire, it is not unreasonable to ask that the candidates be able to campaign in just one or two states per week; it actually occurred, to a fair extent, in 1976, 1980, and 1984. If not exactly a model of deliberative democracy, a campaign of this nature at least allows the candidates some opportunity to address special state or regional concerns, hold rallies, speeches, and debates in front of local audiences, be interviewed on local television, and so on. Such activities become considerably more difficult, however, if the candidates are required to campaign in five or eight states in a single week. The role of campaign volunteers also declines as the primary schedule becomes more compressed.[8]

Concerns of this sort first became widespread in the campaign that preceded Super Tuesday in 1988. When the Southern Legislative Conference first launched its effort to organize a southern regional primary, one of its principal objectives was to force the major presidential candidates to address distinctively southern issues and interests. So far as we can tell, no one seems to believe that it actually accomplished this goal. The weeks immediately preceding Super Tuesday were frequently described as a "tarmac campaign" in which the candidates flew frenetically from one airport to another, rarely venturing beyond the parking toll gates—and thus rarely making contact with real people and their concerns.

In 2000 the campaign that preceded the March 7 extravaganza, when eleven states held their primaries, was described this way:

> The candidates are largely bypassing the small and medium-sized states and concentrating on the larger states, such as New York and California, that have the most delegates. Even there, some critics charge that the candidates don't linger long enough to create much of an impression on voters, or generate substantive debate on issues. In place of the candidates, voters in some states are seeing only their surrogates. . . . And without the candidates, voters can't press them on local issues important to them.[9]

Fred Wertheimer, former head of Common Cause, issued an even harsher judgment on the 2000 campaign: "This has been a disaster for democracy. Voters in some of these early primary states are only going to see the candidates as they pass overhead in their airplanes heading from east to west."[10]

A far-flung, multistate campaign also places a severe strain on the media who cover the candidates. As *Newsday* editor Noel Rubinton noted on the morning of March 7, 2000, "The press is struggling mightily. . . . This year's primary campaign has demanded incredible speed and juggling on the part of the press. But these same attributes are often at odds with quality reporting and constructive political discourse. . . . [Front-loading] guaranteed that the race would be a travel marathon and scheduling meltdown for the candidates, the media, and ultimately the voters."[11]

Effects on Candidate Choice: Locking in the Front-Runner

Besides making the nomination process more chaotic and less well informed, it is widely alleged that front-loading also has important consequences for the types of candidates who are ultimately nominated. Indeed, since front-loading first became a significant issue in the mid-1980s, there have actually been two quite different theories as to what type of candidate is likely to benefit from the new delegate selection calendar.

The more popular of these two theories, especially over the past several election cycles, has been that front-loading works to the advantage of the front-runner. With so many primaries and caucuses jammed together, the argument goes, the only kind of candidate who can run effectively—who can campaign in five or ten different states every week—is someone who is already well known and well financed. Someone who is not a first-tier candidate—even though he or she may be quite experienced and have a solid base of support within the party—cannot participate in what is, for all practical purposes, a national campaign.

If the results of the past several nomination races do not actually prove this theory, they are, at least, clearly consonant with its basic prediction. When the new nomination rules first went into operation in the early 1970s, one of the first and most widely accepted conclusions about the new system was that it greatly advantaged the candidacies of outsiders, insurgents, and other non-front-runners. As the political scientist Jeane Kirkpatrick put it in 1979, "In the past only a predictable number of people who established positions of leadership within the party could win. . . . The moral of the Carter and McGovern experiences is that anyone can win."[12]

Though the image of a wide-open nomination process still persists in some quarters,[13] the record speaks strongly to the contrary. While Kirkpatrick's statement was an accurate description of the way the process seemed to work in the 1970s, Jimmy Carter was, as it turned out, the last real long-shot candidate to win a presidential nomination. Without much fanfare, a system once thought to be quite favorable to outsiders and insurgents has evolved into one that almost invariably confers the presidential nomination on the preelection front-runner.

Consider, in particular, the data presented in table 4-4, in which we use two criteria to identify the front-runner in each contested nomination race since 1972: who was leading in the last national poll of party identifiers conducted before the Iowa caucuses and who had raised the most money in the year before the election. The moral is clear: whatever may have happened back in the 1970s, over the past two decades the American presidential nomination process has not been notably kind to the ambitions of long-shots and outsider candidates. Of all the candidates who have been nominated since 1976, every one of them can plausibly be regarded as, if not the front-runner, at least one of the top-tier candidates.

Table 4-4 *The Fate of Front-Runners in Contested Nomination Races,*
1972–2000

Race	Candidate leading in the last national poll taken before the Iowa caucuses	Candidate raising the most money before election year	Eventual nominee
1972 Democratic	Humphrey	n.a.[a]	McGovern
1976 Democratic	Humphrey	Wallace	Carter
1976 Republican	Ford	Reagan	Ford
1980 Democratic	Carter	Carter	Carter
1980 Republican	Reagan	Connally	Reagan
1984 Democratic	Mondale	Mondale	Mondale
1988 Democratic	Hart	Dukakis	Dukakis
1988 Republican	Bush	Bush	Bush
1992 Democratic	Clinton	Clinton	Clinton
1992 Republican	Bush	Bush	Bush
1996 Republican	Dole	Dole	Dole
2000 Democratic	Gore	Gore	Gore
2000 Republican	Bush	Bush	Bush

Source: Poll results are taken from the Gallup Poll; fund-raising totals are based on Federal Election Commission reports.

a. Accurate data on pre-election-year fund-raising are not available until the 1976 election cycle.

In eight of ten cases, one candidate was leading in both the preelection polls and the fund-raising derby—and in every such case, that candidate went on to win his party's presidential nomination. However important the Carter campaign of 1976 has been in shaping the mythology of the contemporary nomination process, nothing like it has occurred in any race since then.

We are not claiming, we want to emphasize, that front-loading is solely responsible for the increased success rate enjoyed by recent front-runners. A number of other factors are clearly at work. One, which we have developed in more detail elsewhere,[14] is simply that, after the new rules had been in operation for an election cycle or two, the candidates became more familiar with them and understood better what they had to do in order to win. Both McGovern and Carter won, in part, because they understood the new rules environment better than their principal opponents. But as this knowledge became more widely shared, other resources inevitably became more important—and front-runners, almost by definition, tended to have more of these other resources than their opponents.

But front-loading has also played an important role in producing today's front-runner-friendly nomination process. If the task confronting long-shot presidential candidates has never been easy, front-loading makes their

Table 4-5   *Pattern of Contributions Received by Front-Runner and Long-Shot Candidates in Two Contested Nomination Races, 1976 and 1984*[a]

Dollars

Time period	Amount	Percentage of total	Amount	Percentage of total
	Jimmy Carter		Henry Jackson	
January 1–December 31, 1975	957,444	16.0	2,143,703	64.7
January 1–31, 1976	123,442	2.1	112,642	3.4
February 1–29, 1976	408,356	6.8	96,749	2.9
March 1–31, 1976	590,624	9.9	363,155	11.0
April 1–30, 1976	1,055,099	17.7	466,611	14.1
May 1–31, 1976	1,394,744	23.3	95,590	2.9
June 1–30, 1976	1,447,869	24.2	33,706	1.0
Invisible primary total[b]	1,037,084	17.3	2,216,375	66.9
Delegate selection season total[c]	4,940,494	82.7	1,095,781	33.1
	Gary Hart		Walter Mondale	
January 1–December 31, 1983	1,267,351	16.3	9,453,044	62.7
January 1–31, 1984	124,652	1.6	489,543	3.2
February 1–29, 1984	342,009	4.4	800,929	5.3
March 1–31, 1984	3,031,508	38.9	1,286,862	8.5
April 1–30, 1984	1,486,893	19.1	1,066,169	7.1
May 1–31, 1984	912,466	11.7	1,167,299	7.7
June 1–30, 1984	632,144	8.1	810,681	5.4
Invisible primary total[b]	1,616,078	20.7	10,467,334	69.4
Delegate selection season total[c]	6,180,945	79.3	4,607,193	30.6

Source: Compiled from Federal Election Commission reports.

a. Figures include all contributions and transfers from other committees but not loans or federal matching funds.

b. In 1976 invisible primary total includes all contributions received through January 20, 1976. In 1984 it includes all contributions received through February 19, 1984.

c. In 1976 delegate selection season total includes all contributions received between January 21 and June 30, 1976. In 1984 it includes all contributions received between February 20 and June 30, 1984.

lives even more difficult, in at least two major ways: it makes it more difficult for non-front-running candidates to maintain a reliable flow of campaign funds, and it greatly increases the organizational demands upon the non-front-runners.

The Flow of Campaign Funds

The figures in table 4-5 show the total amount of contributions to the campaigns of Jimmy Carter and Henry Jackson, during the 1976 election cycle, and Gary Hart and Walter Mondale, during the 1984 election cycle, broken down by the time period in which the money was received. As befits a long-shot candidate, Carter raised a relatively small amount of money in the year before the election: $957,000, as compared with $2.1 million for Henry Jackson (and $2.9 million for George Wallace). But Carter's inability to raise a lot of money early in the election cycle did not prove to be an insurmountable obstacle to his eventual success. The Carter campaign's fund-raising strategy—in fact, their strategy for dealing with just about every important resource—was to start small and build on their early successes. They did have enough money to wage a vigorous campaign in Iowa and New Hampshire, and if successful there, they believed, they could then raise the money necessary to contest the next round of primaries, which, if they kept winning, would allow them to raise more money for still later primaries, and so on through the final primaries and on into the convention.

To a remarkable extent, the Carter campaign was able to make this strategy work. So, to a lesser extent, was Gary Hart in 1984, another long-shot candidate whose campaign caught fire in the early going. As table 4-5 indicates, the fund-raising pattern of these two candidates was quite different from that of Henry Jackson and Walter Mondale, both of whom were among the front-runners for their party's nomination. Whereas Jackson and Mondale raised most of their money up front, before any of the caucuses or primaries had taken place, the long-shot candidates raised most of their money during the primary season.

What needs to be emphasized is that to raise money in this way, Carter and Hart needed a delegate selection calendar that began in a reasonably slow and gradual manner. In Carter's case, his first significant win came in the Iowa caucuses on January 21.[15] He then had five full weeks to reap the financial benefits of that victory before the next major contest, the New Hampshire primary, which took place on February 24. There was just one primary per week in the four weeks after New Hampshire, and only one of those (the Florida primary on March 9) was really central to Carter's plans. Two major primaries were held on April 6—but then nothing in the two weeks after that. At every stage of the primary and caucus season, in short, Carter had time to raise money from contributors who were impressed by his latest triumph and then apply that money to the next round of primaries.

Front-loading, by contrast, imparts a very different rhythm to the nomination race. Now, a long-shot candidate who wins in Iowa or New Hampshire has little time to raise all of the money that is necessary for waging even a minimally competitive campaign in the dense cluster of primaries that comes immediately after New Hampshire. Given the $1,000 limit that federal law imposed on individual contributions (at least up through 2000), fund-raising in a presidential nomination race is almost inevitably a slow and labor-intensive process. Given that reality, it is almost impossible, in a period of one or two weeks, to raise a large amount of money, deposit it in the bank, and then actually spend it in a productive way.[16]

For a revealing illustration of how front-loading can wreak havoc on the finances of a long-shot candidate, consider the case of Lamar Alexander in 1996.[17] For a candidate who never received more than 4 percent of the vote in the national polls, Alexander put together an exceptionally strong financial team, including six of the past seven Republican National Finance Committee chairs. With a lot of effort, that team managed to raise $11.5 million in 1995. The 1996 race also required a great deal of early spending, however; and by the beginning of the delegate selection season, Alexander would later write, "we were running on empty."[18]

All of that early campaigning finally paid off, however, in Iowa. In the final week before the caucuses, Gramm and Forbes both faded and Alexander finished third—or, as the media almost always described it, "a strong and surprising third." Suddenly, Alexander was a hot story on television and in the newspapers, with a real prospect of winning in New Hampshire. In the first four days after the Iowa caucuses, according to one newspaper tracking poll, Alexander's vote in New Hampshire jumped from 5 percent to 18 percent.[19] Equally important, the Iowa results breathed new life into the campaign's finances. Beginning three days after Iowa, Alexander has written, "contributions started rolling into our Nashville headquarters at the rate of $100,000 a day *without events.*"[20]

Unfortunately, this money came too late to do Alexander any good in New Hampshire: any television ads that would run on the Saturday, Sunday, or Monday before the primary had to have been purchased by Friday. The result was that Alexander was largely absent from the airwaves in the final days of the New Hampshire campaign. Bob Dole, as the frontrunner, was not so financially strapped, and he used his money to run a series of ads attacking Alexander. According to reports later filed with the Federal Election Commission, the Dole campaign spent $459,000 in New Hampshire during February, as compared with just $94,000 for Alexander. Dole's ads did exactly what they were supposed to do, blunting Alexander's momentum just enough so that he finished third, seventy-six hundred votes behind Dole.

Even after its disappointing finish in New Hampshire, the Alexander campaign continued to raise money at the rate of $100,000 a day. But impressive as that figure might have been under other circumstances, it simply was not enough to allow Alexander to run a competitive campaign in the highly front-loaded calendar of 1996, in which twenty-one states held their presidential primaries in the three weeks after New Hampshire. At one point, the Alexander high command estimated that it needed $2.6 million to keep itself going during these three weeks.[21] But $100,000 a day over a three-week period comes up a half million dollars short of this figure.[22] The result was that Dole continued to outspend Alexander whenever his campaign felt the need to do so. In the critical South Carolina primary, for example, Dole spent $685,000 during February and March, as against Alexander's $250,000. As it turned out, Alexander was never a serious factor in any primary after New Hampshire. On March 6, he withdrew from the race.

The moral of this story should be clear: In a front-loaded system, there just is not enough time to win in Iowa or New Hampshire and then raise the money for the next round of primaries. To take advantage of an early breakthrough, a candidate has to have assembled a large war chest before Iowa; and given the federal contribution limits, long-shot candidates can rarely do this. The result in recent years has been that whenever a non-front-runner has won (or done better than expected) in Iowa and New Hampshire, he has usually found himself significantly outspent and out-campaigned by the front-runner in the next round of primaries. This, in brief, is what happened to Dick Gephardt in 1988, Paul Tsongas in 1992, and Lamar Alexander in 1996.

The only non-front-runner in the past several election cycles who managed to beat the front-loading money trap was John McCain. The pattern of McCain's fund-raising during the 2000 nomination race is shown in table 4-6. During the invisible primary, McCain's fund-raising was good, though not spectacular. In 1999 and the first month of 2000, the Arizona senator raised $18.1 million, including almost $2 million that he transferred from his Senate campaign committee. Like Lamar Alexander in 1996, however, McCain found that a contemporary presidential nomination campaign requires a great deal of early spending. Even after receiving more than $2 million in federal matching funds, by the end of January 2000 the McCain campaign had only $350,000 left in its treasury. Then on February 1 McCain beat George Bush in the New Hampshire primary by 18 percentage points. Late that evening, money began pouring into the McCain campaign.

Table 4-6 *Contributions Received by the 2000 John McCain Presidential Campaign, by Time Period*
Dollars

Time period	Amount[a]	Percentage of total
January 1–December 31, 1999	15,585,522	50.4
January 1–31, 2000	2,525,256	8.2
February 1–29, 2000	11,171,953	36.1
March 1–31, 2000	1,653,307	5.3
Invisible primary total[b]	18,110,778	58.5
Primary season total[c]	12,825,260	41.5

Source: Compiled from Federal Election Commission reports.
a. Figures include all contributions and transfers from other committees but not loans or federal matching funds.
b. Includes all contributions received through January 31, 2000. New Hampshire primary was held on February 1.
c. Includes all contributions received between February 1 and March 31, 2000. McCain withdrew from the race on March 9.

Contemporary news reports almost always credited the Internet with enabling McCain to raise so much money so quickly.[23] Shortly after McCain was declared the winner of the New Hampshire primary at 7:00 P.M., according to campaign officials, contributions began flooding into the campaign website at the rate of $20,000 an hour. Hoping to stoke the fires, over the next few days the McCain campaign issued regular reports about how much they had raised over the Internet: $162,000 by early Wednesday morning, $500,000 by Wednesday evening, $1.2 million by Thursday night, $2.2 million in the first week. The pace of Internet donations slowed rather substantially after that (as did press coverage of the phenomenon), but according to the campaign's web manager, McCain raised more than $4 million on the Internet in the month after the New Hampshire primary.[24] Because most of this money came in relatively small donations (the average size was apparently between $110 and $120), that $4 million probably brought in another $2.5 million to $3 million in federal matching funds.

As the figures in table 4-6 indicate, McCain also raised a good deal of money offline during this period. In fact, if the $4 million figure is correct, only about 35 percent of McCain's total fund-raising in the critical month of February 2000 came through his website. But as the preceding discussion should make clear, the principal challenge in a front-loaded system is to raise money quickly, and several features of the Internet may have helped McCain meet this test. First, the campaign website provided a single, easily accessible location for those who considered contributing. (As a further assist to potential donors, McCain mentioned his web address in virtually every interview he gave during this period.) Second, the Internet allowed the McCain campaign to make use of the new contributions much more rapidly than would have been possible had the money been raised in a more traditional fashion. When previous New Hampshire winners had tried to raise money immediately after their victories, they typically had to wait for the donor to write a check and mail it into the campaign, then had to deposit the check in a bank and wait for it to clear. Internet contributions, by contrast, were made by credit card and thus went directly into the campaign treasury, where they could then be spent on advertising, organization, and so on.[25]

So perhaps the Internet will allow future long-shot candidates to reap the financial rewards of an early breakthrough in Iowa or New Hampshire more effectively than Hart, Gephardt, Tsongas, or Alexander did. Yet before we declare that the revolution is here and it works, it is worth calling attention to a number of special features of the 2000 McCain campaign that may not be present for other candidates. First, McCain had the media spotlight pretty much to himself during February: Bush was already a fairly well known quantity, and Gore's narrow win in New Hampshire and a convenient five-week gap in the Democratic schedule guaranteed that nothing much was happening in the other party to compete for the press's attention. By contrast, Gephardt, Tsongas, and Alexander all found that other significant stories were developing in the weeks after their initial breakthrough.[26] Second, McCain himself had an unusually compelling personal story and especially good relations with the media. Finally, as has been shown in chapter 2, New Hampshire's late decision to schedule its primary on February 1 meant that the 2000 primary and caucus calendar was significantly less front-loaded than the one the Republicans had employed in 1996. Even with the Internet and everything else going for him, McCain might have been hard pressed to raise enough money to cope with the calendar that had confronted Lamar Alexander in 1996, when thirteen primaries were held in the first two weeks after New Hampshire. As it was, McCain faced just two primaries in the two weeks after New Hampshire, one of which (Delaware) he chose not to contest.

Organizational Demands

Running for president has always been something of an organizational nightmare, requiring every campaign to navigate its way through fifty-one distinct delegate selection events, each with its own set of laws, rules, customs, and constituencies.[27] When the primaries and caucuses were concentrated near the end of the delegate selection season, however, these tasks were considerably more manageable, for the simple reason that they did not all have to be confronted at once. In organization as in fund-raising, second-tier candidates had the luxury of starting small. In the early stages of the campaign, they needed to be organized in only a small number of states: Iowa, New Hampshire, and perhaps three or four other states with early primaries. If successful in these early events, the non-front-running campaign would then have time to organize and prepare for later primaries. This, in particular, was the pattern of the Carter campaign in 1976.

Front-loading forces candidates to adopt an early battle plan that is considerably more ambitious. Given the current shape of the delegate selection calendar, every candidate who hopes to do well in Iowa or New Hampshire must also be prepared, the moment the votes in New Hampshire have been counted, to run a full-scale national campaign. While this sudden transformation poses a number of challenges for a campaign, it puts an especially severe strain on the campaign organization. Grassroots organizations, of the kind that do door-to-door campaigning or conduct get-out-the-vote drives, simply cannot be put together overnight. If they do not already exist on the day before New Hampshire, they will almost certainly never get established. Though every presidential campaign conducted in a nation of 200 million eligible voters must inevitably rely to a great extent on the mass media, front-loading makes the nomination phase of the campaign even more media centered and, thus, more remote from the typical voter.

From the perspective of a presidential campaign (which is not the only relevant perspective), establishing an extensive grassroots organization is helpful but probably not essential. A candidate who is receiving lots of favorable coverage in the media or advertising heavily on television may be able to win a primary or caucus even if he or she has little or no on-the-ground presence in a state.[28] But certain other organizational tasks cannot be ignored or sloughed off on the media. In particular, every presidential campaign must make sure that it meets two important requirements in every major primary state.

First, the candidate must actually be listed on the ballot. Though write-in campaigns are not unheard of in presidential nomination races, it is obviously much easier to win votes if the candidate's name appears on the official ballot.[29] What a candidate must do to qualify for a primary ballot varies from state to state. In about 40 percent of the states, most candidates are automatically granted ballot access: a state or party official is required, by law, to put together a list of the "major" or "nationally recognized" candidates seeking a party's presidential nomination and then to include all of them on the primary ballot.[30] There remain, however, a considerable number of states in which campaigns must take a more active role in securing ballot access: filing a petition with a few thousand signatures or paying a qualifying fee, and sometimes both. Though such requirements are generally not very onerous, the important point is that the filing deadlines usually occur several months before the primary.[31] Table 4-7 shows two calendars for the 1996 Republican nomination contest: the calendar of primaries and the calendar of filing deadlines. As this table indicates, by the time the New Hampshire primary took place on February 20, the filing deadlines in thirty other states had already passed. For second-tier and long-shot candidates, who are generally short of funds and staff, meeting these filing requirements is at least a nuisance and sometimes a major burden.

Though most second-tier candidates do manage to make it onto the ballot in almost every state, many fail to surmount a second hurdle: filing delegate slates. The problem here is a rather technical one (though no less important for that) and concerns how states that hold presidential primaries actually choose specific persons to serve as national convention delegates. In many states, the presidential preference vote in the primary is used to allocate delegates among the candidates—but the choosing of the individual delegates does not actually take place until several months later, at a state or district convention or a caucus of the candidate's supporters. In other states, however, the rules require each candidate to have a complete list of potential delegates put together before the primary takes place.

The necessity of filing delegate slates before the primary is particularly associated with states that use the so-called direct election method for selecting their delegates. Under a direct election system, the voters first generally vote for one of the presidential candidates in the presidential preference or "beauty contest" line on the ballot. But this vote, though it is usually the one the media focus on, plays no role in selecting delegates. That takes place on a second part of the ballot, where all of the individual candidates for national convention delegate are listed, along with the candidate each supports, and the delegates are voted on and elected as individuals. To win the maximum number of delegates in a direct election primary, then, a presidential campaign must file a full slate of delegate

Table 4-7   *Calendar of Republican Presidential Primaries and Filing Deadlines, 1996*

Date	Calendar of presidential primaries	Calendar of filing deadlines[a]
November 30, 1995		RHODE ISLAND
December 1		MAINE
December 15		NEW HAMPSHIRE
December 22		Georgia
December 26		Maryland
		SOUTH DAKOTA
December 29		NORTH DAKOTA
December 31		SOUTH CAROLINA
January 2, 1996		COLORADO
		Oregon
		Tennessee
		TEXAS
January 4		NEW YORK
January 5		Massachusetts
January 10		OKLAHOMA
January 11		Florida
January 12		California
		LOUISIANA
		Michigan
January 15		Mississippi
		VERMONT
January 17		ILLINOIS
January 18		ARIZONA
		Washington
January 19		Connecticut
		OHIO
January 30		KENTUCKY
		Wisconsin
February 3		WEST VIRGINIA
February 6		North Carolina
February 13		PENNSYLVANIA
February 20	New Hampshire	
February 24	Delaware	
February 27	Arizona	INDIANA
	North Dakota	
	South Dakota	
March 2	South Carolina	
March 5	Colorado	
	Connecticut	
	Georgia	
	Maine	
	Maryland	
	Massachusetts	

(continues)

Table 4-7   *Calendar of Republican Presidential Primaries and Filing Deadlines, 1996 (Continued)*

Date	Calendar of presidential primaries	Calendar of filing deadlines[a]
	Rhode Island	
	Vermont	
March 7, 1996	New York	DISTRICT OF COLUMBIA
March 12	Florida	
	Louisiana	
	Mississippi	
	Oklahoma	
	Oregon	
	Tennessee	
	Texas	
March 13		Nebraska
March 15		ALABAMA
March 16		New Mexico
March 19	Illinois	
	Michigan	
	Ohio	
	Wisconsin	
March 26	California	
	Nevada	
	Washington	
March 29		Idaho
April 2		ARKANSAS
April 11		NEW JERSEY
April 23	Pennsylvania	
May 7	District of Columbia	
	Indiana	
	North Carolina	
May 14	Nebraska	
	West Virginia	
May 21	Arkansas	
May 28	Idaho	
	Kentucky	
June 4	Alabama	
	New Jersey	
	New Mexico	

Source: Compiled from information in *Congressional Quarterly Weekly Report*, August 19, 1995, pp. 2477–604; and Republican National Committee, *Delegate Allocation and Selection Procedures for the 1996 Republican National Convention* (Washington: November 1995).

a. States listed in capital letters are those that do not include major or nationally recognized candidates on the ballot automatically.

candidates. If the campaign neglects to run delegates pledged to its candidate in a particular district, they cannot win delegates in that district—no matter how well they do in the presidential preference vote.

According to most of the campaign professionals we spoke with, putting together a delegate slate is a substantially greater challenge than getting a presidential candidate listed on the primary ballot. Particularly in the larger states, assembling a delegate slate requires a campaign to identify from several dozen to several hundred persons, all of whom must be reliable supporters of the candidate and residents of the state or congressional district in which they are running.[32] Some attention must also be given to questions of racial, ethnic, or other types of diversity (Democratic national rules actually mandate that each candidate's slates be equally divided between men and women), as well as to making sure that nothing in the delegates' personal histories could prove embarrassing to the campaign. All campaigns must grapple with these complexities; but frontrunners, who generally have more money and name recognition and more support from party and elected officials, are obviously in a much stronger position to do so.

The best example of a campaign that failed to meet the challenge of filing full delegate slates—and suffered for its failure—is the Hart campaign in 1984. As noted in the previous chapter, front-loading probably hurt the Mondale campaign as it attempted to come back from its unexpected loss in New Hampshire. But front-loading also provided Mondale with one compensating advantage. In the month and a half immediately after the New Hampshire primary, there was a succession of big-state primaries—including Florida, Illinois, and Pennsylvania—all of which used the direct election system for selecting delegates. Because of their position in the calendar, the deadline for filing delegate slates in each of these states came before the New Hampshire primary, when Hart was still limping along at 1 percent in the national polls and his campaign was struggling just to stay afloat. The upshot was that in every one of these states, the Hart campaign was unable to file complete delegate slates—and thus won significantly fewer delegates than it might have in a less front-loaded system.

Florida provides a particularly good illustration of the problems the Hart campaign encountered. According to state law, Hart, Mondale, and all the other presidential contenders were supposed to file delegate slates in each of Florida's nineteen congressional districts. The Mondale campaign did so; but the Hart organization was unable to field a single candidate for delegate in eight districts and had incomplete slates in five others. To compensate for these deficiencies, the Hart campaign tried, in the final week, to "adopt" some of Reubin Askew's delegates (Askew had withdrawn from the race a few days earlier), but this remedy proved only partially successful. In the end, Hart beat Mondale 39 percent to 33 percent in the preference vote—but it was Mondale who scored a plurality of the delegates, winning sixty-one to Hart's fifty-two (nine others were uncommitted).[33] Though there is no simple way to determine what would have happened if Hart had filed a full set of delegate slates (a number of complicated judgments are required), our best estimate is that the delegate count would have been Hart eighty-five, Mondale thirty-four.[34]

The pattern is similar in Illinois. The Land of Lincoln had at that time twenty-two congressional districts. Hart filed complete delegate slates in just seven of them; he filed partial slates in three others. We estimate that, had Hart filed full slates, he probably would have won twenty-one more delegates in Illinois, Mondale twenty fewer. Given how close the 1984 nomination race turned out to be—when Mondale finally declared victory on the day after the last round of primaries, he had just seven more delegates than the minimum number needed for nomination—these discrepancies are not trivial.

The good news for Democrats is that the difficulties associated with filing delegate slates have been greatly reduced. In 1996 the Democrats added a provision to their national delegate selection rules that requires states using presidential primaries to allocate delegates according to the presidential preference vote and specifically allows candidates who have not filed full slates before the primary to choose any additional delegates they are entitled to through a "special post-primary procedure."[35] But nothing similar exists in the Republican Party, where direct election primaries continue to pose a substantial burden for the non-front-runners.

There is, in the end, a certain irony in criticizing the presidential nomination process on the grounds that it is too favorable to front-runners. Not so many years ago, most commentators (including most political scientists) were attacking the process for precisely the opposite reason: that it did not do enough to advance the candidacies of the nationally known and those with long records of service to the parties, that it gave too much of an advantage to the outsider and the insurgent. Yet the contradiction between these two viewpoints may be more apparent than real.

On the one hand, there is much to be said for a system that does not deliberately stack the deck in favor of outsiders and insurgents, as seemed to be the case with the nomination process of the 1970s. The presidency of Jimmy Carter, in particular, could not help but raise questions about the wisdom of giving a major-party presidential nomination to someone who had been almost entirely unknown to most voters—and even to a substantial segment of his own party's leadership—just twelve months earlier.

So not all front-runners are bad. Indeed, many become front-runners for the eminently sensible reason that they have spent years earning the trust and support of other party leaders. A nomination process that favors front-runners, then, is not the worst thing in the world.

Yet there is, we think, some happy medium between a system that nominates Carter-type candidates and one that poses so many difficult, perhaps insurmountable obstacles to the non-front-runners. Our argument, simply put, is that not all front-runners are the best possible nominees or would make the best possible presidents. Sometimes candidates become front-runners simply because they are flamboyant or famous or controversial or because they happened to do well in the last nominating cycle. What a good nomination process requires—and the present system seems to lack—is some measure of flexibility: some capacity to question and test the front-runner, to ask if he or she really is the right person for the circumstances facing the party and the country, to ensure that the front-runner is not nominated merely by virtue of being the front-runner. And the more front-loaded the system becomes, the more it loses this flexibility.

Effects on Candidate Choice:
The Case of the Unstoppable Momentum

All the evidence we have to date, then, suggests that front-loading tends to help the front-runner. But a second possibility has also been entertained by a number of commentators: that in some circumstances, front-loading might propel a little-known outsider all the way to his or her party's nomination, before the public or the press has any real opportunity to learn much about the candidate or to conduct a thorough assessment of his or her strengths and weaknesses.

The sort of scenario these commentators have in mind is, in many ways, quite familiar: A candidate with little previous exposure in national politics somehow manages to pull off an upset victory in the New Hampshire primary. (Certainly, if we have learned anything about the New Hampshire primary over the years, it is that the results rarely turn out the way we expect.) Suddenly, this candidate is the hottest thing in American politics—a fresh face with, at least for the moment, no blemishes. Eventually, of course, this early glow will start to fade: The media will do more detailed and more balanced reporting about the character and record of the candidate; the candidate's errors and shortcomings will come out (every candidate has them); his or her opponents will begin to counterattack. The problem, under a heavily front-loaded system, is that this new information, these second thoughts, may come too late. By the time the doubts set in, the new candidate may already have locked up the nomination.

Lest the scenario just described be dismissed as entirely fanciful, consider the candidacy of Gary Hart in the Democratic nomination race of 1984. As is well known, Hart went from an asterisk to a front-runner in essentially eight days (for a few of the relevant details, see the top panel in table 3-3). After finishing a quite distant second in the Iowa caucuses, just a few percentage points ahead of George McGovern, he received a huge wave of publicity and press attention that enabled him to come from far behind in the polls and post a comfortable win in New Hampshire.[36] Quite suddenly, the entire Democratic race was turned upside down: Hart was now the front-runner, and the previously unstoppable Mondale campaign was close to collapse.

Eventually, Mondale recovered, won a string of important primaries, and went on to become the party nominee. But—and this is the key point— it took time. As one media scholar has concluded about the press's behavior in the first few weeks after Iowa, "Hart's coverage [during this period] was virtually free of any harsh criticism, unflattering issues, or cynical commentary."[37] Indeed, it was not until about a week and a half after New Hampshire that the initial infatuation with Hart began to wear off. Fortunately for Mondale, under the 1984 delegate selection calendar, he did have at least a little bit of time. In the week immediately following the New Hampshire primary, there was just one Democratic caucus and a single, nonbinding presidential primary. Five more primaries were held in the week after that, but two were in states (Alabama and Georgia) that were unusually strong for Mondale.

Mondale also benefited from a quirk in the way the media reported the results of the March 13 delegate selection events. In addition to the five primaries that took place that day, there were also four state caucuses— but the caucuses all occurred in the West, which meant that their results were not available until after most of the late-night news programs had concluded and most of the major eastern newspapers (including the *New York Times* and the *Washington Post*) had already gone to press. As it turned out, Hart won all four of these caucuses, meaning that he actually won seven of the nine contests on Super Tuesday. But most major news outlets, having only the primary results to work with, reported a fairly balanced and competitive outcome—three wins for Hart, two for Mondale—which seemed to give credence to the Mondale campaign's claims that they were finally starting to slow down Hart's momentum and mount a comeback.[38]

And so, barely, Mondale managed to hang on. But what if the primary calendar had been more front-loaded? What if, as in the 1996 Republican race, there had been four primaries in the week immediately after the New Hampshire primary and nine more in the week after that? A strong case can be made that under this sort of calendar, Hart would have wracked up enough victories in the two weeks after New Hampshire to establish a commanding lead in the delegate count and compel Mondale to withdraw from the race.

This "outsider breakthrough" scenario is, to date, entirely hypothetical. And for reasons developed in the previous section, riding a wave of momentum all the way through to the nomination is not, in the end, as simple as it sounds. But enough candidates have come close to suggest that this possibility needs to be taken seriously—especially because its implications are so plainly troubling.[39] Whatever may be said against individual front-runners, the length of the invisible primary generally guarantees that they will have received at least some measure of public and media scrutiny by the time the first delegates are selected. Long-shot and outsider candidates, by contrast, are much less well known—not only to voters but often also to the reporters who are supposed to cover them. Whatever one's preferences in the Hart-Mondale contest, it is clear that there were a number of serious questions concerning Gary Hart's capacity both as a candidate and as a potential president. Perhaps, as many of Hart's supporters claimed, none of his personal problems would have prevented him from being an effective president. Though we are inclined to disagree with this assertion, we are more emphatic in defending a more limited claim: that the voters did at least have a right to know about these matters before casting their ballots. This, of course, is the same point made earlier in this chapter: that a good presidential selection process ought to allow for second thoughts, for reconsideration, for the possibility that initial impressions may be wrong. And the more front-loaded the system becomes, the less opportunity we all have to do this.

The "Entry Fee" and Candidate Attrition

Up to this point, we have discussed the ways that front-loading affects voter choice among the announced presidential candidates. Front-loading also constrains the voters' options in another important way: by limiting the number of candidates who get into the race at all. If candidates cannot count on raising the money they need after the Iowa caucuses and New Hampshire primary, the logical corollary is that they need to have raised a great deal of money before the delegate selection season begins—and that candidates who cannot raise money in such large quantities may simply decide not to run. In the lead-up to both the 1996 and 2000 nomination races, it was widely argued—by both participants and pundits—that to have any chance of running a competitive campaign, a candidate had to raise between $20 million and $25 million before a single delegate was selected.[40] Though this figure was only an estimate, this is a case in which the perception may be as important as the reality, scaring off candidates who believe they cannot raise this sum of money.

Two points are worth noting about this "entry fee." First, only two types of candidates can generally be expected to raise such money in advance of actually winning a few primaries: wealthy, self-financed candidates, like Steve Forbes, and well-connected political insiders, such as George Bush, Phil Gramm, Bob Dole, and Al Gore. Second, political money is a finite resource, so only a few candidates in any given election cycle will be able to reach such heights of fund-raising. Before the recent changes in the federal contribution limits, one Republican fund-raiser had estimated that the current system required a candidate to find a minimum of eighteen thousand contributors, each of whom would give $1,000, from a donor pool of no more than fifty thousand possible contributors.[41] Several putative Republican candidates in the 2000 election cycle testified that Bush's fund-raising success was less important for the use Bush made of it than for the way it sucked money out of the political world like a vacuum sucking air out of a sealed room. Lamar Alexander, for one, argued that "the problem is not that Bush has raised too much, it's that nobody else can raise enough to compete."[42]

Consequently, many candidates who two decades ago could have made a viable, if not successful, run for their party's nomination are now pre-emptively driven from the race. Some prospective candidates, calculating the improbability that they will be able to reach the minimum threshold for competitiveness, simply stand aside from the outset. Others make the effort, find their situation hopeless, and quickly remove themselves from the race.

A number of factors enter into a potential candidate's decision to get into or stay out of a presidential nomination race, so it is difficult to say for certain how many candidates were kept out of the contest just because of front-loading. But both parties' experience in the 2000 nomination races is surely sufficient to set off some alarm bells. On the Democratic side, the long- and well-established tradition is that whenever a Democratic president is not running for reelection (and sometimes, even when one is), there is always a large and vigorous field of contenders. In 2000, by contrast, Al Gore had just one opponent: former New Jersey senator Bill Bradley. So far as we can determine, there is no other case in the history of the Democratic Party in which an open-seat presidential nomination race attracted just two candidates. Perhaps this was because, as the incumbent vice president, Gore was seen as a prohibitive favorite, with so much support from the party leadership.

Yet it is worth noting that, in late 1998 and early 1999, when a number of other Democrats were debating whether to get into the race, there was a widespread perception that while Gore brought a number of strengths to the campaign, he also had a number of shortcomings. He was generally regarded as a wooden and uninspiring campaigner, and he had been tarnished by the Clinton fund-raising scandals. It is also instructive to compare Gore's experience with that of George H. W. Bush when he sought his party's nomination as the incumbent vice president in 1988. Unlike Gore, Bush had five major opponents, including the Senate minority leader (Bob Dole), a former secretary of state (Alexander Haig), a former congressman and governor (Pete DuPont), and a congressman who had coauthored the Reagan tax cut and was a favorite of the conservative movement (Jack Kemp).

On the Republican side, a much larger number of candidates got into the 2000 race, in the sense that they publicly declared their intention to seek the Republican presidential nomination. But an unusually large number—six of the twelve announced candidates—also exited the race months before the first caucuses were held in Iowa. Among the early retirees were a number of candidates who clearly deserved a more extended hearing, including Lamar Alexander, Elizabeth Dole, House Budget Committee chair John Kasich, and former vice president Dan Quayle.

Compromised Participation

When the McGovern-Fraser Commission first launched the effort to rewrite the rules of the presidential nomination process in the late 1960s, it did so on the basis of an apparent mandate to "give all Democratic voters a full, meaningful, and timely opportunity to participate in the selection of delegates, and, thereby, in the decisions of the Convention itself."[43] Thirty years later, one of the most widely criticized features of the system the reformers spawned is precisely its effect on the extent and quality of voter participation.

As the primary and caucus calendar has become more front-loaded, it has become routine for nomination races to be settled in the early spring. Even with front-loading, this means that lots of states select their delegates at a time when everything of significance has already been decided. In 1996 Robert Dole was widely declared to have a lock on the Republican nomination after winning all eight of the primaries that were held on March 5.[44] All of his major opponents except Pat Buchanan had withdrawn by March 14; Dole finally secured a mathematical majority of his party's national convention delegates on March 26. Depending on which of these dates one chooses to emphasize, at least twelve—and possibly as many as twenty-five—states voted after the race was already over. In 2000 twenty-five states held their primaries after both Bradley and McCain had officially withdrawn.

What effect does this sort of early closure have on voter participation rates? To answer this question, table 4-8 shows voter participation rates in the 1996 and 2000 presidential primaries, broken down by the date on which the primaries were held.[45] Once again, New Hampshire emerges as a special case. If the Granite State's voters receive an extraordinary amount of attention from the candidates and the media, they at least appear to recognize the significance of the role they have been assigned and turn out at a far higher rate than occurs in almost every other state.

Putting New Hampshire aside, voter turnout rates declined as the primary season progressed in two of the three races examined in table 4-8. In the 2000 Republican race, those primaries held from February 8 to March 7 attracted, on average, about 26 percent of the potential Republican electorate to the polls. For primaries held after John McCain's withdrawal on March 9, the average turnout was 16 percent. In 1996 average Republican turnout fell from 22 percent in primaries held from February 24 to March 2, to 18 percent in primaries held during the remainder of March, and then to 14 percent in the April, May, and June primaries. In the 2000 Democratic contest, by contrast, there was essentially no difference in turnout between those states that voted while Bill Bradley was still actively contesting the race and those that voted after Bradley's withdrawal.

Table 4-8   *Average Presidential Primary Turnout by Date,*
1996 and 2000
Units as indicated

Date	Average turnout (percentage)	Number of states
1996 Republican primaries		
February 20 (New Hampshire)	42	1
February 24–March 2	22	5
March 5–26	18	22
April 23–June 4	14	12
2000 Republican primaries		
February 1 (New Hampshire)	52	1
February 8–29	26	6
March 7	26	11
After March 9	16	23
2000 Democratic primaries		
February 1 (New Hampshire)	40	1
March 7	17	11
After March 9	16	22

Perhaps most voters had concluded that the Democratic race was effectively over well before March 7.[46]

In two of three cases, then, the early ending of the presidential nomination race led to a decline in voter participation rates of between 35 and 40 percent in states holding later primaries. Large as this decline may be, it is, from another perspective, surprising that the drop-off was not larger. Given the general difficulty of persuading Americans to vote in elections that matter, why would 15 percent of the eligible voters go to the polls in an election that is apparently meaningless? The answer has to do with what else occurs on the same day as the presidential primary. When states hold their presidential primaries in February or early March, they generally use these elections for the sole purpose of choosing a presidential candidate. Candidates for Congress and for state offices are selected at a second primary, usually held during the summer or early fall. By contrast, states that hold their presidential primaries in April, May, and June usually pick their candidates for other offices at the same time. In 1996, for example, of the fourteen states that held their presidential primaries before March 7, just one (Maryland) used that primary to nominate candidates for Congress. By contrast, of the eleven states that voted after March 26, all but the

District of Columbia also used this primary to select their state and congressional candidates.

So to the question, why would 24 percent of the West Virginia Republican electorate go to the polls in mid-May 1996 to participate in a presidential nomination contest that had been decided a month and a half earlier, the answer is that it probably was not the presidential race that drew them to the polls. Their principal motivation for voting, one suspects, was to help select the party's state and congressional candidates. They cast a vote in the presidential primary because it was at the top of the ballot and involved little or no additional effort.

The Interregnum

One final problem associated with front-loading, though less serious than the others examined here, deserves some attention. Much of the current presidential nominating machinery was designed with the assumption that the nomination contests would continue, if not all the way to the convention, at least through the late spring. As was seen in the previous chapter, however, one clear consequence of front-loading has been to push up the date on which contemporary nomination races get settled, from early June to early March. The result has been to create a peculiar "interregnum"—a period of up to five months during which two persons have become the de facto but not de jure nominees of their parties.

In a purely technical sense, one could argue that this interregnum period is a result not of front-loading per se but of when the primary and caucus calendar begins. That is to say, if both parties were to adopt a rule stating that no primary or caucus could be held before May 1, the resulting system would be just as front-loaded as it is today (in fact, probably even more so), but the interregnum would largely disappear, because the nomination races would now get settled in the first half of June, just a few weeks before the first national convention.[47] Yet it is undeniably the case that the interregnum problem did not exist before front-loading and would almost certainly go away if front-loading could be substantially reversed.

However one chooses to assign the blame for it, the increasingly lengthy period between the effective conclusion of the nomination races and the start of the national conventions poses a number of problems for one or both campaigns. Throughout the 2000 election year, a project emanating out of Harvard University issued regular press releases claiming to find evidence that the late spring and early summer campaign was boring voters and thus depressing turnout in the general election.[48] In fact, though voter interest in the 2000 campaign clearly did decline after the nomination races were settled, there is no reason to think that this has dysfunctional consequences for the political system as a whole or even for the fall campaign, any more than the National Football League is hurt because fans pay no attention during the off-season. A better interpretation of this finding is that it simply shows that voters are reasonable creatures who pay attention to campaigns when something exciting is happening and when the knowledge they acquire from the campaign may actually do them some good—that is, just before the election, as they prepare to cast their ballots.

A more realistic concern, we believe, is that under certain circumstances, one candidate can gain a major advantage from a protracted interregnum period. Once again, money is the root of the evil. Under the federal campaign finance laws, any candidate who accepts matching funds must also agree to a limit on the total amount of money he or she can spend during the nomination phase of the campaign. In a hotly contested race, with a lengthy invisible primary, it frequently happens that one candidate has reached or exceeded that limit by the time his or her party's nomination has been clinched. Thus this candidate will have little or no money available for campaigning until the conclusion of his or her party's national convention, which generally will not occur until four or five months later. If the other party's candidate has not faced any serious opposition and has therefore not had to spend any nomination campaign funds, the result may be a very one-sided campaign during the interregnum period.

Pretty much this scenario played out during the 1996 election. By the end of March, Bob Dole had the Republican nomination locked up—but he had also already spent $28.9 million out of the $30.9 million allowed by law.[49] The Clinton campaign, by contrast, had spent just $9.6 million—and had more than $16 million in cash on hand.[50] The result, according to most observers, was to give the Democrats a considerable advantage over the Republicans during the next five months of the presidential campaign.[51]

Dole was able to keep some kind of campaign going between April and July largely by relying on the Republican Party. After he had locked up the GOP nomination in late March, and especially after he resigned from the Senate in mid-May, Dole took advantage of a series of loopholes in the federal campaign finance laws that allowed him to shift much of the expense of his campaign to the national and state Republican parties. Between May and September, for example, the national party ran $18 million worth of "issue advocacy" advertisements that were designed, as the Republican National Committee chair put it, to "show the differences between Dole and Clinton . . . on the issues facing our country." Though his own campaign had no money to pay for his travel and personal campaigning, Dole was able to make appearances at party fund-raising events throughout the country. The party even managed to place forty-four members of the Dole campaign staff on various party payrolls during this period.[52] As Anthony Corrado, perhaps this country's leading academic authority on campaign finance, commented at the time, the spending limits thus "restricted" the Dole campaign but did not "grind the campaign to a halt."[53]

In future election cycles, however, candidates in Dole's situation may find the going even tougher. The money used to assist the Dole campaign—and similar funds that were spent on behalf of Bill Clinton in 1996 and both Bush and Gore in 2000—was largely soft money: that is to say, money that was not subject to the federal contribution limits and could therefore be raised in relatively large increments. With the passage of the Bipartisan Campaign Reform Act, however, all money that the parties spend to promote their presidential candidates during the interregnum period must be hard money, with no individual allowed to contribute more than $2,000. So though party aid to the presidential candidates will continue, it may be available in somewhat smaller amounts, particularly for the Democrats.[54] If President Bush is unopposed for the 2004 Republican nomination, and if the 2004 Democratic race is effectively over by early March—both of which seem, at this point, quite likely—the Democratic campaign could operate at a serious disadvantage throughout the spring and early summer.

The Other Side of the Ledger

Such is the case against front-loading. Is there anything to be said in its defense?

Perhaps the most common argument made in defense of front-loading—or at least cited as a mitigating factor—is that clustering the primaries and caucuses at the beginning of the delegate selection season helps bring an early end to the nomination contest and thus gives the parties more time to heal any wounds caused by a hard-fought nomination campaign and present a united front for the general election. A party that is deeply divided over its presidential nominee, according to this argument, almost invariably loses in November. Though front-loading obviously does not prevent intraparty divisions, it does make sure that they are not unduly prolonged and gives the parties ample time to undo the damage. As a subcommittee of the Democratic National Committee noted in a recent report:

> The most important part of any primary/caucus schedule is that it needs to identify a strong Democratic nominee early and lead to a Democratic victory in the general election. . . . Consequently, criticism about a front-loaded schedule has to be weighed against a process that seems to be working well. In the last few cycles, the current system has allowed the Democratic Party to identify its presumptive nominee early. As a result, the process has helped the Party unify behind its nominee and focus its resources on the general election.[55]

This line of thinking has also been supported by a number of academic specialists in the parties and elections subfield, who have put forward a body of research often referred to as the "divisive primary hypothesis." According to this theory, having to go through a long and divisive nomination race severely scars whichever candidate eventually wins the nomination and thus makes it more difficult for him or her to achieve victory in the general election. One of the most vigorous exponents of this argument is the political scientist Martin Wattenberg:

> One of the key features of the candidate-centered age is the increasingly difficult task of unifying a political party in November when the various factions within it have been competing so long. Internal animosities stirred up by the reformed nomination process are more likely to continue to hurt the nominee in November. These animosities hurt a candidate not only with his own party's voters but with Independents and the opposition party as well. After all, if members of the candidate's own party find fault with their nominee why should those outside the party view him favorably? . . . A successful presidential campaign now depends on wrapping up the nomination faster and with less lingering bitterness than the opposition.[56]

By significantly shortening the nomination contest, then, front-loading may help promote party unity for the fall campaign.

Two points should be made in response to this argument. In the first place, as we have argued in considerable detail elsewhere, there is little good evidence to show that having a divisive nomination race really does harm a party or candidate in the general election.[57] More precisely, what evidence has been cited in defense of the theory comes from a misspecified model. According to the divisive primary hypothesis, divisions within the party are *created* by a contested nomination race. Rival candidates for the nomination essentially manufacture differences and disagreements that have little or no basis in anything real but that, once excited, linger on to haunt the party in the general election. In our view, it makes considerably more sense to assume (or at least to allow for the possibility) that divisive nomination races are more effect than cause: that bitter, hard-fought nomination races simply *reflect* and *reveal* the problems and divisions that already exist within a party. Divisive primaries may thus be correlated with a weak performance in the general election, but the relationship is spurious. Analyzed from this perspective, most of the evidence offered in support of the divisive primary hypothesis evaporates.

As an example of these two different approaches to the question, consider the Democratic nomination race of 1972. At first glance, the basic facts of this contest might be seen as supporting the divisive primary hypothesis. Three strong and ideologically distinct candidates fought it out through the preconvention campaign, with the eventual winner, George McGovern, receiving just 25 percent of the total primary vote. Several months later, McGovern went down to one of the most lopsided defeats in the history of American presidential elections. But can we therefore conclude that the first circumstance caused the second?

A different interpretation seems to us distinctly more plausible. The Democrats began the 1972 election sharply and crucially divided over two major issues: race and the Vietnam War. The 1972 campaign emphatically did not create these two divisions. The war had been a source of substantial intraparty disagreement for at least six years; and race had been threatening to split the Democrats since the 1940s. Against this background, it is no wonder that the Democrats endured such a remarkably divisive nomination race—and then saw so many Democrats defect to the opposition in November. Indeed, what would have been truly shocking is if the 1972 nomination process had been a calm and unifying affair.

Similarly, we think it greatly mistaken to claim (as some Democrats have) that Jimmy Carter lost the 1980 election because he had to deal with such a bitter and divisive nomination challenge from Ted Kennedy.[58] Carter lost to Reagan because the economy was in terrible shape and because most Americans thought that Carter himself had been a weak and ineffective leader—which are precisely the reasons that Kennedy challenged him in the first place.

Second, even if the evidence supporting the divisive primary hypothesis were a good deal stronger than it is, this would not necessarily mean that the parties would be better off bringing their presidential nomination races to a premature conclusion. Whatever benefits accrue to a party from a shorter nomination contest need to be balanced against all the potential harms associated with front-loading. In particular, as we have argued earlier in this chapter, front-loading greatly increases the likelihood that a party will settle on a nominee before receiving a full discussion of his or her strengths and weaknesses and before many rival candidates have been given an adequate opportunity to make their case to the voters.

In 1992, for example, Ron Brown, then the chairman of the Democratic National Committee, intervened in the Democratic nomination race at several points in an attempt to bring it to an early conclusion.[59] Though Brown's actions perhaps played some role in promoting greater party unity for the general election, they may have done so at a significant cost, pushing the Democrats to rally around a candidate (Bill Clinton) with a number of major personal flaws, many of which may have hurt the party not only in 1992 but also in subsequent elections. It is, in short, an open question as to whether Brown's desire for a quick decision really helped his party in the long run. At the very least, we would argue, there needs to be an appreciation of the potential costs as well as the alleged benefits of shortening the nomination race.

Another argument that has been made in support of front-loading is that it strengthens the political parties and thus helps restore party control over the presidential nomination process. The dense clustering of primaries and caucuses in the contemporary nomination calendar, according to this argument, effectively precludes presidential candidates from setting up their own personal organizations in every state. Instead, candidates must establish some kind of working relationship with the existing state and local party organizations. Thus, it might be argued, state and local party endorsements now count for a lot more than they did in the 1970s and early 1980s.

The only political scientist we know of who deliberately sought to foster front-loading did so primarily on this basis.[60] At the end of his well-received book *Out of Order,* Thomas Patterson recommended a plan that would have condensed the delegate selection season from its current length (about seventeen weeks) to a period of six to eight weeks and eliminated the special positions that Iowa and New Hampshire currently occupy.[61] Patterson claimed a number of benefits for his proposal, but most centered around the idea that it would strengthen political parties. As Patterson put it,

> A shortened campaign with multiple contests on the first Tuesday would encourage presidential hopefuls to build closer ties with their peers in Congress and the states.
>
> Candidates would find it harder to go it alone in this system. Forcing the contenders to spread themselves thinly across several states would encourage them to look for surrogates able to make their case in their absence. The organizational resources of party chairs would be a potentially important factor, as would the support and endorsement of local and state election officials.[62]

Though strengthening the parties is a worthy objective, there are many reasons to view front-loading as a most unsatisfactory method for its accomplishment. In the first place, it is not clear that front-loading has actually increased the role that party leaders and formal party organizations play in the presidential selection process. If anyone has been significantly empowered by recent developments in the nominating process, it has been the media and campaign contributors. Though presidential candidates do solicit the endorsement of state party chairs and other elected officials, they appear to spend a lot more of their time cultivating contributors and reporters and campaigning in the early primary and caucus states.[63]

Moreover, it is difficult to see how state and local parties are helped by a process in which half or more of them hold their primaries and caucuses after the race has been settled and therefore cannot exert any meaningful influence on the outcome. As Walter Stone, Ronald Rapoport, and their collaborators have shown, contested nomination races provide state and local parties with a number of significant "spillover" benefits. People who get involved in a nomination campaign—even if they work for one of the losing candidates—are likely to stay involved, helping out the party in the general election and in future election cycles.[64] By bringing presidential nomination contests to an early conclusion, front-loading may deprive a substantial number of state parties of an important source of activists and volunteers.

Patterson's vision of how campaigns would work under his proposal also strikes us as highly problematic. Though candidates would almost certainly rely more on surrogates, those surrogates are more likely to be family members and celebrities than party leaders. The widespread use of surrogates also seems likely to diminish even further the educational functions of the campaign. If a candidate like Bush or Gore personally campaigns in upstate New York or suburban Chicago, a sizable number of people are likely to turn out for the event, and the local media are likely to give it extensive coverage. When a surrogate assumes those responsibilities, both attendance and media coverage are likely to suffer. Moreover, as we have already noted, while surrogates may be able to make a case for a candidate in general terms, the voters cannot press surrogates to take a stand on issues of local concern or to clarify ambiguities and inconsistencies in the candidate's platform.

Finally, there are other ways to reassert party influence over nominations that do not require front-loading with all its attendant problems. Setting aside a certain number of seats for ex officio "superdelegates," for example, as the Democrats began doing in 1984, would appear to offer some of the same effects without the corresponding negative attributes of front-loading. Altogether, touting front-loading as a corrective for party decline is not unlike "destroying the village in order to save it." Though political scientists routinely caution against putting too much stock in any contrived reform—the law of unintended consequences looms large in any sensible discussion of the nomination process—there is something to be said for addressing problems like the loss of party influence in a straightforward and deliberate way rather than through the indirect and unintentional mechanism of a remarkably haphazard process.

Conclusion

Any attempt to untangle the consequences of front-loading must contend with the complexity of presidential nominations, the small number of cases from which to draw conclusions, and the fact that some consequences have already manifested themselves (for example, the high "entry fee" and the effective disenfranchisement of half of the states) while others are thus far only hypothetical (the potential for runaway momentum to nominate a little-known contender). But all the evidence to date—and all the consequences it is reasonable to expect in the future—argue quite strongly, in our view, that the effects of front-loading on American presidential politics are almost entirely negative. Though a small number of arguments have been made in favor of front-loading, all of them are flawed, we think, in a variety of important ways.

Given all the arguments that can and have been mounted against front-loading, it is a good question why nothing effective has yet been done to reverse or even significantly mitigate it. What alternatives are there to front-loading? What are the pros and cons of each major proposal? Why have none of them been implemented?

CHAPTER FIVE

Proposed
Solutions

The widely shared disparagement of front-loading has produced an almost equally wide array of proposed solutions. In this chapter, for purposes of exposition, we divide these proposals into two broad groups, which we call *comprehensive* and *incremental* solutions. As their names imply, comprehensive proposals call for major, far-reaching changes in the basic operations of the presidential nomination process; incremental proposals make more limited, marginal changes in the existing rules. Both are defensible ways of approaching the front-loading problem and hence deserving of careful attention.

Comprehensive Proposals

We start with the comprehensive proposals, because they have, in general, received the most attention. Four such proposals have dominated recent discussions of the nomination process and its shortcomings: a national primary, a system of regional primaries, the "small-states-first" or Delaware plan, and a national preprimary convention. All four call for substantial changes in the existing system, and they have a corresponding set of advantages and disadvantages. On the positive side, they are more likely to be adequate to the task of actually doing something about front-loading. But precisely because they are so far-reaching, they will probably be more difficult to achieve and more likely to carry the risk of serious unanticipated consequences. Examined on an individual level, some of these proposals, we believe, will not work as advertised, while others would almost certainly fail to deal with important dimensions of the front-loading problem.

National Primary

Of all the major reform proposals, the national primary is both the simplest and, in many ways, the most radical. It is also the oldest of the nominating changes under discussion, having been proposed by Woodrow Wilson and other Progressives long before front-loading became an issue.[1] In general, national primary plans call for a primary election to be held on the same day in all fifty states and the District of Columbia, but there are at least three different ways in which the results of that vote could be used to determine a party's presidential nominee.

—In a plurality-rule election, a single, national election would be held in each party, and whichever candidate won the most votes would become the party's presidential candidate. Though the party might hold a national convention for other purposes—to adopt a platform, to ratify the vice presidential choice, to rally the party faithful—the convention would no longer be necessary and would not play any role, even a purely formal one, in the presidential nomination process.

—In a majority-rule election, as in the plurality-rule election plan, a single national election would be held, but to become the party's presidential nominee a candidate would be required to win some minimum percentage of the votes cast in the primary (usually 50 percent, but in some proposals 40 or 45 percent). If no candidate received that many votes, a runoff election would be held between the top two finishers in the first election. Most recent national primary proposals have used some version of the majority-rule election.

—A third variant would couple a national primary with a delegate convention much like the ones currently in use. Rather than a simple nationwide vote, the national primary would actually consist of fifty-one separate state primaries, all held on the same day, each of which would be used to select delegates to a national convention. As in the present system, those delegates would select the presidential candidate by ballot at the convention, with a majority of the delegate votes necessary to win the nomination.[2]

Whatever the precise format, a national primary has at least two advantages to recommend it. It is simple, and it would treat all states equally.[3]

In particular, it would guarantee that no state had the kind of outsized, disproportionate role now played by Iowa and New Hampshire and that no state would hold its primary after the effective nomination decision had already been made. In exchange, however, a national primary suffers from a long list of maladies that make it a highly questionable option. Above all, it would take most of the problems associated with front-loading—all except the disenfranchisement of late-voting states—and make them exponentially worse.

Indeed, an often-repeated complaint about front-loading is precisely that it makes the existing system too much like a national primary. If voters have little opportunity for reflection and second thoughts in the current system, they would have far less in a national primary. If the candidate fields are truncated and the importance of campaign money is inflated by the high entry fee of the current arrangement, the entry fee for a national primary would be millions of dollars higher. If front-runners have a disproportionate advantage now, that advantage would only grow as candidates struggled to campaign in fifty states at once. If campaigns meet a low standard of quality today because of the need to shift so quickly into wholesale politics, one can only imagine how little opportunity there would be for retail campaigning or discussion of local issues in a national primary.

These problems should hardly be surprising, because a national primary represents, in a sense, the most thoroughgoing front-loading and compression possible, with delegate selection in all states being moved, in effect, to the very first date on the calendar. In short, though the national primary might satisfy a primordial urge for order and rationality, it would almost certainly not resolve or even alleviate most of the difficulties created by front-loading.

Depending on which specific plan is adopted, a national primary could also lead to a result that the current system, even with its highly front-loaded calendar, generally avoids: the nomination of a candidate who is supported by a small but highly committed minority but is unacceptable to a large segment of the party. The kind of situation that could easily lead to such a result is nicely illustrated by the Democratic nomination race of 1988. After Gary Hart's withdrawal from the race in May 1987, the Democratic field consisted of Jesse Jackson and six other candidates, none of whom was particularly well known outside of his own state or region. Because Jackson was well known, and because he attracted strong support from African Americans and a narrow slice of white liberals, national polls that asked Democratic identifiers whom they wanted as their party's next presidential candidate consistently showed Jackson in the lead. Had a national primary been conducted at this point, it seems quite likely that Jackson would have won it, even though he probably would have received just 25 or 30 percent of the vote—and even though his presence at the head of the ticket would clearly have caused major problems for his party.

The sequential nature of the current primary system, by comparison, generally prevents this sort of problem from occurring. A fringe candidate who has the support of only 25 or 30 percent of his party's voters may win some early primaries when the rest of the vote is divided among a large number of other candidates. But as their lack of support among the voters becomes evident, some of these candidates will fade or drop out, and the mainstream of the party will usually coalesce around a more acceptable alternative. In 1988, for example, Jesse Jackson did just fine as long as the field stayed divided. As of March 15, Jackson was actually his party's leading vote-getter in the primaries, having won 27 percent of the total vote to 25 percent for Dukakis. He had also won a plurality of the vote in five states. Once Bruce Babbitt, Dick Gephardt, and Paul Simon dropped out, however, the limits on Jackson's vote became obvious. In the last fourteen primaries, Jackson won only once (in the District of Columbia) and lost the preference vote to Dukakis by a two-to-one margin (60 percent to 31 percent).

It is precisely to avoid this problem that most recent national primary proposals have been structured along the lines of the majority-rule election, requiring the winner to achieve some minimum percentage of the total vote and calling for a runoff election if no candidate crosses that threshold. Yet runoff elections carry problems of their own. In those states that already use runoff elections, the evidence is clear that interest and participation in the second election are usually lower than they were in the first election.[4] Moreover, because most recent national primary proposals call for the first-round primary to be held in the last half of August or the first week in September, Americans might face the routine prospect of holding three national elections over a period of just seventy days.[5] Finally, although holding a runoff between the top two finishers makes it more likely that at least one of the finalists will be minimally acceptable to most party voters, it by no means guarantees that result. In a highly divided field, both of the top finishers may appeal to narrow segments of the party or have serious flaws that make them problematic candidates in the general election. In 1988, for example, the top two Democratic candidates in most of the national polls conducted just before the Iowa caucuses were Jesse Jackson and Gary Hart (who had rejoined the race in mid-December).

Regional Primaries

Another widely discussed option is the use of regional primaries. Again, there are a number of forms that a regional primary system might take, and they are different enough that they cannot be lumped together.

One option is for a group of contiguous states to agree among themselves that they will all hold their primaries on the same day. If enough states join such groups, it might lead, in the end, to a nomination calendar that consists principally of regional primaries. (Exactly how many such regions would be difficult to say.)

A number of regional primaries have already been established in this way (see chapter 2). The best known is the southern Super Tuesday, which goes back in some form to 1980 (three southern states voted together that year) and culminated in 1988, when fourteen southern and border-South states all held their primaries on the same day. (In the past several election cycles, most southern primaries have been spread over two different Tuesdays.) In both 1996 and 2000 all of the New England states except New Hampshire banded together to hold what was sometimes called the "Yankee primary." In 1996 (but not in 2000) Illinois, Michigan, Wisconsin, and Ohio all held their primaries on the same day (the press dubbed it "Big Ten Tuesday"). After the front-loading epidemic of 1996, many other regions made noises about creating similar events. Proponents spoke of a Rocky Mountain primary, a Prairie States primary, a Mid-Atlantic primary, and a Pacific Coast primary. As it turned out, however, California's move to the front undid all such calculations, and none of these additional regional primaries came to pass.

Establishing regional primaries through this type of voluntary, disaggregated process has two major weaknesses. To begin with, whatever its other advantages, the record to date indicates quite clearly that this is not a cure for front-loading. In fact, regional primaries of this sort have actually accelerated the move to the front. When a group of neighboring states begins to talk about scheduling their primaries on the same day, they do not pick a date near the end of the delegate selection season. Instead, they invariably think about moving their primaries to a date near the beginning of the calendar. When the Southern Legislative Conference pushed for a southern Super Tuesday in 1988, it is no accident that they set the date of this event for March 8: that was the earliest date permitted under Democratic Party rules. Of the fourteen southern states that ultimately held their primaries that day, four moved their primaries forward in the calendar by at least a month and a half; not one moved to a later date.

Moreover, even if five or ten neighboring states do agree to hold their primaries on the same day, there is nothing in the current system to guarantee that they will have that date all to themselves. Particularly if the date falls near the beginning of the delegate selection season, other states may hold their primaries or caucuses at the same time—and thus undercut all of the purported advantages of having a regional primary. In fact, such a fate has befallen both the southern and New England regional primaries. In 1988 the fourteen southern states voting on March 8 were joined by two New England primaries and three western state caucuses. This nonsouthern leavening greatly aided the cause of Michael Dukakis, who won both primaries and two of the three caucuses and was thus able to project himself as one of the big winners on Super Tuesday, even though he had run rather poorly in much of the South.[6] In 2000 New England's five primaries were almost entirely ignored when California, New York, and Ohio all decided to vote on the same day.

Because of the difficulties associated with creating regional primaries in this sort of disaggregated way, most recent regional primary proposals would use a more centralized process, in which some central agency or authority would put together a complete regional primary calendar, assigning states to specific regions and assigning regions to specific dates. Three such plans have received particular attention. The first major regional primary proposal was developed by then-senator Robert Packwood of Oregon, who first filed the legislation for it in 1972.[7] Under the Packwood plan, all states would be divided into five regions: Northeast, Midwest, South, Great Plains, and Far West.[8] The first regional primary would be held on the second Tuesday in March. Seventy days before that date, the Federal Election Commission would determine by lot which region went first. The other regions would vote on the second Tuesdays of April, May, June, and July. Again, which region voted when would be determined by lot.

In recent years, the most publicized regional primary proposal is one put forward by the National Association of Secretaries of State (NASS) in February 1999.[9] The NASS plan specifically exempts Iowa and New Hampshire, which would be allowed to hold the first caucus and first primary, respectively, with each of these states getting a week all to itself, just as in the present system. All other states would be assigned to one of four regions: East, South, Midwest, and West. The first region would hold its primary on the first Tuesday after the first Monday in March, with the other regions voting on the first Tuesday after the first Monday in April, May, and June, respectively. Every four years, the order of the regions would rotate, so that whatever region voted in March in the previous election cycle would now vote in June, the region that previously voted in April would vote in March, and so on.

A third major proposal would establish a system of time-zone primaries. As its name implies, this plan calls for the states to form regional groupings by time zone: Eastern, Central, Mountain, and Pacific.[10] As in the Packwood and NASS proposals, each of these time zones would have a specific date (or in some proposals a specific week) on which to hold its primary, with the next time zone voting one month later. The order of the time zones would rotate or be determined by lot.[11]

The regional primary idea has strengths that have made it attractive to a variety of analysts. It cannot be easily dismissed that the nation's secretaries of state, the chief elections officers of the United States, have endorsed it. A regional primary plan should make campaigning easier and more efficient for the candidates by cutting down on travel time and allowing them to advertise in media markets that cross state lines. It also holds out the hope of forcing candidates to confront the particular, often unique problems of each region in turn.

The regional primary idea also has a number of important disadvantages, however. To begin with, it is by no means clear that a regional primary system would actually reduce front-loading: it depends entirely on how the system is designed. The NASS proposal provides a good example of the problem. The NASS calendar allots separate weeks to Iowa and New Hampshire—and then, one week later, the first region would vote. In other words, one week after the New Hampshire primary, delegates would be selected in twelve different states on the same day. By contrast, the 1996 calendar, so widely criticized for its front-loaded character, had only four primaries in the week after New Hampshire. The NASS calendar would open up a bit after that: there would be a month off before the next region voted, whereas the 1996 calendar had twenty more primaries in the next three weeks. But this would be small consolation to all the candidates who could not afford to campaign in twelve states, even twelve contiguous states, just one week after the race began and who would therefore not be around when the second region went to the polls.

In theory, of course, this problem can be remedied: in particular, the number of regions could simply be increased. Yet it is striking that the vast majority of existing regional primary proposals do not take this sort of precaution: most such proposals establish four or at most six regions— effectively guaranteeing that most of the problems associated with front-loading would continue under the new system. Front-runners would still have enormous advantages, the entry fee would be little altered, and campaign quality probably would not improve much.

Nor would a regional primary system prevent a large number of states from being effectively disenfranchised. If anything, it might make things worse. Though it is impossible to say for certain what campaigns would look like under a regional primary plan, given the dynamics of primary competition it seems highly likely that most races would be settled by the end of the second or, at the latest, the third regional primary. In assessing the "small-states-first" plan, which also divides the states into four groups, California secretary of state Bill Jones has noted, "Based on the last 20 years of presidential primaries as well as the 2000 primary season, the states at the end of the primary calendar will never have a chance to matter in the process."[12] His criticism applies with equal force to a regional primary system.

This means that half of the states might regularly be removed from meaningful participation. Of course, the same thing happens in the current system—but under a regional primary plan, whole regions would be disenfranchised. At least in the current system, there are usually a few primaries from every region before the race is locked up. A system based on time zones would partially mitigate this problem (that, indeed, is the principal attraction of this plan) because both the Eastern and Central time zones include states from more than one region (the Eastern zone includes states in the Northeast, South, and Midwest; the Central zone includes both midwestern and southern states). However, this is not true of the Mountain and Pacific time zones.

A time-zone plan has one other shortcoming that is particularly relevant to a study of front-loading. Whereas the regions in most regional primary plans are designed to be roughly equivalent in population and hence numbers of delegates, the time zones differ enormously in this regard. As shown in table 5-1, 49 percent of all Americans live in the Eastern time zone, as compared with just 6 percent living in the Mountain

Table 5-1 *Distribution of Population and Delegates in Various Regional Primary Plans*
Units as indicated

Plan	Number of states	2000 population Number[a]	%	Delegates to the 2000 Democratic convention Number	%	Delegates to the 2000 Republican convention Number	%
Time-zone plan							
Eastern	22	137	49	2,104	49	930	46
Central	16	81	29	1,237	29	640	31
Mountain	7	16	6	245	6	193	9
Pacific	6	47	17	668	16	277	14
Packwood plan							
Northeast	10	54	19	933	22	364	18
Midwest	6	46	16	705	17	305	15
South	10	62	22	849	20	449	22
Great Plains	12	56	20	854	20	452	22
West	13	63	22	913	21	470	23
NASS plan[b]							
Northeast	12	61	22	1,074	26	411	21
South	13	92	33	1,182	28	649	32
Midwest	11	61	22	999	24	468	23
West	13	63	23	913	22	470	24
Delaware plan							
Group 1 (smallest states)	13	11	4	333	8	235	12
Group 2	13	35	12	590	14	356	17
Group 3	13	68	24	1,063	25	477	23
Group (largest states)	12	167	59	2,268	53	972	48

a. In millions.
b. Excludes Iowa and New Hampshire.

time zone. This means that any year in which the Eastern time zone leads off the nomination calendar will be radically front-loaded: half of all the delegates will be selected on the first day. It is difficult to see how such a system would differ from a national primary, save that it would be less representative of the entire American population.

Another serious problem associated with regional primaries is that they would confer a significant advantage on any candidate who happened to be particularly strong in whatever region voted first.[13] As table 5-2 indicates, region is an important variable in explaining primary outcomes. Over the last several decades, almost every major presidential candidate

Table 5-2   *Average Primary Vote in Recent Presidential Nomination Races, by Region*[a]

Percent

Race	Northeast	South	Midwest	West
1976 Republican				
Ford	60	44	53	35
Reagan	38	55	46	63
Number of states	(4)	(6)	(7)	(4)
1976 Democratic				
Carter[b]	35	62	47	21
Number of states	(6)	(6)	(7)	(5)
1980 Republican[c]				
Reagan	38	65	56	54
Bush	45	24	24	35
Number of states	(5)	(8)	(6)	(1)
1980 Democratic				
Carter	41	70	56	45
Kennedy	53	18	36	38
Number of states	(9)	(8)	(7)	(5)
1984 Democratic				
Mondale	38	33	37	33
Hart	33	29	46	48
Jackson	21	24	13	13
Number of states	(9)	(6)	(5)	(3)
1988 Democratic[d]				
Dukakis	57	18	27	. . .
Jackson	26	29	22	. . .
Gore	7	35	8	. . .
Number of states	(5)	(12)	(4)	(0)
1992 Democratic[e]				
Clinton	27	65	40	27
Tsongas	47	19	18	26
Brown	17	9	20	29
Number of states	(4)	(8)	(4)	(1)

a. Regions are those contained in the plan of the National Association of Secretaries of State.

b. Carter was the only Democratic candidate in 1976 who contested enough primaries to make this sort of analysis feasible.

c. Averages are based on those primaries conducted through May 20. On May 26 Bush withdrew from the race.

d. Averages are based on those primaries conducted through April 19. On April 21 Gore withdrew from the race.

e. Averages are based on those primaries conducted through March 17. On March 19 Tsongas withdrew from the race.

has done significantly better in one region than in the others. In 1976, for example, Gerald Ford won 60 percent of the vote in the average northeastern primary, as against 35 percent in the average western primary. In the same year, Jimmy Carter won, on average, 62 percent of the vote in the South, 35 percent in the Northeast, and 21 percent in the West. In 1980 Edward Kennedy won 53 percent of the vote in the average northeastern primary, but only 18 percent in the southern primaries.[14]

In the contemporary presidential nomination process, the order in which primaries are held matters. Indeed, as we have shown in chapter 3, that is why front-loading developed in the first place. Unless all momentum effects, for some unexplained reason, suddenly disappear under a regional primary system, which region goes first could have important implications for which candidate gets nominated. If the 1976 Republican nomination contest had begun with a western regional primary, it might have dealt a severe blow to Gerald Ford's candidacy, whereas a process that began with an eastern regional primary might have greatly lengthened the odds against Ronald Reagan. In 1992 Bill Clinton's candidacy would likely have been doomed if the southern states had voted last: for the first five weeks of that year's delegate selection season, Clinton won not a single primary or caucus outside the South. Supporters of regional primaries implicitly acknowledge this problem, for regional primary proposals invariably include a provision that either rotates the order in which regions vote or determines that order by lot. But rotation and lotteries do not eliminate this problem; they merely ensure that the direction and recipient of the distortion will vary, in a random manner, from one election cycle to the next.

Small States First

Another way of rearranging the primary calendar is the "small-states-first" proposal, otherwise known as the Delaware plan. After years dominated by discussion of the national and regional primary models, the Delaware plan gained center stage in 2000. Indeed, it became so popular that a special commission of the Republican National Committee recommended that the party adopt it. For a variety of reasons discussed in the next chapter, the plan was pulled from consideration just days before the Republican national convention in Philadelphia. Nevertheless, it remains a potent proposal and will almost certainly continue to be part of the national discussion, not least because it is the only one of the four plans considered here that was explicitly designed to deal with the problem of front-loading.

Under the Delaware plan, the nation is divided into four groups of states, based on their population (see table 5-3). Those four groups would vote by order of ascending population—smallest states first, biggest states

Table 5-3   *State Groupings under the Delaware Plan*

Group 1[a]	Group 2	Group 3	Group 4
Alaska	Arkansas	Alabama	California
Delaware	Connecticut	Arizona	Florida
District of Columbia	Iowa	Colorado	Georgia
Hawaii	Kansas	Indiana	Illinois
Idaho	Mississippi	Kentucky	Michigan
Maine	Nebraska	Louisiana	New Jersey
Montana	Nevada	Maryland	New York
New Hampshire	New Mexico	Massachusetts	North Carolina
North Dakota	Oklahoma	Minnesota	Ohio
Rhode Island	Oregon	Missouri	Pennsylvania
South Dakota	South Carolina	Tennessee	Virginia
Vermont	Utah	Washington	Texas
Wyoming	West Virginia	Wisconsin	

Source: Advisory Commission on the Presidential Nominating Process, *Nominating Future Presidents: A Review of the Republican Process* (Washington: Republican National Committee, 2000), p. 37.
a. American Samoa, Guam, Puerto Rico, and the Virgin Islands are also included in Group 1.

last. More specifically, the Republican task force recommended that the twelve smallest states and the District of Columbia—group 1—be allowed to conduct their primary or caucus anytime on or after the first Tuesday in March. The thirteen next smallest states—group 2—could start to select their delegates on the first Tuesday in April, the third group on the first Tuesday in May, and the final group—the twelve largest states—on the first Tuesday in June. The groups in the Delaware plan, it is important to note, are designed to include roughly equal numbers of states; since the groups are based on population, they are dramatically unequal in terms of the number of people and delegates they take in. The final group contains about 60 percent of the U.S. population and about half of the delegates attending both parties' national conventions (see table 5-1).

Supporters of the Delaware plan claim four major advantages for it. First, because the small states would vote first, they argue, the entry fee would diminish. In the early going, candidates would do most of their campaigning in states like Wyoming, South Dakota, and Rhode Island, where a competitive campaign could be mounted for a fraction of what it would require in California or New York. Second, having the small states vote first would also permit more "retail politics" and personal campaigning and would reduce the importance of the mass media. Third, unlike those in a regional primary system, the groups in the Delaware plan are based on population and therefore include states from all over the country. Finally, by preventing the large states from voting before the final month of the campaign, the Delaware plan holds out the hope that a contested nomination race would no longer end a few weeks after it begins. Because half of the delegates would not be selected until the final month, no candidate could clinch the nomination or build up an insurmountable delegate lead in the first couple of months, no matter how well he or she did.

Unfortunately, we think there is strong reason to doubt that the Delaware plan would work as advertised. To begin with, though the plan officially establishes a month-long window for each group of states to hold their primaries and caucuses, it is surely unrealistic to think that the states would spread themselves out evenly over the entire month. A much more likely result, we think, would be front-loading within each month, such that almost all of the smallest states would vote on or shortly after the first Tuesday in March, most of the states in group 2 would vote on the first Tuesday in April, and so forth. To the extent that this occurs, it raises doubts about whether the Delaware plan really would reduce the so-called entry fee for presidential candidates. Though the small states vote first, there are still thirteen of them (counting the District of Columbia), and any candidate who hoped to establish that he or she was a serious contender with nationwide appeal would probably feel some pressure to mount a major campaign in most of the thirteen.

Equally important, because the Delaware plan groups states by population rather than geography, it also forgoes all of the increased efficiency and reduced travel burdens that regional primary advocates claim as one of the principal selling points for their plan. As the *Los Angeles Times* has editorialized, the Delaware plan "would impose a nightmare travel burden on the candidates as they roamed the first month from Maine to Wyoming to Rhode Island to North Dakota to shake hands with very few voters. In effect, each month would mean another nationwide primary."[15]

As this quotation indicates, there is also reason to doubt whether campaign quality would improve much under the Delaware plan. Probably each of the states in group 1 would receive some measure of personal campaigning from the candidates. (As a rough index of how much, take all the time now spent by the candidates in Iowa, add in all the time spent in New Hampshire, and divide by 13.) This would not greatly diminish the importance of television, though it would probably give a little more opportunity for lesser-known candidates to make their mark. But it is difficult to see how the campaign preceding the kickoff dates for groups 2, 3, and 4 would differ much from the campaign that preceded Super Tuesday in 1988.

Similar questions can be raised about how long the nomination race would last under the Delaware plan. Mathematically, it is true, no candidate could clinch his party's nomination until the fourth group of states had begun to select its delegates. But delegate numbers alone are hardly the whole story in the contemporary presidential nomination process. As we have shown in chapter 3, the major reason so many candidates drop out of the race shortly after the first delegates are selected is not that one of their opponents has clinched the nomination but that they themselves do not have the money necessary to continue campaigning. Even candidates who are not so hard-pressed financially will often exit the race simply because they have fared so poorly in a succession of primaries and caucuses as to make it clear that the voters simply have no interest in their candidacy. In 1996, for example, Steve Forbes plainly had the money to stay in the race all the way to the convention. By the night of March 12, however, Forbes had lost seventeen consecutive primaries to Bob Dole, during which he had won, on average, 13 percent of the vote to Dole's 47 percent.[16] Not surprisingly, on March 14 Forbes withdrew from the race.

Whatever the precise set of causes and circumstances, the bottom line is that most losing presidential candidates exit the race before the winner has mathematically clinched the nomination. In 1992 Bill Clinton did not claim a majority of the convention delegates until June 2—but all of his opponents except Jerry Brown had withdrawn by March 19. In 1996 Bob Dole did not clinch his party's nomination until March 26—but all of his opponents except Pat Buchanan had dropped out by March 14. In 2000 John McCain and Bill Bradley both withdrew from the race on March 9—but neither George W. Bush nor Al Gore achieved a mathematical majority until March 14. As a practical matter, then, it seems highly unlikely under the Delaware plan that either party's presidential nomination race will still be up for grabs when the fourth group of states finally gets its chance to vote.

As noted earlier, the same thing is likely to happen under a regional primary system. Given the rotation and lottery provisions that those systems invariably employ, however, each region at least periodically gets an opportunity to cast a meaningful vote. (This is one thing that rotation does accomplish.) Under the Delaware plan, by contrast, the twelve largest states, which contain almost 60 percent of the U.S. population, are condemned to regular irrelevance.

If the nomination race does not last all the way to the end of the delegate selection season, increased attention will naturally focus on the states

Table 5-4   *Demographic Differences between the Group 1 States in the Delaware Plan and All Other States*
Units as indicated

Characteristic	Average in thirteen smallest states	Average for all other states
Percent black	7	12
Percent Hispanic	4	9
Percent living in metropolitan areas	52	73
Percent of labor force who are union members	14	13
Percent below poverty line	12	13
Percent of population over 25 with a college degree	22	19
Median household income (dollars)	36,173	36,534
Number of states	(13)	(38)

Source: Data taken from U.S. Census Bureau, *County and City Data Book: 2000*, 13th ed. (Government Printing Office, 2001), pp. 3, 4, and 7; and U.S. Census Bureau, *State and Metropolitan Area Data Book, 1997–1998*, 5th ed. (Government Printing Office, 1998), pp. 3 and 23.

that vote early in the Delaware plan, particularly the states in group 1. Here, too, the plan is problematic. As shown in table 5-4, the states in group 1 are not a microcosm of the United States as a whole. They differ from the other thirty-eight states in a number of important ways. In particular, they have fewer African Americans and Hispanics and fewer people living in metropolitan areas.[17] Given the significant role each of these groups plays in Democratic Party politics, it seems most unlikely that the Delaware plan will ever be an appealing option for the Democrats.[18]

Even in regional terms, the smallest states are not as diverse as advocates of the Delaware plan seem to think. Though the states in group 1 might seem, at first glance, to be spread all over the map, they actually are clustered in three major clumps: New England, the upper Great Plains and Rocky Mountain area, and the noncontinental United States (Alaska and Hawaii). Notably, there is not a single southern state in the group and none from the industrial Midwest.[19]

National Preprimary Convention

The final comprehensive proposal we consider here does not so much eliminate front-loading as attempt to make it irrelevant. As its name implies, a national preprimary convention plan would reverse the order of present arrangements: the national convention would come first, followed by a national primary.

Though a number of versions of the preprimary convention plan have been put forward, the best known is probably the one proposed by Thomas Cronin and Robert Loevy in 1983.[20] Under the Cronin-Loevy plan, 75 percent of the delegates to the national convention would be selected through a four-step caucus procedure that would begin with a nationwide day of precinct caucuses on the first Monday in May. At every stage of the caucus system, those seeking to become delegates to the next stage would be able to state a preference for a particular candidate or declare themselves uncommitted. Those national convention delegates who did state a preference when they were elected would be required to vote for that candidate on the first ballot. The other 25 percent of the national convention delegates would be party and elected officials who "might be nominated by the state central committees."[21] These delegates would be unbound.

The national convention itself would have two ballots. After the first ballot, all candidates except the top three finishers would be eliminated. On the second ballot, any candidate who received at least 25 or 30 percent of the votes would be placed on the national primary ballot.[22] The primary would take place in September. If only one candidate exceeded the 25 or 30 percent threshold, the national primary would be dispensed with.

In a formal sense, then, the preprimary convention plan does not eliminate or even reduce front-loading: in fact, it specifically calls for a national primary. What it does attempt to do is make front-loading less important, as the task of screening and winnowing a large field of candidates would no longer be performed by the primaries. The national primary would, instead, have the much more manageable task of choosing between two or at most three contenders, each of whom would have already demonstrated some significant level of national support.

As this description may suggest, the most important questions that need to be asked about a national preprimary convention plan concern the way the delegates to that convention would be selected. There are two general possibilities—and both are likely to create significant problems. One option is to have most or all of the delegates selected ex officio: that is, to have the convention consist primarily or exclusively of members of Congress, governors, state legislators, state party chairs, big city mayors, and so on.[23] The difficulty with this mode of selection is that it so clearly conflicts with the plebiscitary, participatory ethos that dominates the contemporary era that it would face serious legitimacy problems.

These problems would appear to be especially critical for the Democrats. In a party that depends to a substantial extent on the votes of women

Table 5-5   *Selected Demographic Traits of Three Categories of Likely Ex Officio Delegates If a National Preprimary Convention Had Been Held in 2000*
Units as indicated

Deletage category	Total number	Men Number	%	Women Number	%	African Americans Number	%	Hispanics Number	%
Democrats									
House members	211	172	82	39	18	36	17	15	7
Senators	45	39	87	6	13	0	0	0	0
Governors	18	17	94	1	6	0	0	0	0
Total	274	228	83	44	17	36	13	15	5
Republicans									
House members	223	206	92	17	8	1	*	3	1
Senators	55	52	95	3	5	0	0	0	0
Governors	30	28	93	2	7	0	0	0	0
Total	308	286	93	22	7	1	*	3	1

Source: Data on House and Senate members taken from *CQ Weekly*, January 9, 1999, p. 62. Data on governors based on reports in Michael Barone and Grant Ujifusa, *The Almanac of American Politics 2000* (Washington: National Journal, 1999); and Michael Barone and Richard E. Cohen, *The Almanac of American Politics 2002* (Washington: National Journal, 2001).
*Less than one-half of one percent.

and minorities, most categories of ex officio delegates would consist largely of white males. Consider, for example, the data presented in table 5-5, which shows the demographic composition of three groups that would almost certainly be included in any preprimary convention plan: governors, U.S. senators, and members of the U.S. House of Representatives. Of the 274 Democrats who were members of one of these three groups in 2000, fully 83 percent were men. African Americans and Hispanics were represented reasonably well among Democratic House members, though not among senators and governors. On the Republican side, though identity politics have generally not been as important in the GOP as in the Democratic Party, many Republicans might nevertheless balk at a system that gives such important powers to a group that was, at least in 2000, 93 percent male and 99 percent white.

Perhaps because of the problems just discussed, some versions of the preprimary convention plan choose most of the convention delegates in a second way: through a national caucus process in which every interested party member can participate. This is the principal vehicle for delegate selection used in the Cronin-Loevy plan. Remarkably, Cronin and Loevy seem to believe that the campaign preceding these caucuses would be a rather short and decorous affair. This seems to us most unlikely. Since the delegates selected at these caucuses could nominate the party's next presidential candidate—and will, at the very least, substantially narrow the field of candidates who can participate in the national primary—the nationwide caucus day would in all probability be preceded by a lengthy and quite expensive campaign: a little like the campaign that currently precedes the Iowa caucuses, only on a national scale. Had the Cronin-Loevy plan been in operation in 2000, for example, Bush, McCain, Bradley, and Gore would plainly not have waited until the day after the May caucuses to launch their campaigns. To the contrary, they would have spent at least a year, and possibly far longer, trying to identify, persuade, and organize potential caucus attendees in all fifty states.

Thus while supporters of the national preprimary convention plan almost always claim that one advantage of their proposal would be to shorten the nomination campaign, we think it highly unlikely that the plan would have that effect. A better description of what would happen is that the current system, in which candidates compete in a sequence of distinct primaries and caucuses, would be replaced by a single, national day of caucuses and a national primary several months after that. In terms of the problems associated with front-loading, it is not at all clear that the country would benefit from the change. Any presidential candidate who hoped to have a reasonable prospect of winning the nomination would almost certainly have to run a nationwide precaucus campaign, with active organizations operating in almost every state.[24] A national caucus day, in short, would probably be characterized by most of the same disadvantages we identified earlier with regard to a national primary: a huge, possibly prohibitive advantage for the early front-runners and a very substantial entry fee.

In response to this criticism, Cronin and Loevy argue that the "cost of entering state caucuses is significantly, perhaps four times, lower than entering state primaries."[25] While there does seem to be a general consensus that campaigning in caucuses is cheaper than campaigning in primaries (though it is not clear that the advantage is quite as large as Cronin and Loevy suggest),[26] that conclusion is derived from experience under the current system, in which caucuses tend to be held in small, rural states and receive less media attention than primaries.[27] But in a system in which all states use caucuses—where caucuses are the only game in town—it is by no means certain that caucuses would continue to be so inexpensive.

Consider, as an obvious counterexample, the present-day Iowa caucuses, which have often been described as "the functional equivalent of a primary."[28] Whatever else may be said of the Iowa caucuses, running a full-scale campaign in them is not cheap. In 1996 Dole spent $969,000 in Iowa, Alexander $590,000, Gramm $898,000, Buchanan $847,000. Steve Forbes, by some estimates, dropped $4 million there.[29] Obviously, no one state would see such an incredible concentration of resources if caucuses were held in all fifty states on the same day, just as one cannot accurately predict the costs of a national primary by extrapolating from the amounts of money currently spent in New Hampshire. But the Iowa figures are sufficient to prove that caucuses are not invariably a low-budget affair and at least to raise a question about whether participating in a national day of caucuses might be prohibitively expensive for all but the most well-funded candidates.

Many of the other purported advantages of a caucus system might prove equally elusive if all states used caucuses and held them on the same day. For example, Cronin and Loevy claim that their proposal "will require presidential candidates to meet with party and elected local leaders and to build coalitions at the grass-roots level—not just appear in television spot ads."[30] We are much less certain this would be the case. It depends, one suspects, on how large the turnout at these caucuses would be. If the total turnout is between 1 and 3 percent, as is true of most current caucuses, it is at least conceivable that the candidates will be able to do much of their campaigning in person and not rely too heavily on the mass media.[31] If turnout expands to about 10 percent, however, as it has in Iowa, and if lots of weakly affiliated party members get drawn into the caucuses by all the excitement and publicity (as has also happened in Iowa), the number of potential caucus participants will simply be too large for personal campaigning to matter very much. In a nation of 200 million potential voters, a national campaign may inevitably be a mass media campaign.

All of the questions and controversies surrounding the nature of these nationwide caucuses are accentuated by one additional uncertainty: until the system has been up and running for a few years, it will be unclear just what role the national convention will play in the larger nomination process. Supporters of this proposal almost always refer to it as a *preprimary* convention plan, which implies that a primary will follow the convention. In fact, as our more detailed description of the Cronin-Loevy plan indicates, this is not necessarily the case. If one candidate gets more than 70 or 75 percent of the convention vote, the primary will not take place.[32] Will the cancellation of the national primary be a rarity—or the norm? Will the national convention merely serve as a preliminary screening device—or will it, in most cases, have the final say? It is difficult to answer these questions in advance, but it does seem likely that in many situations, great pressure will develop, at least within the party leadership, to settle the nomination early and thus avoid all the expense and potential divisiveness of a national primary battle. And this will lead to even greater concern with the way delegates to the national convention are selected.

Incremental Proposals

If front-loading cannot be cured by major surgery, perhaps the remedy lies in a series of smaller, less drastic therapies. Alternatively, to continue the medical analogy, perhaps front-loading cannot be cured at all, and instead we should think about ways to make the patient a little more comfortable. Though they have received less attention than the national and regional primary schemes, there are a number of other proposals that attempt to get at the problem by making more limited changes in some of the existing rules.

Incentive Plans

If front-loading developed because states saw major advantages in moving to the front of the calendar, one way to reverse or at least slow down the process might be to offer some kind of explicit benefit to any state that would schedule its primary or caucus near the end of the delegate selection season. The first major proposal of this kind was one considered—though ultimately rejected—by the Hunt Commission in the early 1980s. At that time, one of the major rules changes sought by a number of large states was to eliminate the provision in the national Democratic rules that required all states to use proportional representation—that is, to allocate delegates in direct proportion to the preference vote in the primary. As the commission struggled to develop a compromise on this issue, one suggestion was to tie delegate allocation rules to a state's position in the calendar: a state could adopt some alternative to proportional representation (such as direct election or winner-take-more) only if it scheduled its primary after a given date, such as the third Tuesday in April. Partly because of the particular combination of interests that dominated the Hunt Commission and partly because front-loading was then still at an early stage of development, the proposal was never adopted.[33]

It was not until a decade and a half later that an incentive-based proposal was actually given a try. This time, the initiative came from the Republicans. In January 1996 Republican National Committee chairman Haley Barbour appointed a special Task Force on Primaries and Caucuses to look into possible changes in the party's rules that might stem the front-loading tide.[34] The task force recommended the creation of a system of "bonus delegates," under which states that agreed to hold later primaries and caucuses would get more delegates. As finally approved by the 1996 Republican National Convention (the rule did not go into effect until the 2000 nomination cycle), states holding their primaries or caucuses between March 15 and April 14 would have the size of their national convention delegation increased by 5 percent; states holding their primaries or caucuses between April 15 and May 14 would get 7.5 percent more delegates; and states selecting their delegates on May 15 or later would get a 10 percent bonus.[35]

The plan adopted by the Republicans in 1996 was an interesting experiment, nicely consonant with basic party principles. Unfortunately, it had one major drawback: it did not work. By early 1998 it was clear that lots of states would be moving their primaries forward and few would be going in the other direction. The final scorecard on the Republican reforms of 1996 is as follows: of the forty states holding Republican presidential primaries in both 1996 and 2000, twenty-eight had the same position in the calendar both years, eight moved to an earlier date, and just four moved to a later date.[36]

The lesson to be drawn from this episode is not, of course, that incentive systems per se do not work but that this particular incentive was simply not sufficient to outweigh all the benefits states believed they would obtain by moving their primaries or caucuses to the front of the calendar. At one level, the bonuses were simply not large enough to alter the fundamental dynamics of the nomination process. Despite the additional delegates awarded to the nine states that held their primaries after May 14, a sufficient number of delegates could still be acquired in the early going that George Bush was able to clinch the Republican nomination on March 14. And if the nomination was already decided before a state held its primary, having a few additional delegates was just not very valuable. At best, it allowed the state parties to reward a few more of their members by sending them to Philadelphia as national convention delegates. Moreover, because the national Democratic Party did not adopt a similar bonus plan, a state with a Democratic governor or state legislature had no reason to move its primary date back and thus risk being caught on the wrong side of the line dividing the relevant from the irrelevant states.

The key question is this: Are there any incentives that are both large enough to reverse or at least arrest front-loading and within the realm of political plausibility? The outlook, it must be said, is not bright. In late March 2000 Bill Brock, who chaired the most recent Republican reform commission, conjectured that no state was likely to move its primary date back "for less than a 50 percent bonus, and probably not even then."[37] Perhaps if some of the other incremental changes discussed here were also adopted, a bonus delegate system might make some contribution to an attack on front-loading. By itself, however, it is plainly not adequate to the task.

In retrospect, we think that a reasonably constructed incentive system would probably have been most effective if it had been adopted when front-loading was still at a comparatively early stage of development. In 1980 or 1984, when at least two major candidates generally stayed in the race until late May or early June, a bonus delegate system might have provided just enough counterweight to convince many large states to resist the pressures that were pushing them to the front of the calendar. Unfortunately, that insight is not of much help in solving our current problems.

Changing the Campaign Finance Laws

At a number of points we have emphasized the critical role of the campaign finance laws in causing front-loading and producing some of its more deleterious consequences (see chapters 3 and 4). It is a lack of money that forces so many candidates to withdraw from the race at a comparatively early stage in the process, prevents non-front-runners from taking advantage of their early successes in Iowa and New Hampshire, and discourages many otherwise viable candidates from getting into the race at all. This suggests that one important way to mitigate the effects of front-loading would be to make it easier for candidates to raise money. This could be accomplished in at least two different ways.

The first would be to increase the contribution limits that have been established by the federal campaign finance laws. In 1974 that limit was set at $1,000 for each individual contributor.[38] By the end of the 1976 campaign, the first held under the new law, observers from across the political spectrum were arguing that the limit had been set too low. The distinguished journalist Jules Witcover, for example, concluded his book on the 1976 election by recommending that the individual contribution limit be raised from $1,000 to $5,000. As Witcover noted, "If $1000 will not buy a candidate's soul, . . . neither is $5000 likely to."[39] In 1982 the same recommendation was made by a Campaign Finance Study Group organized by the Institute of Politics at Harvard. As their final report concluded, "Candidates for the presidency are not permitted to spend enough money to meet the vast demands of a national campaign. The limitations upon expenditures have become increasingly restrictive and have spawned a whole series of serious problems of definition, allocation and enforcement."[40]

To make matters worse, though the total amount of money that a candidate was allowed to spend during the nomination campaign was indexed to inflation, the contribution limit was not. By 2000 the real purchasing power of $1,000 had declined by more than 70 percent. Inevitably, this increased the difficulty of funding a competitive campaign, in the simple sense that for any given amount of real spending, the candidates needed to locate a much larger number of contributors. In 1976, for example, a candidate who wanted to spend $10 million on his nomination campaign (about 75 percent of the legal limit) needed a minimum of eight thousand contributors.[41] By 2000 a candidate who wanted to raise the same amount, in real terms, would have had to get money from more than twenty-four thousand contributors.

Yet it was not until 2002 that Congress made any move at all toward rectifying this problem. As part of the Bipartisan Campaign Reform Act (BCRA), the individual contribution limit for all federal candidates was increased to $2,000; that limit is also now indexed to inflation. As the figures in the preceding paragraph indicate, this increase does not come close to undoing the effects of inflation since 1974: to meet that goal, the contribution limit should have been raised to about $3,500. Still less does the new limit hit the target recommended by Witcover twenty-five years earlier.

Thus, though we think this reform is clearly in the right direction, it is unclear how much practical effect it will have in either allowing more candidates to raise the $20 million entry fee or in helping candidates who cannot raise this sum before the Iowa caucuses to raise a large amount of money quickly once the delegate selection season has started. To get some purchase on the former question, consider table 5-6, which shows the amount of money raised in 1995 by the top six candidates for the 1996

Table 5-6   *Estimated Effect of Increasing the Contribution Limit on Pre-Election-Year Fund-Raising in the 1996 Republican Nomination Race*
Millions of dollars

Candidate	Total contributions during 1995	Estimated increase[a]	New total
Dole	24.52	6.13	30.65
Gramm	20.76	5.19	25.95
Forbes	17.97	0.38[b]	18.35
Alexander	11.52	2.88	14.40
Buchanan	7.22	1.80	9.02
Lugar	5.90	1.48	7.38

Source: Contribution data taken from Anthony Corrado, "Financing the 1996 Elections," in Gerald M. Pomper, ed., *The Election of 1996: Reports and Interpretations* (Chatham, N.J.: Chatham House, 1997), table 4.2, p. 143.

a. Increase based on the assumption that if the contribution limit were increased to $2,000, total contributions would increase by 25 percent.

b. For Forbes, the 25 percent increase was applied only to money that he did not contribute himself ($1,507,910).

Republican presidential nomination. Under the laws that existed at that time, two candidates—Dole and Gramm—made it across the $20 million threshold. As the next two months would demonstrate, Forbes clearly could have raised that much if he had wanted to. The others all fell at least $8 million short of that goal.

How will the typical contributor respond to the new limits established by the BCRA? Since the law did not go into effect until the day after the 2002 elections, any answer given to this question is necessarily speculative. Indeed, we know of only one relevant bit of data that bears directly on this issue. In early 2001 a group of political scientists conducted a survey of people who had contributed to the nomination campaigns of the major Democratic and Republican presidential candidates in 2000.[42] One of the questions in that survey asked contributors to predict how their own giving would be affected if the contribution limit were raised to $2,000. Twenty-two percent of the respondents said they would give more, 2 percent said they would give less, and the rest said they would not change their level of contributing.

Unfortunately, the survey did not specifically ask contributors *how much* more or less they would give; but if one assumes that all donors who said they would give more will double the size of their contributions and that all donors who said they would give less will cut their contributions in half, the total contributions to both parties' candidates would go up by about 25 percent. In the middle column of table 5-6, we apply this 25 percent estimate to the actual fund-raising totals of the 1996 candidates. A higher contribution limit, it appears, would have added about $2.9 million to Lamar Alexander's war chest and about $1.8 million to the Buchanan campaign. Both candidates thereby inch a bit closer to the $20 million threshold, though they remain well short of the mark.

As the authors of the study note, the responses to this survey question probably represent a "minimum estimate" of what donors will actually do. Many contributors who said their giving would be unaffected will no doubt behave differently when a campaign is under way and they are being pressured to ante up. If the estimates in table 5-6 are even approximately correct, however, it appears that the new contribution limit will not ease too many of the fund-raising problems associated with front-loading. To do that would probably require a larger increase in the contribution limit.

Another possible finance change, and one that would probably be less toxic to the campaign finance reform lobby, would be to increase the amount of federal matching funds that go to the candidates. At present, once a candidate has fulfilled certain minimum conditions, any individual contribution he or she receives will be matched, up to $250, by an equal amount from the federal government.[43] In most recent nomination races, about a third of all the money spent by the candidates has come from these matching funds.[44] In December 1999 Barbara Norrander recommended that the matching ratio be increased, such that the federal government would match individual contributions on a 3:1 or 4:1 basis rather than the current 1:1 ratio.[45] As shown in table 5-7, this change would have had a more significant effect on the fund-raising of the non-front-running candidates in the 1996 Republican race than an increase in the contribution limits. Tripling the matching ratio would have added about $4.6 million to the Lugar campaign, $6.4 million to the Alexander campaign, and almost $8.0 million to the Buchanan war chest. Given the recent increase in the individual contribution limit, a second change may also be in order: matching all contributions up to the level of $500, rather than the current $250.[46]

Two final points are worth noting about changes in the campaign finance laws. First, as the data in tables 5-5 and 5-6 indicate, though raising the contribution limit or tripling the matching-fund ratio would have put more money in the hands of second-tier and non-front-running candidates, it would have added even more to the campaign coffers of the front-

Table 5-7   *Estimated Effect of Tripling the Matching Fund Ratio on Pre-Election-Year Fund-Raising in the 1996 Republican Nomination Race*
Millions of dollars

Candidate	Initial matching entitlement	Estimated increase	New total[a]
Dole	9.26	18.52	43.04
Gramm	6.65	13.30	34.06
Forbes	0[b]	0	17.97
Alexander	3.23	6.46	17.98
Buchanan	3.98	7.96	15.18
Lugar	2.28	4.56	10.46

Source: Data on initial matching entitlements taken from Anthony Corrado, "Financing the 1996 Elections," in Gerald M. Pomper, ed., *The Election of 1996: Reports and Interpretations* (Chatham, N.J.: Chatham House, 1997), table 4.2, p. 143.

a. Total is the sum of the estimated increase and the total contributions the candidate received during 1995 (see table 5-6).

b. Forbes spent more than $50,000 of his own money on his campaign and was therefore ineligible for matching funds.

runners. Nevertheless, we think that the non-front-runners would be the clear net beneficiaries of these reforms. As the analysis in chapters 3 and 4 has shown, the principal challenge in a front-loaded system is not to provide equal resources to all candidates (which would, in any event, be enormously difficult to do) but to give non-front-runners the minimum amount of money necessary to get into the game, have some reasonable opportunity to get their message out to the voters, and not feel compelled to withdraw a few days after the New Hampshire primary.[47] In the current argot of campaign finance, we seek "floors without ceilings." A system that meets this goal would not meet everyone's criterion of a "level playing field," but it would, we believe, be a considerable improvement over the current system.

Second, neither of these proposals, it is fair to say, currently stands any chance of being enacted on its own. Conservatives and Republicans would staunchly resist any attempt to get the government more involved in funding campaigns; liberals and Democrats are unlikely to agree to another increase in the individual contribution limit, especially one coming so soon after the last increase. Under the right conditions, however, it may be possible to link the two proposals together and thereby put together a more broad-based coalition for change.

Table 5-8   *Effect of Delegate Allocation Rules on the 1992*
Nomination Races[a]
Number of delegates won, except as indicated

| | | | | Results under winner-take-all | | Results under proportional representation | |
| | Number of primaries | Actual results | | | | | |
Candidate	won	Number	%	Number	%	Number	%
Republicans							
Bush	37	1,547	94	1,654	100	1,251	76
Buchanan	0	75	5	0	0	355	21
Other[b]	0	32	2	0	0	48	3
Democrats[c]							
Clinton	18	1,008	63	1,600	100	1,009	63
Brown	0	415	26	0	0	423	26
Other[b]	0	177	11	0	0	168	10

Source: Actual results are based on contemporary reports in *Congressional Quarterly Weekly Report* and the *New York Times*.

a. Winner-take-all and proportional representation estimates are based on statewide results. Most states actually apply winner-take-all or proportional representation rules at the congressional district level.

b. Includes both delegates pledged to other candidates and uncommitted delegates.

c. Last eighteen primaries only.

Promoting Proportional Representation

Another recommendation made by the Republicans' Advisory Commission on the Presidential Nominating Process was that all states use proportional representation as the means of allocating delegates among the candidates in primaries and caucuses. When proportional representation is not used, when states employ a winner-take-all or direct election allocation system, the argument goes, a candidate who wins a few early primaries can sometimes convert a relatively narrow edge in the preference vote into a quite substantial lead in the delegate count. With proportional allocation rules, by contrast, losing candidates generally receive at least some share of the delegates in each primary.[48] Proportional representation thus makes it more difficult for the front-runner to achieve a mathematical majority of the convention delegates, thereby prolonging the competition and giving other candidates a greater chance to mount a comeback.

For a good example of how these rules operate, consider the nomination races of 1992. On the Republican side, incumbent president George Bush and challenger Pat Buchanan squared off against each other in thirty-seven primaries; Bush won every one of them. As shown in table 5-8, had every Republican primary used proportional representation, Buchanan would have received 355 delegates, 22 percent of the total. In fact, because most Republican primaries used some version of winner-take-all (most often, winner-take-all at the congressional district level), Buchanan won just 75 delegates, 4 percent of the total. In the Democratic race, what started out as a quite competitive contest became, in early April, a remarkably one-sided affair: Bill Clinton won every one of the last eighteen Democratic primaries. Had the Democrats allowed states to use winner-take-all rules, Clinton would have won all of the 1,600 delegates at stake in these eighteen states. Under the actual rules, which required states to use a proportional allocation system, Clinton won just 1,008 delegates (63 percent of the total), and Jerry Brown won 415 (26 percent). Quite clearly, proportional representation rules do give more delegates to losing candidates.[49]

That said, there are strong reasons, both empirical and theoretical, to doubt that the greater use of proportional allocation rules will significantly alleviate the effects of front-loading. On the empirical side, the most compelling argument against proportional representation is the simple fact that since 1992 the Democrats have required all states, primary and caucus, to use proportional allocation rules—yet there is no evidence to indicate that the Democratic nomination calendar is less front-loaded than the Republican calendar or that Democratic nomination races last longer than Republican contests.[50]

On a more theoretical level, the case for proportional representation has, we think, two major flaws. First, just as we have argued in connection with the Delaware plan, proponents of proportional representation place too much emphasis on the mathematical delegate count and make insufficient allowance for all the other factors that determine the course of a contested nomination race. The fact that his principal opponent has yet to clinch a majority of the convention delegates is of little consolation to a candidate if he has no money available to continue campaigning or if he has lost so many consecutive primaries that his candidacy lacks all credibility with the voters and the media. To repeat the point made earlier, most candidates exit the presidential nomination race—and most races are declared over by the media—long before the winning candidate clinches a mathematical majority of the delegates.

Yet even with respect to the narrow mathematics of the delegate count, the argument in favor of proportional representation is problematic in a second important way.[51] Though proportional allocation rules generally work to the disadvantage of whichever candidate is winning most of the primaries, this is only half of the story. Proportional representation also

Table 5-9   *Effect of Delegate Allocation Rules on the Final Day of Primaries in the 1980 Democratic Nomination Race*[a]
Number of delegates won, except as indicated

Candidate	Number of primaries won	Actual results		Results under winner-take-all		Results under proportional representation	
		Number	%	Number	%	Number	%
Carter	3	323	46	215	31	330	47
Kennedy	5	372	53	481	69	366	53
Other[b]	0	1	0	0	0	0	0

Source: Actual results are based on contemporary reports in *Congressional Quarterly Weekly Report* and the *New York Times*.
   a. Winner-take-all and proportional representation estimates are based on statewide results. Most states actually apply winner-take-all or proportional representation rules at the congressional district level.
   b. Includes both delegates pledged to other candidates and uncommitted delegates.

makes it more difficult for losing candidates to catch up. Consider the situation of a front-running candidate who, having done well in the first several weeks of the primary season, stands only a few hundred delegates shy of the nomination, with five or ten major primaries still to be held. Under a proportional representation system, a candidate in this position is all but assured the nomination. Even if the candidate loses most or all of the remaining primaries, proportional representation rules guarantee that he or she will still pick up a sizable number of delegates. But a winner-take-all system, even if it helped the front-runner at an earlier stage of the race, gives the second- or third-place candidate some lingering cause for hope. Under winner-take-all rules, a front-runner who falters in the final primaries can be shut out in the delegate hunt, thus allowing his or her chief rival to stage a dramatic comeback. Proportional representation rules, by contrast, essentially make dramatic comebacks impossible.

The 1980 Democratic nomination contest provides a good example of this phenomenon. The primary season that year ended on June 3, when eight states selected their national convention delegations. Starting the day well behind Jimmy Carter in the delegate count, Edward Kennedy won five of these last eight primaries, including those held in California and New Jersey. As shown in table 5-9, had these states used winner-take-all rules, Kennedy would have beaten Carter in the June 3 delegate count by a substantial margin: 481 to 215. Under the rules actually in operation, however—all eight states used proportional representation—Kennedy gained surprisingly little advantage from his five victories. He won just 372 delegates that day to Carter's 323.

For those who are interested in trying to use delegate allocation rules to counter the effects of front-loading, a better alternative than requiring that all states use proportional representation is to adopt the suggestion originally entertained by the Hunt Commission in the early 1980s: to prohibit winner-take-all primaries in the early stages of the race but allow that option for later-voting states.[52] Like a system of bonus delegates, that change by itself is unlikely to have much effect, but in combination with other reforms it might make some contribution to solving the problem.

Easing the Strain on the Campaigns

There are, finally, a number of small steps that might be taken to ease some of the more difficult problems that campaigns face as they try to grapple with a severely front-loaded calendar. These include

—increasing the number of states that grant automatic ballot access to all "nationally recognized" candidates,

—having the Republicans adopt some version of the Democrats' rule, under which candidates who fail to file full delegate slates may select delegates to which they are otherwise entitled through some kind of special postprimary procedure,

—moving the start of the delegate selection window back to the beginning of March or even April, to reduce the length of the interregnum period,

—amending the campaign finance laws to allow candidates to raise and spend more money during the interregnum.

Conclusion

We end this chapter on a pessimistic note. We are not particularly dazzled by any of the proposals examined in this chapter. On the one hand, none of the "comprehensive" plans are likely to remedy most of the real problems associated with front-loading. Many of them are also likely to spawn a host of new problems. The incremental proposals, by contrast, are almost certainly safer, in the sense that they are unlikely to generate serious but unanticipated negative consequences. But it is unclear whether any of them are potent enough to have more than a marginal effect on front-loading. In some cases, to repeat the metaphor used earlier, these proposals would probably just make the patient a little more comfortable.

CHAPTER SIX

The Politics of Nomination Reform

For a body of writing that has been produced largely by political scientists, the existing literature on reforming the presidential nomination process is strikingly apolitical. Most of it approaches the topic as if it were a purely technical matter of finding the right solution to a suitably defined problem in engineering. All of the things that political scientists routinely insist are important in every other area of public policy—interests and opinions, power and authority—have been almost entirely ignored. In particular, surprisingly little attention has been given to the question of how any of the major reform proposals would be implemented and enforced.[1] This chapter begins to redress that imbalance by examining the political and governmental context within which reforms of the nominating process must take place.

Perhaps the most salient feature of that context—and one of the greatest obstacles to reform—is the extreme fragmentation of authority over the presidential nomination process. Indeed, it is not unreasonable to say that the process is not a single system at all but rather a complex weave of rules and laws from a multitude of sources. Among the entities that have a hand in setting the rules of the process are the following:

—The two national parties, which promulgate general delegate selection guidelines

—The fifty state governments, which are generally responsible for the laws establishing presidential primaries and for regulating many other aspects of the structure and activities of state political parties

—The hundred state parties (fifty Republican and fifty Democratic), under whose auspices presidential caucuses are usually held and which sometimes have some measure of control over primaries

—The federal government, which enacted the campaign finance laws and, according to some sources, may have the authority to set up a national or regional primary system

—The courts, especially the U.S. Supreme Court, whose decisions with regard to campaign finance and the legal autonomy of the parties are responsible for some of the most important features of the current regime

Thus even if we could decide that a national or regional primary system is the best way to reshape the current system, there would remain another important question: Who exactly should create and enforce this new process, and how should they go about doing it? Three basic possibilities have been advanced in regard to this question: the states, the federal government, and the national parties. Some proposals may actually require action by all three entities.

Public Opinion

As background to that discussion, however, we begin with a brief look at public opinion. Though pollsters have rarely asked Americans what they think about the presidential nomination process (as distinct from the candidates competing in it), the survey materials that are available are sufficient to establish two major conclusions.

The first and most fundamental point to recognize is that reforming the presidential nomination process is just not something that most Americans care much about. When Americans are asked what is wrong with the country or what issues they want the president and Congress to deal with, the nomination process is not the sort of thing that comes readily to mind. One particularly compelling demonstration of this point comes from the American National Election Studies (ANES), a series of academic election surveys conducted by the University of Michigan. In almost every election year since 1960, the ANES has included some version of the question originally developed by the Gallup poll, asking respondents what they think is "the most important problem facing the country." Though the questionnaires allow interviewers to record up to three different problems for each respondent, so far as we can tell, in the entire history of the ANES, no one has ever answered this question by claiming that the travails of the presidential nomination process are the country's most important problem.

Many readers, we suspect, will not be terribly surprised to hear that fixing the presidential nomination process does not rank high on the public's scale of priorities. As the preceding pages testify, the nomination process is a complex set of rules and procedures, not easily reducible to simple slogans or solutions, without an obvious villain. Even when a nomination race is in progress, the process (as distinct from the candidates and the contest) receives relatively little media attention. But the same cannot be said of an issue that is, in numerous ways, closely related to the presidential selection process: campaign finance. The role of money in politics receives an enormous amount of press coverage, and almost all of this coverage is organized around a simple and highly moralistic theme: that money from wealthy individuals and special interests is corrupting the American political system. Yet even here, the public simply refuses to buy in to all the hype: no matter how much the press talks about it, no matter how much they insist that limiting the role of money in politics is the key to solving many of our other problems, the evidence clearly indicates that campaign finance reform has never been a particularly important concern of the American public.

In 1997, for example, a CBS–*New York Times* poll asked respondents which of four issues—the economy, education, campaign finance, or crime—was "most important right now."[2] Forty-two percent said crime, 32 percent chose education, and 19 percent said the economy. Only 4 percent said campaign finance. In 1998 a question posed by the survey research firm Market Strategies offered a different list of issues—tax reform, health care reform, campaign finance reform, and Social Security— and asked which was "most important to address right now." Again, campaign finance finished last, and by a substantial margin: 33 percent said health care, 27 percent Social Security, 26 percent tax reform, 7 percent campaign finance. In a similar vein, the Harris poll regularly asks its samples, "What do you think are the two most important issues for the government to address?" In thirty-one separate polls conducted over the past eight years, the largest number of Americans to mention "campaign finance" was 3 percent. In most surveys, it winds up as an asterisk (that is, the issue is mentioned by less than one-half of one percent of all respondents).

Particularly impressive are the results of a January 2000 Gallup poll that asked respondents to assess the importance of twenty-five separate issues, including education, health care, taxes, poverty, race relations, and crime. Remarkably, "campaign finance reform" ranked twenty-fourth on the list; the only issue it beat out was "policy concerning gays and lesbians." John McCain's candidacy, which drew so much attention to the campaign finance issue, did nothing to change this situation. In January 2001 Gallup presented respondents with a list of fourteen possible goals for the new administration and asked what priority each goal should have. This time, "improving the way political campaigns are financed" ranked dead last.

Given this general lack of public interest in the subject, it seems clear that any survey data purporting to measure public views on the presidential nomination process need to be treated with some caution. As survey analysts have long recognized, respondents will frequently provide answers to questions even if they have never given the subject much previous thought and have little long-term commitment to their responses.[3] Questions on the presidential nomination process seem especially apt to produce these sorts of "nonattitudes."

Yet one attitude about the nomination process comes through sufficiently clearly, in a variety of question wordings, as to suggest that it represents a strongly held predisposition. Simply put, the public supports public participation in and control of the presidential selection process. It is considerably more skeptical about, if not downright hostile toward, proposals that seek to increase the power of party leaders or other elite groups. In an analysis of a *Los Angeles Times* survey conducted in December 1979, William Schneider and I. A. Lewis reached a conclusion that is still valid today:

> The closer the process comes to popular democratic expression, the more satisfactory it seems, while the closer the process moves toward self-interest and entrenched bureaucracy, the less it is approved of. . . . Any changes or reforms are likely to meet public opposition unless they are "democratic" in nature. There does not seem to be any significant popular constituency for "de-forming" the candidate selection process and increasing the role of elite groups such as party leaders and contributors.[4]

That such an outlook exists should come as no surprise; it reflects two other attitudes that have long been part of American political culture: a generalized support for democracy and a pronounced ambivalence about political parties.[5]

Another symptom of this outlook is the strong support Americans have long shown for a national primary system. Beginning in 1952, the Gallup poll has periodically asked Americans if they favor having "presidential candidates chosen by the voters in a nationwide primary election instead of by political party conventions as at present." Across fifteen separate surveys, 67 percent of the public, on average, have supported a national primary; just 20 percent have opposed it. This does not mean, of course, that Americans have actually tried to itemize the pluses and minuses of a national primary, as we attempted to do in the previous chapter. Americans support a national primary, we think, simply because it seems to be the most direct and overtly democratic system available.

Reform by the States

To return to the question raised earlier in this chapter: Suppose that we have decided on the best way to remodel the presidential nomination process. Who should implement and enforce this new system?

Some reform proposals have been advanced under the proposition that the states should enter into voluntary agreements to rearrange their primary schedules. A good example is the proposal made in 1999 by the National Association of Secretaries of State. The NASS put together a Model Presidential Primary law, which it then urged each state to adopt. By passing that legislation, a state would pledge to "participate in a rotating regional presidential primary system" as defined later in the bill.[6]

The problem with this approach is that it requires full, or almost full, cooperation from all fifty states. If even a relatively small number of states decide not to go along, the system is likely to collapse. Consider all the things that might occur under the NASS plan (or any other plan that uses this approach) to short-circuit the system:

—Some of the states that are not scheduled to vote until the final grouping might decide that they are unwilling to wait that long and move their primaries up to the date set for the first or second grouping.

—One or two large states—California, New York, Texas, or Florida— might conclude that the system treats them unfairly, since the rotation schedule gives them no more weight than any other state, and opt out of the system entirely.

—Though the NASS hoped to get forty-eight states and the District of Columbia to participate in one of the four regional primaries, the plan specifically exempted Iowa and New Hampshire, allowing those two states to continue holding the first caucuses and first primary "prior to the commencement of the rotation schedule."[7] As experience under the current system amply indicates, many other states would no doubt feel that such an arrangement was manifestly unfair and hence decide that they too should schedule their primary or caucus sometime before the first regional primary takes place.

As these examples illustrate—lots of others could be added to the list—the problem with this approach to reform is that it relies entirely on voluntary cooperation. States that fail to pass the legislation—or pass it and then renege—suffer no penalties or sanctions. Though the country as a whole might be better off if this reform were implemented, it is in the immediate interest of each state not to cooperate. Indeed, as we have argued in chapter 3, it was precisely this "tragedy of the commons" that led to front-loading in the first place.

In addition to each state's desire to maximize its own benefits from the nomination process, efforts to create a new calendar by voluntary agreement among the states can also be undermined by the simple difficulty of getting fifty separate states to take any kind of action at all. Given the lack of public concern with the issue and the press of other priorities, as well as the other, more parochial considerations that inevitably affect each state's politics, persuading a substantial number of states to adopt the necessary legislation can be a significant hurdle.

A good example of this latter problem was the attempt to create a Rocky Mountain regional primary for the 2000 nomination cycle.[8] After observing the heavily front-loaded calendar of 1996 in operation, many leaders in state government concluded that the best way to combat front-loading—or at least to preserve their own states' influence in the process—was to create a series of new regional primaries through decentralized and voluntary cooperation. The most notable of these efforts was launched in early 1998, when the governors of Arizona, Colorado, Idaho, Montana, Nevada, New Mexico, Utah, and Wyoming announced their intention to establish a common primary date. The total delegate strength of these eight states roughly equaled the number of delegates assigned to California, and the governors hoped that combining their primaries would force presidential candidates to pay attention to western states and western issues. After California announced that it would hold its primary on March 7, Utah governor Mike Leavitt, who was spearheading the effort, set the date of the Rocky Mountain primary for March 10, halfway between the new Titanic Tuesday and the old, southern Super Tuesday.

In the end, however, only three states—Colorado, Utah, and Wyoming—actually voted together on March 10. What is especially noteworthy for present purposes is that the Rocky Mountain regional primary failed to materialize not because any of the nonparticipating states thought that a regional primary was a bad idea but because of simple fragmentation and parochialism. States declined to join the regional primary for a remarkable assortment of reasons. Arizona opted out because its primary was already set for an even earlier date in the nomination season (February 22), a date that had brought the state considerable attention from the candidates and the media in 1996. Some Arizona Republicans also reportedly wanted an early date to give a boost to the campaign of home-state candidate John McCain. In Nevada and New Mexico, the regional primary bill seems to have been defeated, at least in part, because of partisan tensions between a Republican governor and a Democratic legislature. Democrats in several states were concerned that a March 10 primary date might put the state in conflict with national Democratic rules.[9] Every state worried about the cost of holding a separate presidential primary—or about the disruption to state politics that would result from selecting its state and local candidates in mid-March.

Federal Legislation

Precisely because of the difficulty of relying on the states, many authorities have come to the conclusion that if reform is to have any real prospect of succeeding, it must be accomplished through federal legislation. Since the early 1900s more than three hundred bills have been introduced in Congress calling for some sort of national primary or nationalized system of delegate selection. In the 106th Congress, two more bills were added to the list. One (S. 1789) would have established a system of four rotating regional primaries corresponding to the Northeast, South, Midwest, and West. The other (H.R. 4014) would have established six primary dates on which a mix of states from different regions would vote. Neither bill proceeded past the hearing stage.[10]

Though some of these bills have specifically called for a constitutional amendment, many were ordinary legislation: that is to say, they sought to create a new nomination process by using the existing powers of the federal government.[11] It is, however, far from clear that the federal government has the constitutional authority to regulate or reform the presidential nomination process. Indeed, two separate constitutional challenges can be raised against any federal legislation on this subject.

First, does the federal government have the power to impose a national or regional primary system upon the states? Does the federal government, in other words, have the authority to tell the states that they must hold a presidential primary, or when they can hold it, or how precisely they are to use this primary to select or bind convention delegates? Three provisions in the Constitution are particularly relevant to these questions:

—Article II, section 1: "Each State shall appoint, in such Manner as the Legislature thereof may direct, a Number of Electors, equal to the whole Number of Senators and Representatives to which the State may be entitled in the Congress."

—Article II, section 1: "The Congress may determine the Time of chusing the Electors, and the Day on which they shall give their Votes; which Day shall be the same throughout the United States."

—Article I, section 4: "The Times, Places and Manner of holding Elections for Senators and Representatives, shall be prescribed in each State by the Legislature thereof; but the Congress may at any time by Law make or alter such Regulations, except as to the Places of chusing Senators."

As these clauses indicate, the federal government is given very little power generally to regulate the presidential selection process, particularly in comparison with the broad powers it is given over congressional elections. Most important details with respect to presidential elections are specifically left to the discretion of the state legislatures. Congress does have the authority to determine the time of "chusing the electors," but this clause quite clearly relates only to the selection of members of the electoral college. The entire presidential nomination process—anything that the parties or anyone else does to influence the effective set of choices available to the electoral college—would appear to be completely extraconstitutional. Certainly the Constitution gives Congress no explicit authority to regulate that process.

As is often the case in constitutional law, however, the text of the Constitution is one thing; what lawyers and judges do with it is something else. In fact, there are a small number of Supreme Court cases that, according to some scholars, may provide a basis for extensive federal intervention into the presidential nomination process.

The seminal case in this area is *Burroughs* v. *United States*, which was decided in 1934. At issue in this case was the constitutionality of the Federal Corrupt Practices Act of 1925, which required any committee that raised or spent money to influence a presidential election in two or more states to file periodic disclosure reports. Though the Court made no attempt to argue that the Constitution had expressly granted such powers to Congress, it nevertheless upheld the act as a valid exercise of Congress's general authority to protect and safeguard the procedures that were essential to the government's continued existence. As the Court put it,

> The President is vested with the executive power of the nation. The importance of his election and the vital character of its relationship to and effect upon the welfare and safety of the whole people cannot be too strongly stated. To say that Congress is without power to pass appropriate legislation to safeguard such an election from the improper use of money to influence the result is to deny to the nation in a vital particular the power of self protection. Congress, undoubtedly, possesses that power, as it possesses every other power essential to preserve the departments and institutions of the general government from impairment or destruction, whether threatened by force or by corruption.[12]

Though *Burroughs* is invariably cited by supporters of federal primary legislation, it is important to note the narrowness of the Court's actual ruling in this case. The Court did not claim that Congress had the general authority to rewrite the rules of the presidential selection process anytime it believed that it could make the system work better. The Court merely said that Congress had the power to protect the fundamental integrity of the presidential election process whenever it was threatened by what the Court called "the two great natural and historical enemies of all republics, open violence and insidious corruption."[13] It was this same power that the Court relied upon in *Buckley* v. *Valeo*, when it upheld Congress's general capacity to regulate campaign finance during the nomination phase of a presidential election.[14]

Some authorities, however, have used the *Burroughs* decision to argue that Congress possesses quite sweeping powers to regulate and control presidential elections. The best-known and most frequently cited example of such an argument occurs in the case of *Oregon* v. *Mitchell*. In early 1970 Congress passed a voting rights act that, among other things, lowered the voting age to eighteen in all federal elections, presidential as well as congressional. A number of states, including Oregon, claimed that the act took away from them "powers reserved to the States by the Constitution to control their own elections." In announcing the judgment of the Court, Justice Hugo Black not only upheld that portion of the act but also argued that Congress had an almost unlimited authority to govern presidential elections:

> I would hold, as have a long line of decisions in this Court, that Congress has ultimate supervisory power over congressional elections. Similarly, it is the prerogative of Congress to oversee the conduct of presidential and vice presidential elections and to set the qualifications for voters for electors for those offices. It cannot be seriously contended that Congress has less power over the conduct of presidential elections than it has over congressional elections.[15]

Since the Court had earlier ruled that Congress's authority over congressional elections extended to primaries as well as general elections,[16] Black's opinion would seem to provide a basis for virtually any kind of regulatory scheme Congress chooses to adopt with respect to the presidential nomination process.

Not to put too fine a point on it, but Black's opinion (which, it is important to note, was not the opinion of the Court)[17] is a travesty of legal reasoning. Indeed, there is not much real reasoning in it—just a rather bluff assertion that Black cannot imagine the Framers writing the Constitution according to a different set of principles from those he would have employed if he had been given the job. The actual text of the Constitution, however, leaves little room to doubt that the Framers did, in fact, give Congress much greater control over congressional elections than over presidential elections. As the clauses quoted above clearly indicate, Congress was given power to control the "times, places, and manner" of congressional elections but only the "time" of choosing presidential electors. This difference cannot legitimately be called meaningless or unimportant. As the debates at the constitutional convention show, and as James Madison was to argue in Federalist 39, the Constitution was deliberately designed so that some offices in the new government had a national character while others embodied the "federal" principle. The latter accordingly gave a greater role to the states—and correspondingly more limited powers to the national government.

A second difference between the clauses regarding congressional and presidential elections is also significant. Article I, section 4, gives Congress the authority to regulate various aspects of congressional "elections," a provision that, as noted earlier, the Court has reasonably interpreted as applying to primary as well as general elections. The grant of power in Article II, section 1, by contrast, is considerably more limited, allowing Congress to set the time of "chusing the electors" (that is, the members of the electoral college), a phrase that cannot reasonably be construed as extending to the nomination phase of presidential elections, when the parties are choosing their candidates.

It is, then, an open question whether Congress has the constitutional authority to impose a national or regional primary system upon the states. A straightforward reading of the relevant constitutional provisions, we think, strongly suggests that it does not, but as we have indicated, there are other ways of reading the Constitution that would permit a more expansive construction of congressional power. None of the major precedents conclusively settle the issue.

As noted earlier, there are two major reasons to question whether the federal government has the constitutional authority to regulate or reform the presidential nomination process. In the second case, what is at issue is not federalism—that is, whether the federal government can impose its will on the state governments—but whether *any* government can control the activities of a political party, an entity that many view as a private association, whose internal operations are protected from outside interference by the First Amendment. Political parties are, of course, mentioned nowhere in the original text of the Constitution. As parties emerged and developed during the last decade of the eighteenth century and the first half of the nineteenth century, they were accordingly treated as entirely private organizations, whose decisions and procedures were beyond the scope of governmental regulation. As V. O. Key has noted of this early period, "It was no more illegal to commit fraud in the party caucus . . . than it would be to do so in the election of officers of a drinking club."[18] As parties became more powerful, however, they were gradually subjected to extensive legal regulation.[19] "By 1920," as Austin Ranney has noted, "most states had adopted a succession of mandatory statutes regulating every major aspect of the parties' structures and operations."[20]

Though these laws and regulations were enacted by state legislatures, the courts did nothing to obstruct the trend. In certain respects, in fact, they reinforced it. Of particular significance was a series of Supreme Court decisions known collectively as the white primary cases. Through the first several decades of the twentieth century, most southern states openly and explicitly banned blacks from participating in Democratic Party primaries. Had this occurred in a general election, it would plainly have been a violation of the Fifteenth Amendment and hence unconstitutional.[21] But what about a primary election? Was a primary an instance of "state action" and thus subject to the strictures of the Constitution, or was the Democratic Party simply a "voluntary association," as the southern state parties themselves maintained, that had a First Amendment right to select its own members and limit participation in organizational decisions in any way it found suitable? After dancing around this question for a number of years, in *Smith* v. *Allwright* (1944) the Court finally and definitively came down in opposition to the white primary. "Primary elections," the Court argued,

> are conducted by the party under state statutory authority. . . . This statutory system for the selection of party nominees for inclusion on the general election ballot makes the party which is required to follow these legislative directions *an agency of the state* in so far as it determines the participants in a primary election. The party takes its character as a state agency from the duties imposed upon it by state statutes; the duties do not become matters of private law because they are performed by a political party.[22]

As this quotation indicates, in the *Smith* case the Court derived its finding that political parties were a public agency from the fact that the primaries were held under governmental auspices and the parties were already deeply enmeshed in a state regulatory system. In this sense, the decision arguably had little to say about how parties should be regarded when they act independent of state law. In the decade after *Smith* v. *Allwright*, however, an additional series of white primary cases came close to answering this last question by asserting, in strikingly unqualified terms, that parties are a public agency, no matter what the law says.

The most noteworthy of these cases was *Rice* v. *Elmore*, decided by the Fourth Circuit Court of Appeals in 1947. Shortly after the *Smith* v. *Allwright* decision was announced, the South Carolina legislature repealed all of that state's laws relating to primary elections; the Democratic Party then conducted its own primaries, under rules set by the party itself. Not surprisingly, one of those rules prohibited blacks from participating. Yet even in this new, radically privatized form, the appellate court rejected the argument that the Democratic Party was a "voluntary political association" whose activities were beyond the reach of the Fifteenth Amendment. As the court put it,

> The fundamental error in defendant's position consists in the premise that a political party is a mere private aggregation of individuals, like a country club, and that the primary is a mere piece of party machinery. The party may, indeed, have been a mere private aggregation of individuals in the early days of the Republic, but with the

passage of the years, political parties have become in effect state institutions, governmental agencies through which sovereign power is exercised by the people.[23]

In other words, parties are public agencies simply because they are powerful, because they play such an important role in the selection of public officials.

Rice v. *Elmore* was never reviewed by the Supreme Court; but six years later, the Court came close to ratifying its central thesis. At issue in *Terry* v. *Adams* was a group called the Jaybird Democratic Association, which ran its own primaries, with no governmental sanction or cooperation, in Fort Bend County, Texas. As in South Carolina, these primaries excluded blacks from voting. The Court ruled that these primaries did violate the Fifteenth Amendment, but the case's value as a precedent for future decisions was undercut by the fact that a majority of the Court was unable to agree as to why exactly that amendment applied.[24]

Through the first six decades of the twentieth century, in short, courts gave every indication that they regarded political parties as public entities, subject to whatever regulations a state chose to impose upon them.[25] Beginning in the early 1970s, however, the pendulum began to swing back in the opposite direction.

The seminal case in this new line of thinking was *Cousins* v. *Wigoda*, decided in 1975. The *Cousins* case emerged out of a battle between two groups of delegates, both of whom claimed to represent the Chicago area at the 1972 Democratic National Convention. One group, the Wigoda delegates, had been elected in the 1972 Illinois Democratic primary, many by overwhelming margins. But a second group, the Cousins delegates, claimed that they deserved to be seated at the convention because the first group had failed to adhere to the new "slate-making" and affirmative action guidelines that had been established by the McGovern-Fraser Commission. Eventually, the Democratic National Convention chose to seat the second group; contempt proceedings were then initiated against the Cousins delegates on the grounds that they had violated Illinois law, which required delegates to be selected via the Democratic primary.

The Supreme Court, however, sided with the Cousins delegates, ruling that "the National Democratic Party and its adherents enjoy a constitutionally protected right of association" that overrode any interest the state had in protecting the integrity of its electoral processes:

> If the qualifications and eligibility of delegates to National Political
> Party Conventions were left to state law each of the fifty states could

establish the qualifications of its delegates to the various party conventions without regard to party policy, an obviously intolerable result. . . . The Convention serves the pervasive national interest in the selection of candidates for national office, and this national interest is greater than any interest of an individual state.[26]

Since then, the Supreme Court has quite consistently upheld the claims of political parties almost every time they have come in conflict with state law.[27] In 1981 it overruled the Wisconsin Supreme Court's attempt to assert the supremacy of that state's "open primary" law against national Democratic rules. In 1986 the Court allowed the Connecticut Republican Party to open up its primaries to independent voters, even though state law limited primaries to registered party members. In 1989 the Court invalidated California laws that dictated the organization and composition of party governing bodies and prohibited those bodies from making endorsements before a primary. In 2000 it declared the "blanket primary" unconstitutional.[28]

Yet if the general principle has been clearly established, the precise boundaries of party autonomy remain rather murky. The general mode of analysis the Court has used in these cases first requires it to determine whether the burden on the parties' First Amendment rights is mild or severe. If severe, the law may still be upheld if it is "narrowly tailored to serve a compelling state interest." Though the Court has repeatedly made clear that it accords considerable importance to the parties' freedom of political association, particularly as it relates to the parties' "basic function" of nominating candidates for public office, it is not so easy to say, in any given instance, what constitutes a "compelling state interest."[29]

Suppose, then, that Congress were to adopt a law establishing a national or regional primary system. Could one or both parties opt out of the system on the grounds that they thought the law unwise or harmful to the party's interests and that they had a First Amendment right to determine their own nomination procedures? There is, at present, no clear answer to this question.[30] The Court has made clear, in two different cases, that national party rules take precedence over *state* law, but as the passage from *Cousins* v. *Wigoda* quoted earlier suggests, part of the Court's concern was with the possibility that the sheer diversity of state laws and practices could undermine the integrity of a national party convention. Perhaps the Court would look more favorably on a uniform national regulation.[31]

If a national or regional primary plan cannot be established by ordinary federal legislation, Congress could still enact such a system through constitutional amendment. The problem with going the amendment route, of course, is that it would make it considerably more difficult to get any reform enacted. To pass a constitutional amendment requires not only a two-thirds majority in both houses of Congress but also the approval of three-fourths of the state legislatures or conventions in three-fourths of the states. As simple testimony to how difficult this is, it is worth recalling that over the past 210 years, just seventeen amendments have been added to the Constitution.[32]

Another major problem with federal regulation of the presidential nomination process, however it is instituted, is the potential rigidity it is likely to introduce into the system. All of the major comprehensive proposals discussed in the previous chapter represent substantial departures from the current system, whose full consequences are difficult to predict. Given that fact, and the fact that changes in technology, candidate behavior, and media organization and practices may soon introduce further important changes in the process, it is likely that any legislation that Congress passes will soon need to be modified. As the chairman of the 2000 Republican advisory commission noted, "Whatever our proposed 'solution,' it would at best be out of date in a decade. The world is simply changing too rapidly."[33]

Yet the clear record of federal legislation in this area indicates that such laws are difficult to pass, even when there is widespread dissatisfaction with the current system. Over the past ninety years, more than three hundred bills have been introduced in Congress calling for some sort of national primary or nationalized system of delegate selection, yet none has even come close to being enacted.[34] In the specific area of campaign finance, the system established in 1974 was widely criticized almost from the beginning, yet only two major amendments to the 1974 law have been passed in the twenty-eight years since then—and one of these was essentially forced upon Congress when the U.S. Supreme Court declared large parts of the original legislation unconstitutional.

There are a number of reasons for this uninspiring record. One important factor, we think, is the public's general lack of concern with the issue. Representatives and senators often seek reelection by portraying themselves as zealous advocates of health care, education, national security, or tax relief, but it is difficult to imagine any incumbent trying to build a career around the claim that he or she is Congress's leading champion of reforms in the presidential nomination process. As a result, it appears that most of those who have introduced legislation in this area have regarded it as a distinctly secondary concern, easily thrust aside in the face of more pressing issues.

A wonderful example of this problem can be found in an article written some years ago by the political scientist Michael Nelson. Having reached the decision that a national primary was the best way to reform the presidential nomination process, Nelson called up Senator Lowell Weicker (R-Conn.), the sponsor of a national primary bill, to ask about its current prospects. After first being informed that the senator's press secretary knew nothing about the bill, Nelson met with Weicker himself. The senator then told him that "he did not know if his bill had attracted any cosponsors, did not know if there were comparable bills being looked at in the House of Representatives, and was not sure whether hearings had been scheduled on it in the Senate."[35]

To take another plausible scenario, suppose that the new federal law, once in operation, is found to confer some kind of advantage on one party over the other in terms of its prospects of winning the general election.[36] Changing federal law, unlike party rules, generally requires some cooperation from both parties, particularly when Congress is as closely divided between the parties as it has been in recent years. Neither party, we think it fair to say, would readily agree to surrender such an advantage. As a result, one party might be stuck with a nomination process that it had no capacity to change or abandon, even though, in the opinion of most party members, that process was doing the party serious harm. In either case, it seems particularly unwise to enact a major reform of the nomination process in a way that would be so difficult to change if the new system were found to be seriously deficient.

Reform by the National Parties

If there is one group that clearly does have a direct, continuing interest in the structure and functioning of the presidential nomination process, it is the political parties. The presidential selection system is central to the parties' national existence (indeed, for many years, it was virtually the only thing either of the major parties did as a national entity) and may have strong and important effects on the parties' electoral fortunes. If Congress and the general public are prone to lose sight of the nomination process in the press of other business, the same cannot be said of the parties. In that sense, parties would seem to be the most natural agency to pursue nomination reforms.

Moreover, as the preceding discussion should make clear, the national parties do have the legal right to set up their delegate selection rules in pretty much whatever way they wish. In particular, both *Cousins v. Wigoda* and *Democratic Party of the United States* v. *Wisconsin* declare, in remarkably broad terms, that state laws are not binding on national party conventions.

The key question with regard to the parties is whether, in practice, they have the ability to enforce their national rules upon the states. National party rules, it is important to emphasize, are not self-executing. If state laws cannot bind the national conventions, neither can national parties issue binding orders to state legislatures or even state parties. The only concrete power the national parties have—their sole real enforcement tool— is their control over the seating of convention delegates. If a state selects its delegates in a way that the national party believes violates that party's delegate selection rules, the party can refuse to seat those delegates at its national convention. In practice, however, this can be a difficult power to wield. Consider three case studies.

The McGovern-Fraser Commission

On the positive side, the "reforms" of the McGovern-Fraser Commission—the "greatest systematic change in presidential nominating procedures in all of American history"[37]—were brought about by national party initiative. Not a bit of federal legislation was necessary; and though some state legislatures or state parties might have changed their delegate selection procedures even in the absence of a national party mandate, there is little doubt that the changes would have been far less thoroughgoing and would have included far fewer states had the national party not been applying pressure in the same direction.

Whatever one thinks of the wisdom of the McGovern-Fraser guidelines, their implementation represents, in its own way, a remarkable achievement. In February 1970, when the commission first sent out so-called compliance letters to all of the state party chairmen, every state was held to be in violation of at least six of the eighteen guidelines. Yet "by the time the last delegates had been selected, the fifty states and the District of Columbia were in conformity with 905 of the 918 commission guidelines, a success rate of 98.6 percent. Only two of the nonconformities . . . were accurately classed as serious. In 94 percent of the states, or 99 percent of the guidelines, reform was essentially achieved."[38]

A number of factors help explain why the national Democratic Party was so successful in getting the state parties to implement the new delegate selection rules.[39] First, there already existed within most states a solid nucleus of individuals and groups who were favorably disposed toward reform and actively embraced the commission's handiwork. Second, even among those party "regulars" who opposed some of the new rules, there was a widespread sense that dealing with credentials disputes at the 1968 convention had been a long and divisive experience and that some kind of "precise, advance standards"[40] were needed to make sure that the same thing did not happen again. Finally, given the emotionally heated character of American politics generally in the early 1970s and the strident moral tone of the New Politics movement, a plausible threat existed that the national party just might apply its full enforcement powers against those states that refused to implement the guidelines. That threat gained additional credibility from the fact that one state delegation had been entirely excluded from the 1968 convention for failing to comply with an earlier set of antidiscrimination rules.

Whatever the exact set of causes, the result was not only a dramatic reshaping of the presidential nomination process but an equally far-reaching change in the federal structure of the Democratic Party. As William Crotty has noted, "The party reform movement altered the power distributions within the Democratic party in an even more fundamental way. The historic relationship between the national party and its state and local units was altered, and before reform had run its course, dramatically reversed."[41]

Showdown in New Hampshire and Iowa

The Democrats' first serious attempt to enforce their delegate selection "window" came during the 1984 nomination cycle.[42] As drafted by the Hunt Commission and approved by the Democratic National Committee, the 1984 window rule required all caucuses and primaries to be held between the second Tuesday in March (March 13) and the second Tuesday in June, except that New Hampshire was allowed to hold its primary seven days before the start of the window (March 6) and Iowa could hold its caucuses fifteen days in advance (February 27). Everything seemed to be in order until New Hampshire noticed that Vermont had scheduled a nonbinding presidential preference vote for March 6 as part of its Town Meeting Day. Since New Hampshire state law required its primary to be held one week ahead of "any similar event," Granite State officials now insisted that they had to move their primary up another week, to February 28. The national Democratic Party disagreed, arguing that because the Vermont primary did not select any delegates, it was not a "similar event." Protests from national party officials notwithstanding, New Hampshire did move its primary to February 28, at which point Iowa moved its caucuses to February 20. When the national party refused to approve the new dates, the result was a test of wills that lasted for more than a year.

At one level, there was no doubt that the national party had legal authority on its side. The Democrats were not bound to follow New Hampshire law. They had every right to refuse to seat the delegates selected in these rescheduled events and to select a new set of delegates through some alternative procedure that did comply with party rules. The more significant question was whether the national party had the will to enforce its legal rights, and on this score, New Hampshire and Iowa held most of the high cards. Party leaders in both states could (and did) plausibly claim that any attempt to desanction the Iowa caucuses or the New Hampshire primary would be bitterly resented by local residents and party activists, seriously hampering the party's efforts to carry those states in the general election and possibly costing the Democrats control of the Senate. (Both Iowa and New Hampshire had hotly contested Senate races that year.) The states also essentially blackmailed the presidential candidates into endorsing their position. In late October 1983, while attending a Democratic state convention in New Hampshire, the candidates were asked to sign a letter pledging to support the dates preferred by the states and not to participate in any alternative delegate selection events organized by the national party. "Rather than risk antagonizing Democrats" in these crucial early states, all but one of the Democratic candidates signed on.[43]

After several attempts at compromise fell through, Iowa and New Hampshire went ahead and held their caucuses and primary on their preferred dates, even though they were both in violation of national party rules. Yet no one seemed to notice or care. The candidates all showed up, just as they had promised, and engaged in their usual frenzied courtship of the local electorates. The media substantially overreported both events, as usual, with barely a passing mention of the fact that they might be beyond the pale. For the next month or so, national party leaders continued to talk about the possibility of holding a second round of elections in both states, but there was never any real prospect that they would follow through on their threats.[44] In May the Democratic National Committee finally and officially relented and agreed to seat the Iowa and New Hampshire delegations.

In short, the 1984 confrontation between the national Democratic Party and the states of Iowa and New Hampshire ended in a total victory for the two states. Having been granted a privileged position in the nomination calendar by the Hunt Commission, the two states had demanded even more and then shown little willingness to compromise. Yet in the end, the national party gave into them on every count.

Wisconsin's Open Primary

The McGovern-Fraser Commission not only tried to open up the Democratic Party's presidential nomination process to any party member who wanted to participate; it also sought to exclude members of other political parties and unaffiliated voters who had no desire to join the party.[45] As this goal was worked out by subsequent reform commissions, it did not require states to institute party registration, but it did prohibit the kind of open primary in which any registered voter could participate in either party's primary without even having to make a public declaration of his or her party affiliation or preference.[46] Since 1903 the Wisconsin presidential primary had been operating under just such a rule. Voters in the Wisconsin primary were effectively given both a Republican and a Democratic ballot, and though they could vote in only one party's primary, they made that decision in the privacy of the voting booth.[47]

The national Democratic Party—more specifically, the party's Compliance Review Commission (CRC)—had informed Wisconsin as early as December 1973 that its primary was in violation of party rules and needed to be revised. Yet Wisconsin showed not the slightest willingness to comply. Though Democrats held almost two-thirds of the seats in the state assembly, that body refused even to debate a bill that would have repealed the open primary provision. The state senate, equally dominated by Democrats, took up the bill and promptly rejected it. Nor did the state party abide by the CRC's suggestion that they begin to organize an alternative plan for delegate selection, one that did conform to the national party rules. Instead, the state's Democratic governor, legislative leaders, and state party chair filed suit against the Democratic National Committee (DNC), hoping to force the national party to accept whatever delegates were selected in the state's primary. That behavior notwithstanding, in early March 1976, just a month before the primary, the CRC actually granted Wisconsin an exemption from the rules on the grounds that they had made a "good faith effort" to change the state law. As with New Hampshire and Iowa, the presidential candidates were critical actors in this decision. Morris Udall, who had emerged as the strongest candidate from the party's liberal wing, needed a state in which he could win a primary, and Wisconsin, with its Progressive heritage, looked to be a favorable venue. Hence a bloc of party "reformers" who normally voted for strict enforcement of the rules voted this time to give Wisconsin an exemption.

Almost exactly the same thing happened in 1980. The national party again held that Wisconsin's open primary was in violation of the party rules. (Indeed, the 1980 rules actually included a provision that specifically prohibited the party from granting any state an exemption from the rule limiting participation in primaries and caucuses to Democrats.) Nevertheless, the Wisconsin state party again insisted that they would select their delegates by open primary and then tried to get the presidential candidates to pledge their support for the state's position. Meanwhile, in January 1980, the Wisconsin Supreme Court ruled in favor of the state in its suit against the DNC. With time running out, the DNC Executive Committee voted once again to grant Wisconsin an exemption.

In early 1981, as noted earlier in this chapter, the U.S. Supreme Court resolved any legal questions by ruling decisively against the state's claim that the national party was legally required to recognize the delegates selected in accord with Wisconsin law. Bolstered by that decision, the Democratic National Committee rejected all further attempts to allow Wisconsin's open primary to play a role in selecting national convention delegates. In February 1983 the state party finally threw in the towel and formally voted to ask the state legislature to make the needed changes in the law. Even then, the state legislature, still firmly in Democratic hands, refused to change the open primary provision. The result was that Wisconsin did hold an open presidential primary in 1984, but, at least on the Democratic side, it was a purely advisory affair. Delegate selection was accomplished through a caucus-convention process organized by the state party that began four days after the primary.

In its struggle with the Wisconsin open primary, then, the national party fared better than it had in its efforts to enforce the window against Iowa and New Hampshire—but not much better. Wisconsin won an exemption from the national rules in both 1976 and 1980, even though a strict reading of the rules suggests that neither exemption was justified. Even in 1984 the national party was unable to achieve what was, presumably, its ideal solution. The Wisconsin delegates to the 1984 Democratic National Convention were selected through a process that was not open to Republican or unaffiliated voters, but the Wisconsin primary law was never changed.

Had the Democrats won the White House in 1984, it is possible that they would have been satisfied with this partial victory. As it was, national party leaders interpreted Walter Mondale's forty-nine-state loss as a sign that it was time to bring to an end the party's long-running attempt to solve its presidential election woes by rewriting its delegate selection rules. The Democrats did form one last party reform commission—the so-called Fairness Commission—but its spirit was summed up this way by one member: "We've reached a consensus in the party that we should not fight over rules any further."[48] As an adviser to the commission put it, "The commission tried to remove spurs causing great pain to the party without reopening debate on larger principles."[49] As one reflection of this attitude, the party rewrote the section of its delegate selection rules concerning participation by those who were not party members so that the Wisconsin primary could fit within the rules. And thus it has been in every subsequent election cycle.

These last two cases are probably not representative of the national Democratic Party's experience over the past three decades. As Gary Wekkin has noted, in the relationship between national and state parties, "cooperation is more common than conflict. . . . All state parties comply with most DNC rules."[50] But these cases do make the simple point that full state compliance with national party rules is not always a given. Applied to the specific case of front-loading, whether the states will go along with any package of reforms promulgated by the national parties will depend, we think, on three factors: what the parties ask the states to do—and how much that conflicts with the needs and interests of the individual states; how hard the national party works to promote state compliance—and whether states that are not inclined to cooperate see a credible threat that real sanctions will be applied against them; and the extent to which other party elites, particularly presidential candidates, work to support or undercut the reforms.

Other Obstacles to Party-Based Reforms

Issues of power and compliance aside, there are a number of other problems with using the national parties as the principal agents for reforming the presidential nomination process. First, parties are notoriously—and properly—suspicious of any changes that might affect their ability to compete in the general election. Parties have a number of concerns when it comes to designing the nomination process, but their most important consideration is that the system help—or at least not hinder—their chances of winning the White House. This has made both parties somewhat reluctant to tackle the front-loading issue on their own. Though both parties clearly see front-loading as a problem, both also entertain the belief that if one party's nomination race were to last into May or June while the other party settled on a nominee in February or March, the former party would labor under a significant disadvantage in the general election.

A good example of this dilemma occurred during the summer of 2000.[51] In early May of that year, a special commission set up by the chairman of the Republican National Committee (RNC) had recommended that the party adopt the small-states-first or Delaware plan for its 2004 presidential nomination (for further details, see chapter 5). That recommendation was later approved by both the rules committee of the Republican National Committee and the full RNC. On the Friday before the opening of the Republican national convention, however, the convention rules committee, acting at the behest of the Bush campaign, voted to kill the proposal. Though there were a number of reasons why the Bush campaign came out against the Delaware plan, one of the most important considerations was the potential dangers that the plan might pose for the Republicans' competitive position vis-à-vis the Democrats. As one Republican strategist put it at the time, "Their nominee would emerge in March, we're still fighting until May or June. It gives them a tremendous advantage in the general election. . . . They could finish in March, be raising money and be ready to pounce on us."[52]

Similarly, the Democratic committee that recommended moving up the start of their delegate selection window from March to February for the 2004 election cycle seems to have recognized that this decision would almost certainly increase front-loading. Yet they felt they had no choice: in 2000 only Republican primaries had taken place between February 1 and March 7, giving that party, according to many Democrats, a distinct advantage in media exposure and primary voter participation.

Second, party-initiated reforms are unlikely to carry much weight with governors or state legislators from the other party. As noted in the previous chapter, one reason the Republican "bonus delegate" plan had so little apparent effect on front-loading was that the bonuses applied only to Republican convention delegations. Presidential primary dates are established by state legislatures, and there was plainly no incentive for Democratic legislators to move back their primary to help their partisan opposition. By contrast, one reason the Democrats were so successful at implementing the McGovern-Fraser guidelines is that the Democrats then controlled a large proportion of the country's governorships and state legislatures.[53]

There is, of course, a way to cope with both of these problems: get the two major parties to agree on a common reform program. Yet this solution is not as simple as it might appear at first glance. In the first place, differences in party ideology sometimes mean that the parties will disagree about the elements that ought to go into a properly designed nomination process. For many years, for example, Republicans were noticeably more reluctant than Democrats to impose nominating reforms through national party mandates (the 2000 reform proposals were, in this respect, a sharp break with party tradition). While a number of factors may have contributed to this reluctance, to a large extent it was simply a reflection of the Republicans' long-standing principles concerning states' rights and the dangers of centralized power. On the other hand, any effort to raise the individual contribution limit, as the Republicans have recommended, is likely to encounter stiff resistance from Democrats, largely because of their philosophical beliefs about the role of wealth in American politics.

Both parties also hope that the nomination process will give adequate voice and proper representation to the groups that constitute their core supporters. Given the different makeup of the Democratic and Republican coalitions, the parties may thus have divergent views about which states ought to go first or how the process should deal with various political or demographic minorities. As noted in chapter 5, the Delaware plan, which was thought by the Brock Commission to be the best of all the plans they considered, would be significantly less appealing to Democrats since it shunts so many of their core constituencies to the back of the calendar.

Any attempt to have the parties agree on a common program for reforming the presidential nomination process must also come to terms with the different ways in which each party adopts its delegate selection rules. On the Republican side, delegate selection rules are set by the previous national convention: the rules for 2004, for example, were adopted by the 2000 convention. Between conventions, the Republican National Committee has no authority to alter or amend these rules. On the Democratic side, by contrast, it is the Democratic National Committee that sets the party's delegate selection rules, usually about ten to fifteen months after the conclusion of the previous presidential general election. (The Democratic rules for 2004 were approved at a meeting of the DNC held in mid-January 2002.)

Obviously, getting the parties to agree on a common set of reforms becomes more difficult if the two parties proceed according to different timetables. Beyond that, there are, we believe, substantial problems with trying to institute major changes in a party's delegate selection rules at a national convention. Because national conventions come at the height of a presidential campaign, it is all too easy to subordinate all rules disputes to the narrow question of what will help the presidential candidate in the November voting. Another reason the Bush campaign killed the recommendations of the Brock Commission was simply that they did not want a highly divisive issue such as the Delaware plan spoiling a convention that was otherwise designed to be one long encomium to the nominee. As one analyst put it, Bush "was not about to do anything to interfere with the convention's carefully crafted ambience—and particularly something that would give news-hungry reporters even the tiniest morsel of red meat on which to chew."[54]

In 1988, to take another example, Jesse Jackson and his supporters were anxious to make a number of major changes in the Democratic Party's delegate selection rules, which they regarded as unfair to Jackson's candidacy and black interests more generally. The Dukakis campaign essentially granted Jackson just about everything he wanted, not because they agreed with his demands or felt they were in the best interests of the party but because changing the rules seemed to be the easiest way to buy off Jackson and gain his cooperation for the fall campaign.[55] Fortunately for the Democratic Party, the national committee had the authority to override the convention resolutions and adopt its own rules.[56]

The Role of the Candidates

Finally, it is appropriate to say a few words about the role of the presidential candidates in the reform process. At one point, candidates and their supporters were seen as central actors in the writing of delegate selection rules. Particularly during the late 1970s and early 1980s, when the Democrats created a major party reform commission after every election, would-be candidates and their advisers often intervened in the work of these commissions, in an attempt to devise a set of rules that would be favorable to their own campaigns. In 1977–78, for example, representatives of the Carter White House played a major role in the deliberations of the Winograd Commission, with the clear intention of trying to ease the president's road to renomination. In 1981–82 supporters of both Edward Kennedy and Walter Mondale, the early front-runners for the 1984 Democratic nomination, were actively involved in the Hunt Commission. Not surprisingly, both groups sought rules that would enhance the nomination prospects of front-running candidates, particularly those who had strong ties to other party leaders and the regular party organizations.

Such behavior led some observers to portray the rules-writing process as little more than a product of the narrow interests of the likely candidates.[57] As one student of the presidential nomination process argued in 1987, "Rigging the rules . . . is nothing new to American politics, or to presidential nominating campaigns. . . . What the series of recent reform commissions did, however, was to legitimize and institutionalize this politicking. Rules were no longer constants from one election to the next; instead they became a variable to be manipulated by candidates and interest groups. The opening skirmish in the battle for the party's nomination is now fought in a reform commission."[58]

In fact, even when candidate influence was supposedly at its high point, the Democratic rules were shaped by a lot more than the perceived interests of the major contenders. In 1977–78 the Carter White House reportedly sought three major changes in the Democratic rules: a significantly shorter nomination season, a tighter filing deadline for primary states, and an increase in the "threshold" level, the minimum percentage of the vote a candidate had to receive to win any delegates.[59] Yet even though their candidate was the incumbent president, the Carter forces were eventually forced to compromise on every one of these issues. For example, the Winograd Commission originally approved a proposal requiring all candidates who wanted to be included on a state primary ballot to file their nomination papers between fifty-five and seventy-five days before the primary. When this provoked substantial opposition, the filing period was expanded to run from thirty to ninety days before the primary, a rule with which almost every state was already in compliance.[60] Similarly, though the Hunt Commission did adopt a number of major rules changes that were seen as favorable to front-runners and party regulars, this was not simply because such changes were thought to help Kennedy and Mondale.[61] To the contrary, by the early 1980s there had emerged within the party a broad consensus that the first wave of reforms had overshot the mark and that something needed to be done to get the established party leadership more involved in the presidential nomination process.[62]

Moreover, however successful Carter and Mondale may have been in getting the Democratic Party to adopt their preferred set of rules, it is not obvious that they actually drew much benefit from their labors. Like party reform as a whole, the consequences of the new rules were difficult to predict—and sometimes seemed to hurt the candidate who had pushed hardest for their adoption. The 1980 threshold rule, for example, was designed to help Carter deal with "minor" or "fringe" candidates who received a small percentage of the vote (which is what, as of 1977, the Carter strategists expected to face in 1980). It offered no protection from a challenge of the sort eventually presented by Edward Kennedy. In 1984, as we have seen, the Mondale campaign's efforts to front-load the schedule almost forced their candidate into an early withdrawal.

Perhaps in response to this less-than-inspiring record, presidential candidates have generally not been major players in the rules-writing efforts that have taken place since 1984. Though Gary Hart and Jesse Jackson both pushed for the creation of another Democratic reform commission after the 1984 campaign (it was eventually called the Fairness Commission), neither of them took an active role in its deliberations—nor did the commission accommodate any of their major grievances.[63] Similarly, we know of no evidence that Bill Clinton made any attempt to tinker with his party's rules in either 1992 or 1996 or that Al Gore sought to tilt the playing field in his own favor in anticipation of the 2000 or 2004 nomination races. On the Republican side, the Dole campaign was strikingly uninvolved in the proceedings of the 1996 task force that devised the bonus delegate system. In 2000 the Bush campaign did act to kill the Delaware plan just a few days before the opening of the Republican convention. Yet there is little evidence that it did so because it thought the plan would affect its own chances of winning renomination in 2004. The Delaware plan was shelved because it threatened to be a source of division and distraction during the 2000 convention and because many Republicans genuinely thought it was not in the best interests of the party.

In general, then, there is no reason to think that the presidential candidates will be a uniquely obstructive force in the effort to devise a remedy for front-loading. The evidence to date suggests that front-loading has worked to the advantage of the front-runners; but that need not invariably be the case. As things actually worked out, the heavily front-loaded calendar of 1996 probably provided some advantage to the Dole campaign, but if Lamar Alexander had received seventy-six hundred more votes in New Hampshire, front-loading might have made it impossible for Dole to recover. Against that background, we think it unlikely that some future nomination front-runner will wage an active battle to retain front-loading. A more likely assessment has been provided by the chair of the 1996 Republican task force: "I have not talked to one presidential candidate who doesn't think this process has problems. They all think something has to be done."[64]

Conclusion

Two overriding conclusions emerge from the analysis in this chapter. First, none of the methods of implementing and enforcing reforms of the presidential nomination process is foolproof. All have their problems and limitations. Second, those who seek to reform the system—whether they be elected officials, party leaders, or scholars—should give more attention to such issues in the future. Books and articles on the nomination process often include a list of qualities or objectives that a properly designed presidential selection system ought to embody: that it produce competent candidates, that it be seen as legitimate by the general public, that it strengthen (or at least not weaken) the political parties. One other item needs to be added to such lists: that the proposed reform be one that could be implemented and enforced with a minimum of difficulty. A plan that requires voluntary cooperation from all fifty states or that asks the federal government to exercise powers it does not constitutionally possess is not very helpful, no matter how attractive that plan may be on other grounds.

CHAPTER SEVEN

Conclusion

Given all the difficulties and constraints discussed in the preceding two chapters, two questions need to be addressed. What realistically can be done about front-loading? And who should do it?

A Choice of Agents

Let us begin with the latter question. We believe quite strongly that the fundamental responsibility for reforming the presidential nomination process ought to rest with the political parties. We have reached this conclusion for two principal reasons. First, there are serious questions about whether the federal government has the constitutional authority to regulate the presidential nomination process. In our view, it does not. Second, if the initial set of reforms needs to be updated or revised, as seems highly probable, Congress is much less likely than the political parties to undertake that task in a timely manner. Congressional legislation is likely to be rigid and difficult to change in an area in which flexibility and adaptability seem particularly necessary.

The political parties, of course, have their own weaknesses as an agent of reform. In particular, the national parties have sometimes had difficulty getting state legislatures and state parties to comply with their rules. Whether the national parties will have the same problem in their efforts to combat front-loading depends, to a large extent, on what exactly they ask the states to do. At a minimum, it is important to formulate a plan that is perceived as treating all states fairly and equitably.

To bolster the parties' enforcement capabilities, we think it particularly desirable for the parties to try to reach agreement on a common program of reforms. Having the parties adopt a common program will strengthen the national parties' hand in at least three ways. First, as we saw in Iowa's and New Hampshire's successful attempt to evade the Democratic window, when a state party refuses to go along with a national rule, one of its principal lines of defense is to claim that if the national party insists on enforcing the rule, it will only generate hostility among state voters and party activists and thus weaken the party in the general election. Though this can be a quite credible argument if only one party is trying to enforce a particular rule, it plainly loses much of its potency if both parties are cracking the whip. Second, any incentive-based reforms—any proposals that try to combat front-loading by giving states a positive incentive to hold their primaries later in the year—lose much of their persuasive impact if they apply to only one party. A legislature under Democratic control has no reason to move back the date of the state primary if all the benefits of that decision go to the Republicans.

Third, even if the national parties mandate that states adopt a particular procedure or refrain from a given practice, if that mandate is included in only one party's rules, it is all too easy for a state party to resist—and then blame its failure to comply on the other party. When New Hampshire fought to move its primary up an additional week in 1984, for example, state Democratic officials did everything they could to support that effort—and then told national party officials they were unable to change the new primary date because Republican elected officials would not go along with it. Again, this excuse becomes less tenable if the reforms are required by both parties.

Ease of enforcement aside, the 2000 nomination campaign showed, we think, that while the two major national parties can disagree about a lot of rules-related issues, having different delegate selection calendars is likely to produce a good deal of mischief—for both parties. On the one side, the Democrats had that peculiar five-week gap between the New Hampshire primary and the eleven primaries held on March 7, during which media attention focused overwhelmingly on the Republican race and which therefore made it all but impossible for Bill Bradley to get his campaign back on track, even though he had just barely lost to Al Gore in New Hampshire. Meanwhile, given the absence of meaningful contests on the Democratic side, huge numbers of independents and Democrats came flooding into the Republican primaries, almost nominating a candidate who, as subsequent events have shown, was substantially out of step with the mainstream of his party and has even apparently contemplated leaving the Republicans and running for president as an independent. In Michigan, to take a particularly glaring example, one of every six votes in the Republican primary was cast by a self-identified Democrat, about four or five times the normal level of crossover voting. Though the American presidential nomination process can easily tolerate disagreements between Republicans and Democrats on such matters as affirmative action, a strong case can be made that the parties should seek agreement on a common calendar.

One of the prime obstacles to getting the parties to agree on a common reform program is the fact that the parties operate on different timetables and that the Republicans adopt their rules in what is, in effect, the middle of the general election campaign, when both parties are distracted by other concerns and the prospects for interparty cooperation are probably at their lowest (see chapter 6). Accordingly, an important first step in the reform process is for the 2004 Republican convention to adopt one of the recommendations made by the Brock Commission: "that the Republican National Committee be given the authority to modify the Rules of the Republican Party between national conventions."[1]

Two Pathways to Reform

So much for the who and how of reform. But what precisely should the national parties do? There are, we believe, two plausible pathways to combating front-loading. Depending on how serious one thinks the front-loading problem is, how much one worries about the prospect of unanticipated negative consequences, and how much political support can be mustered within each party's governing bodies, the parties can either take a series of small steps that will hopefully mitigate the problem and allow candidates and voters to deal with its consequences more effectively or adopt a more comprehensive approach to the problem, including a centrally coordinated calendar of primaries and caucuses.

In chapter 5 we analyzed a number of what we called incremental solutions, most of which would probably not be very effective if pursued in isolation but which together hold out some prospect of arresting and perhaps reversing front-loading—or at least allowing the principal actors in the nomination process to cope with it more effectively. Specifically, we think there is a strong case to be made for all of the following proposals:

—Substantially increasing the individual contribution limits for presidential nomination campaigns, as well as increasing the matching fund ratio from its present 1:1 level to 3:1 or 4:1

—Increasing the Republican bonus delegate formula to the levels originally proposed by the 1996 Task Force on Primaries and Caucuses and applying the same formula (or something along the same lines) to the Democratic convention

—Allowing states to use a winner-take-all or winner-take-more system of delegate allocation only if they schedule their primaries and caucuses after a particular date—say, April 15

—Trying to increase the number of states that grant automatic ballot access to all nationally recognized candidates

—Having the Republicans adopt some version of the Democrats' rule under which candidates who fail to file full delegate slates may select delegates to which they are otherwise entitled through some kind of special postprimary procedure

—Moving the start of the delegate selection window back a month or two, to reduce the length of the interregnum period

—Amending the campaign finance laws to allow candidates to raise and spend more money during the interregnum period

Some of these recommendations will offend the sensibilities of purists in both parties. Some Republicans, for example, will bridle at any attempt to limit the freedom of states to adopt whatever delegate allocation system they want, no matter when they schedule their primaries or caucuses. Some Democrats, by contrast, will object to any suggestion that proportional representation be watered down or abandoned, even if it helps promote some other valued end. Such principled objections notwithstanding, the proposals just listed are unlikely, we think, to produce any serious negative consequences. The real question is whether they are potent enough to have much impact on a problem that has reached such an advanced stage of development as front-loading has. As indicated in chapter 5, there is ample reason to be pessimistic.

The one of these proposals that may go beyond the merely incremental—the one on which we would probably place most emphasis—is the first. (Unfortunately, it is also one the parties cannot implement on their own: new federal legislation would be required.) Campaign finance is a key factor both in explaining why front-loading developed and in account-ing for some of its more negative consequences. Making it easier for the candidates to raise money would lower the bar that now discourages many plausible contenders from getting into the race—or forces them to make an early exit. It would also give candidates who do well in the early going a better chance of raising the money they need to contest the next round of primaries and caucuses.

In addition, increasing the flow of money to presidential candidates would allow them to make better use of the invisible primary by spending less time meeting with contributors and more time trying to engage the concerns of ordinary voters. During the year that precedes the first prima-ries and caucuses, a remarkable amount of a candidate's time is devoted entirely to fund-raising. As Lamar Alexander has reasonably argued,

> To raise $10 million in 1995 for the Alexander for President cam-paign, I traveled to 250 fund-raising events. . . . This is about one event per campaign day. This took 70 per cent of all my time. As a result, I became unusually well acquainted with a great many good Americans capable of giving $1,000 (who probably represent a cross section of about one per cent of all the people in the country). Wouldn't I have been a better candidate—and the country better off had I been elected—if I had spent more time traveling around America and visiting allies abroad?[2]

Obviously, any proposal to increase the amount of money that is spent on presidential campaigns, particularly if it involves raising the contribu-tion limits, cuts against the grain of much recent commentary on the American system of campaign finance. Over the past several decades, a small army of editorial writers, investigative reporters, and "watchdog" groups have deluged the country with cries of alarm about the huge amounts of money raised and spent by candidates for public office and its poten-tially corrupting effects on public policymaking. While these are undeni-ably valid concerns, most such critiques, in our judgment, have done the nation a signal disservice by failing to recognize another moral impera-tive: candidates must be allowed a reasonable opportunity to raise the money needed to get their message out to the electorate. Though a num-ber of worthwhile proposals have been made for reducing the costs of campaigning, the cumulative effect of such changes is likely to be rather limited, particularly in the context of a presidential nomination race.[3]

The unavoidable fact is that running for president is expensive. It is expensive because the United States is a very large country, both in terms of population and geographic expanse, and because, contrary to a good deal of civic mythology, most voters are not terribly interested in politics or campaigns and therefore must be contacted through relatively costly technologies and communications media (for example, buying thirty-second advertisements on television rather than simply making a set of position papers available on the Internet). Though it is easy to be appalled by candidates who spend $65 million to win a single seat in the U.S. Senate, the far more typical experience in this country is that candidates cannot raise the amount of money that most professionals believe is necessary to run even a minimally effective campaign. While reducing the corrupting influence of money is a valid objective, in the realm of presidential nomination campaigns the greater problem at the moment, we believe, is the difficulty that so many candidates have in raising the money necessary to get into the game at all.

As we have suggested at several points in chapter 4, all of the incremental proposals listed above may not be sufficient to alter the fundamental dynamics of the current system, particularly if (as seems likely) Congress is simply unwilling to make further changes in the campaign finance laws. Assuming this to be the case, more drastic surgery may be required. In particular, it may be necessary to abandon one of the key features of the current nomination process—the autonomous, uncoordinated way that states decide when to schedule their primaries and caucuses—and move toward some kind of centrally directed calendar. This is, in some respects, a radical departure from past practice, and yet there is precedent for such a step. One of the few powers the federal government has explicitly been given over presidential elections is the authority to "determine the Time of chusing" the members of the electoral college. The Constitution further mandates that those members then cast their votes on the same day throughout the country. While these provisions do not provide anything like a constitutional basis for federal regulation of the nomination process, they do show the Framers' understanding of the critical importance of timing and sequence in a nationwide election process. When a large number of states are given the opportunity to vote or otherwise register their preferences for a single office, those states that go first may have a significant impact on the behavior of later-voting states.[4]

Though it is not our purpose to present a detailed proposal for revising the delegate selection calendar, the analysis of the past several chapters does suggest several desirable features that ought to be included in such a plan:

—It should start small. Small need not mean one state, much less one state the size of New Hampshire. But given all the features of the current system that favor front-runners, there is great value in making sure that the calendar does not begin with eight or ten primaries on the same day, as is the case with many regional primary proposals. While we do not want a system that regularly confers presidential nominations on long-shots and outsiders, neither do we want one that confuses celebrity with merit and does not give small-state governors or non-mediagenic senators at least some reasonable opportunity to make a case for their candidacies.

—It should deliberately incorporate a mix of regions in the early going. One of the key flaws of a regional primary system is that it may give a significant advantage to a candidate who is unusually strong in whatever region happens to go first. To make sure this does not happen, a centrally coordinated nomination calendar ought to include a mix of regions through-out the delegate selection season, but especially in its early stages.

—It should not attempt to compress the delegate selection season. One of the most common complaints about the presidential nomination pro-cess is simply that it takes too long: that it compels too many top political leaders to abandon or give short shrift to their governing responsibilities and spend months or even years out on the campaign trail. While we generally agree with this criticism, we think it a grave misunderstanding to believe that the process can be significantly shortened by compressing the delegate selection season, which currently lasts about sixteen weeks, to six or eight weeks. The reason the nomination process takes so long is not the length of the formal primary and caucus schedule but the much longer period of informal campaigning (the so-called invisible primary) that precedes it. The shorter the delegate selection season, the more front-loading will increase, as the same number of primaries and caucuses are distributed among a smaller number of possible dates. So unless one delib-erately wants to encourage front-loading, there is, we think, little to be gained by compressing the delegate selection calendar.

—It should make some attempt to accommodate states seeking greater autonomy and flexibility, so long as they are willing to schedule their primaries toward the end of the delegate selection season. Any attempt to move to a centrally directed nomination calendar will no doubt provoke opposition from some states that will object to having to reschedule their primaries every four years or to holding two different primary elections, one for presidential nomination purposes, the other for state and congressional candidates. To some extent, these complaints need to be taken with a grain of salt. Many states already reschedule their primaries almost every election cycle to preserve or enhance their influence on the nomination races. In 1996 twenty-two states had separate primaries for president and all other offices. For those states that find this an intolerable burden, however, the system can provide a remedy. A state can hold its primary at the same point in the calendar every four years and can use this primary to nominate all candidates who will appear on the November ballot—so long as it is willing to hold that primary near the end of the delegate selection season. That is to say, it will be necessary to have central planning and coordination only for the first two months or so of the nomination calendar. Any state that is willing to wait until, say, May 1 can be allowed to schedule its primary or caucus entirely at its own discretion.

A Brief Word about Iowa and New Hampshire

No examination of the front-loading issue is complete without at least some attention to the question of what to do about Iowa and New Hampshire. New Hampshire has held the first primary in every presidential nomination race since 1920; Iowa has actually been preceded by another caucus state on several occasions (at least on the Republican side), but in six of the past seven election cycles, it has been the first major publicized showdown between the candidates.[5] More to the immediate point, both states have fought very hard to keep that status—and are likely to continue doing so in any future version of the nomination process.

Is the presidential nomination process better for the way it starts out? Are Iowa and New Hampshire, on balance, a positive or a negative influence? The arguments most often made in favor of starting off the process in Iowa and New Hampshire relate to their size. In 2000, according to the census, New Hampshire was the tenth smallest of the fifty states, home to just 1,235,000 people. To translate this into the hard currency of votes, even with New Hampshire's relatively high turnout rate (see table 4-8), total turnout in its 2000 Democratic primary was 154,000 votes, as compared with 284,000 in Georgia, 507,000 in Maryland, and 2,654,000 in California. John McCain's candidacy spurred an unusually large turnout on the Republican side in 2000; yet even in this case, just 238,000 votes were cast in the GOP primary. Given the large number of candidates running in the typical New Hampshire primary, this means that it is generally possible to win the primary by attracting between 55,000 and 90,000 votes. In comparison with the Granite State, Iowa is, in fact, not all that small. In 2000 Iowa ranked thirtieth in terms of population. But because it uses a caucus system rather than a primary, and the turnout tends to be far smaller at caucuses than in primaries, the number of individuals participating in the Iowa precinct caucuses is generally a good deal smaller than the turnout for the New Hampshire primary. In 2000 just 87,000 Republicans and 61,000 Democrats showed up for the Iowa caucuses.

The relatively small electorates in New Hampshire and Iowa are said to benefit the presidential nomination process in two principal ways. First, small electorates mean that all candidates are compelled to engage in a certain amount of "retail" politicking: meeting with voters in small groups, listening to the concerns of ordinary voters, breaking beyond the frequently limited perspectives of Washington-based commentators and consultants. Niall Palmer, a British admirer of the New Hampshire primary, has stated this argument: "The size of the state and its demographic spread dictate a town-by-town, door-to-door strategy that is now defunct in larger states such as Ohio or California. This affords ordinary voters the chance to question candidates at close quarters and compels candidates to think on their feet."[6]

Second, having the process start off in Iowa and New Hampshire gives a boost to candidates who are not able to raise huge sums of money during the invisible primary or who are not fortunate enough to be classified as one of the early front-runners. To quote Palmer again,

> New Hampshire aids not only the voter but also the small-scale candidacies of a Kefauver, a McCarthy, a Carter, a Hart or an Alexander. Candidates with little chance of serious attention in regional primaries have two opportunities in Iowa and New Hampshire to improve their financial and polling positions. They find fertile ground in New Hampshire since the state can still be organized on a shoestring budget. In addition, only in the two early states can flaws in the campaigns of front-runners be effectively exploited. . . . The closing of the Iowa–New Hampshire opportunity would signal the complete dominance of wealthy, big-name candidacies.[7]

Arguments of the type just quoted are, we think, largely a matter of balance: of assessing how Iowa and New Hampshire fit into the nomination process as a whole. If the nomination calendar still looked as it did in 1960 or 1976, we would be inclined to see the Iowa–New Hampshire kickoff in less favorable terms, since the calendar then afforded other opportunities for less well known candidates to get a hearing and win a breakthrough primary and did not require candidates to raise a huge amount of money before any delegates were selected. As the system has become more front-loaded, however, the value of Iowa and New Hampshire has increased. As Palmer correctly notes, the campaign in these two states provides a welcome and needed contrast to what will happen on the day after New Hampshire. However front-loaded the calendar has become in week 3, it continues to "start small" in weeks 1 and 2.

Yet it should also be clear that the nomination process pays a price for all the attention lavished on these two states. All of Iowa's and New Hampshire's idiosyncrasies and peculiarities are magnified and given national consequence. As has long been noted, there are significant demographic differences between Iowa and New Hampshire and the rest of the country, differences that ought to be of particular concern to Democrats since several of the national party's most important constituencies are almost entirely absent from both of the leadoff states.[8] In every recent presidential election, blacks have accounted for about one of every five Democratic votes—yet blacks constitute only about 1 percent of the Iowa Democratic caucus participants or New Hampshire primary voters. In addition, neither state has what could plausibly be called a big city. Among other things, these differences go a long way toward explaining why Walter Mondale fared so poorly in New Hampshire—and why Gary Hart did so well there: almost all of the groups that made up Mondale's core voters were underrepresented in New Hampshire.[9]

As New Hampshire's defenders are quick to note in reply, no state is perfectly representative of the country as a whole; all states have their distinctive traits and local or regional peculiarities.[10] Yet this argument is telling only if the nomination process must somehow begin in just one caucus state and just one primary state. Having two or even three states vote in each of the first several weeks of the calendar would arguably retain all of the advantages of starting small, without making the idiosyncrasies of any one state an important variable in the presidential selection process.

Moreover, even if it is finally decided that it is best to start the process off with a single caucus and a single primary, the more telling question is why it has to be the same two states in every election cycle. For the location of the first caucus and the first primary not only helps determine which candidates do well in the early going; it also has a major effect on what gets discussed by the presidential contenders. For reasons both practical and moral, candidates talk about the issues that are important to the people whose votes they are soliciting. The economic, social, and demographic peculiarities of Iowa and New Hampshire thus get translated into the agenda of presidential politics. Meanwhile, groups and constituencies that are not present in these two states are, for that reason, much less likely to hear the candidates address their distinctive issues and concerns.

A good example of this latter phenomenon is provided by the campaign of Bill Bradley in 2000. When Bradley launched his run for the White House in late 1998, he indicated that one of the major issues he wanted to talk about was the role of race in American life. Yet so far as we can tell from contemporary press coverage of the campaign, Bradley did not, in fact, actually spend much time addressing this issue. The principal reason he did not talk much about race was that he did so much of his early campaigning in Iowa and New Hampshire, two states with almost no black residents. In a similar vein, several recent Democratic nomination races (most notably, that of 1988) have included an extended dialogue on the problems facing contemporary American farmers. That issue was, of course, unavoidable, given all the time the candidates spent in Iowa. By contrast, the problems of big cities almost never get discussed in the nomination campaigns of either party. Though there are a number of reasons for this void, a sufficient explanation is the absence of big cities in both Iowa and New Hampshire.

Ever since the presidential campaign of Jesse Jackson in 1984, black politicians and civil rights leaders have often complained that the presidential nomination process does not give adequate attention to their distinctive issues and concerns. For those who are convinced that this grievance is legitimate, we think that one of the more effective remedies would be to make sure that the delegate selection calendar periodically begins in a state that has a sizable black population.

What can and should be done, then, about Iowa and New Hampshire? So long as we restrict our focus to incremental solutions, the answer, we think, is: very little. Over the past several election cycles, politicos in Iowa and New Hampshire have proved very successful at retaining their first-in-the-nation position by, in effect, blackmailing the candidates. In the 1996 election cycle, for example, when both Arizona and Delaware attempted to encroach on New Hampshire's turf, New Hampshire Republicans demanded that all of the major candidates sign a pledge "supporting the Granite State's right to stay one week ahead of any other primary contest. At a state party meeting in January 1995, [New Hampshire state party chair Steve] Duprey warned candidates refusing to support New Hampshire not to bother campaigning there during 1996."[11] Certain that New Hampshire would hold its early and much-reported primary, much less certain that other states would be around when it mattered, all but one candidate knuckled under.

Yet even if there is, at present, little real prospect of dislodging these two states from their preeminent position, we think it a mistake to add the national party's sanction to this state of affairs, as the Democrats have done in every election since 1984, by granting Iowa and New Hampshire a specific exemption from the timing rule that is not available to any other state. This manifest inequality would seem to be a clear violation of principles the Democrats would uphold in virtually every other context, and the party has plainly had some difficulty justifying it. Though Democratic Party documents sometimes refer to the "historical position of these two states,"[12] the fact is that in 1982, when the Democrats first wrote this exemption into their national delegate selection rules, Iowa's "tradition" of holding the first caucuses in the nation was all of ten years old. If Iowa and New Hampshire are determined to go first, they should be required to win that distinction on their own initiative (which they are probably capable of doing), without having the weight of the national party thrown in against any state that might challenge them and thereby introduce a bit of variety into the early nomination calendar.

It is more difficult to say what would or should happen if the national parties were to move toward a centrally coordinated calendar, as outlined earlier. No doubt Iowa and New Hampshire would both continue to insist that they deserve an exemption from the schedule that applies to everyone else; and as the NASS plan and the current Democratic rules testify, it is possible that the parties will go along, if only because they doubt their capacity to secure cooperation from these two states on any other basis. Given all the other difficulties facing any attempt to redesign the delegate selection calendar, a case clearly can be made that adding in a full-fledged battle against Iowa and New Hampshire is just not worth the effort.

If a new approach to primary and caucus scheduling is to succeed, however, it must be one that is seen as treating all states fairly and equitably, and it is difficult to believe that a system that grants special exemptions to two states, both of which have used their existing powers in a rather high-handed way, would meet that test. For reasons both practical and principled, then, we are inclined to think that any centrally devised calendar should not accord special treatment to Iowa and New Hampshire—or to any other two states. If the nomination process begins with a series of weeks in which a very small number of states are allowed to hold their primaries or caucuses, the states that get to fill these coveted positions should be determined by lottery or rotation, not by perpetual fiat.

Conclusion

It is, in retrospect, not terribly surprising that our political system would have so much trouble coping with front-loading, for front-loading poses difficult issues of authority and autonomy along two long-standing fault lines in American politics. On the one hand, it raises questions about the public versus private character of political parties; on the other hand, it requires judgments about the proper line of division between national versus state authority and decisionmaking.

Given all these difficulties, many observers will no doubt insist that the best course is to do nothing. The current system, it will be said, has functioned at some minimum level of effectiveness; it has yet to produce a real "disaster." Why not leave well enough alone? As the late Everett Carll Ladd put it in an essay written in 1994,

> I emphatically do not believe that our present system of picking presidential nominees is perfect. But neither do I think it is a walking disaster. It is like American political institutions generally—sound in many regards, but with shortcomings. Through ill-advised tinkering, one could certainly make things worse. And, I further argue, there is, quite literally, nothing that we can do to the present system of picking presidential nominees that can make things significantly better—in terms of a responsible and responsive democracy—that starts with the nominating system itself. . . . Messy and vulgar, to be sure, the system is working, better than we are often prepared to acknowledge, responding to the public's claims and the nation's needs.[13]

In a congressional hearing on the presidential nomination process conducted in 1986, the late Richard Scammon, then director of the Elections Research Center, came to a similar conclusion: "Frankly, I would just leave it alone. I would respond with Dean Atchison's (sic) comments once to President Truman: 'Have you ever thought, Mr. President, of doing nothing?'"[14]

Though we think caution and restraint are generally good advice when evaluating proposals that seek to "reform" major political institutions, that path seems ill suited to the particular case of front-loading. As we have argued at some length in chapter 4, front-loading is already having a number of decidedly negative effects on the nomination process.

Has it, to borrow Ladd's terminology, produced a "disaster" yet? Probably not—but that depends on what constitutes a disaster. Front-loading has been a dominant characteristic of the presidential nomination process for only about fourteen years.[15] During that time, there clearly are ample grounds for questioning the wisdom or appropriateness of many major-party nomination decisions. In 1988 the Republicans selected a candidate who seems to have had stunningly little interest in or solid convictions about domestic issues. In 1992 the Democrats chose a standard-bearer with some obvious personal gifts—and some equally significant personal problems. In 1996, after having just won control of Congress for the first time in forty years, the Republicans nominated a candidate who clearly had major problems running a national campaign and communicating with the voters.

None of these choices, most observers would probably agree, had obviously catastrophic consequences for the country (though some might argue differently about Clinton's failure to get after terrorism more aggressively). By most criteria, the American economy and the U.S. position in world affairs are in a stronger position today than they were in the mid-1980s. But this seems to us less a commentary on the adequacy of the nomination process than on the nature of the American political system as a whole. In the United States, both the political system and the party system have proved to be remarkably stable and adaptable. No matter who gets nominated or elected, no matter what they do in office, we somehow manage to muddle through.

Even when the shortcomings of the presidential nomination process seem particularly egregious—when the process plainly fails to live up to some of the standards that have conventionally been proposed for judging its effectiveness—the political parties (and the country) have a knack for rolling with the punches. One such standard, for example, is that the parties should select candidates who have a broad appeal to the electorate, particularly within the candidate's own party, and thus have some reasonable prospect of winning the general election. In 1972, however, the Democrats nominated a presidential candidate who was widely perceived as both personally weak and vacillating and far to the left of the average voter on almost every issue. The result was one of the most lopsided losses in the history of American presidential elections, in which, according to the American National Election Study survey, 42 percent of all Democratic identifiers voted for the Republican candidate. Yet most of the Democratic congressional candidates did just fine in 1972, and even the party's presidential wing proved to be sufficiently robust to elect a Democratic president just four years later.

In 1976, to take another example, the Democrats nominated a one-term governor with almost no previous experience in national politics. He had a very rocky four years in office; by 1980 the economy was in deep recession, and American foreign policy was, according to most observers, in serious disarray. As a result, he was decisively defeated in his quest for reelection—and took a lot of Democratic congressional candidates down with him. Yet the economy recovered, and just ten years later the cold war was over. As for the Democrats, they never lost control of the House of Representatives and by 1988 were once again competitive at the presidential level.

The fact that "things have worked out" in the past, however, seems to us to provide little cause for complacency. The challenges facing American national government are likely to be very great in the years ahead. Though it is generally not possible to draw a close, direct link between the effective operation of any particular political process or subsystem and the successful handling of a specific policy problem, both the U.S. Constitution and the discipline of political science are based on the belief that properly designed political institutions are more likely to solve problems than malfunctioning ones. The study and analysis of political institutions thus requires caution but also vigilance. Even if they do not result in obvious catastrophes, there clearly are instances in which important components of the political system function less well than they should, in which certain problems or tendencies would seem to cry out for correction. And while there is no simple way to determine when a problem has reached this point, front-loading seems to us to be well beyond the threshold.

On Measuring
Front-Loading

Given that we have devoted an entire book to the subject, a few words are clearly in order about how—and how not—to measure front-loading. As the discussion in chapter 2 should indicate, we view front-loading as a matter of how primaries and caucuses are concentrated within the delegate selection season. More specifically, front-loading occurs when primaries and caucuses are bunched together at the beginning of the delegate selection calendar, as opposed to being spread out evenly or being concentrated near the end of the process. To operationalize that definition, we have presented, in tables 2-2 and 2-3, two measures of front-loading, both of which indicate when delegate selection activity occurs relative to the first primary of each election cycle. The first measure is simply the number of primaries that took place in each week. The second—which is, we believe, the single best measure of front-loading available—is the cumulative percentage of delegates that had been selected by the end of each week in the primary season.

An alternative strategy, frequently used by both scholars and journalists, tries to measure front-loading by counting up the number of primaries that were held or the percentage of delegates that had been selected by some particular date in the election year, such as March 31.[1] A measure of this type will be equivalent to the kind of measure we use *if the primary season begins on the same day in every election cycle.* But as the narrative in chapter 2 indicates, this has not been the case. The primary season now begins almost a month and a half earlier than it did in the 1950s and

1960s. Before 1972 the New Hampshire primary was held on the second Tuesday in March. In 2000 New Hampshire selected its national convention delegates on February 1.

Measures based on the number of primaries occurring before or after a particular date thus confuse two matters that need to be more carefully distinguished: when primaries take place in an election year and how thickly the primaries are clustered at the beginning of the delegate selection season, regardless of when that season begins. To appreciate the distinction, imagine that the entire 1996 primary schedule were simply moved back one month, with New Hampshire voting on March 20 (instead of February 20) and California holding its primary on April 26. (For the actual 1996 Republican calendar, see table 2-5.) By our measures, such a move would have no effect at all on how front-loaded the system is; but if one measures front-loading on the basis of how many primaries occur before March 31, shifting the schedule in this way would make the system dramatically less front-loaded.

In the end, of course, choosing between these two measures is not a matter of deciding which one best captures the essence of the Platonic form of front-loading but rather of determining which one has more analytical and substantive utility. And as we believe we have shown in chapter 4, the major problems associated with front-loading almost all derive from the heavy concentration of primaries in the early weeks of the delegate selection season, not from when that season takes place. The need to raise huge sums of money during the invisible primary, for example, occurs because once the primary calendar begins, there simply is not enough time for a long-shot candidate who does well in Iowa and New Hampshire to raise enough money to run a competitive campaign in the next round of primaries. This would be true regardless of whether the Iowa caucuses and the New Hampshire primary take place in January, February, March, or April. Indeed, of all the problems discussed in chapter 4, the only one that would be affected by moving the start of the primary calendar back one month is what we have called the interregnum, the increasingly lengthy period between the effective end of the nomination races and the start of the national conventions.

For reasons that are discussed more fully in chapter 2, the frontloading measures presented in tables 2-2 and 2-3 are limited to delegates who were selected by primary. Primaries, it is worth noting, can be used to "select" delegates in two ways. In some cases, candidates for national convention delegate are actually listed on the ballot, either individually or as a slate, and are elected directly by the voters. In other states, a caucus-convention system is used to designate which particular individuals will attend the convention, but these delegates are allocated among the candidates or are pledged to vote for various candidates on the basis of how well those candidates did in the primary.[2] In either case, one can say that the primary voters have some meaningful control over a state's national convention delegation; hence, all such delegates are included in tables 2-2 and 2-3. States that held purely advisory primaries—in which the primary results played no role at all in the delegate selection process—are not included.

To assist those who may be interested in checking or replicating our results, one final point is worth mentioning. Some of the figures in tables 2-2 and 2-3 differ in small ways from an earlier presentation of these data.[3] The difference between these two sets of tables is a result of a change in the criterion that was used for defining the beginning and end of a week. In the earlier article, weeks begin on Wednesday and end on Tuesday, which is, in our experience, the way most candidates, reporters, and political practitioners think about time. In this book, we adopt the more conventional standard, in which weeks begin on Sunday and end on Saturday.

Specification of the Regression Equations in Tables 3-4 and 3-5

This appendix provides details on the construction of the regression equations shown in tables 3-4 and 3-5. For the equations in table 3-4, the dependent variable is the total amount of money spent by all candidates for that party's presidential nomination. All spending data are taken from Federal Election Commission reports.[1]

The independent variables are defined as follows:

—*Date of primary or caucus:* The date of the first primary or caucus in a party's delegate selection season (in most of the races analyzed in table 3-4, it was the Iowa caucuses)[2] was considered to be day 1. The date of every other primary or caucus was based on the number of days that had passed since that first event. In 1984, for example, February 20, the date of the Iowa caucuses, was designated as day 1; the New Hampshire primary, on February 28, took place on day 9; and the California primary, on June 5, occurred on day 107.

It is not difficult to identify the date on which Democratic and Republican primaries and Democratic caucuses are held; Republican caucuses, however, are a different story. Unlike the Democratic Party, the GOP has no requirement that all of the caucuses in a state be held on the same day. In some cases, a state's Republican caucuses may stretch over a period of several months. To deal with this problem, we used the following rule: Where Republican caucuses extended over a period of one week or less, we used the midpoint of that period as the date of the caucuses. For caucuses that extended over a longer period, we coded the date as a missing value and thus excluded that state from the equation. This explains why the equations for Democratic spending in table 3-4 all have an N of 51 (fifty states plus the District of Columbia), whereas the Republican equation has an N of 42 in 1980 and 45 in 1988.

—*Number of convention delegates:* The data can be found in a variety of sources.

—*Selection system used:* A dummy variable coded 1 for states that used primaries, 0 for caucus-convention states. States that held purely advisory primaries that played no role in the actual selection of delegates were coded 0.

—*Iowa and New Hampshire:* Separate dummy variables were used for each state.

For the equations in table 3-5, the dependent variable is the total amount of media coverage each state received. For 1980, we use Robinson and Sheehan's count of the total number of seconds each state received on the *CBS Evening News*.[3] For 1988 and 1992, we use the total number of stories on all three networks in which each state was mentioned, as counted by the Center for Media and Public Affairs.[4] For all three years, these data record the coverage received in both parties combined; separate data for Republicans or Democrats are unavailable. Hence the equations must be set up so as to take into account the influence of both parties' nomination races.

To explain how and why we defined the independent variables, consider a highly simplified model, in which the coverage of each state's Democratic primary or caucus depends entirely on the date on which it is held, and similarly for Republican delegate selection events. That is to say,

$$\text{Democratic Coverage} = a_1 + b_1{}^*\text{Democratic Date}$$

and

$$\text{Republican Coverage} = a_2 + b_2{}^*\text{Republican Date.}$$

Then,

$$\text{Total Coverage} = (a_1 + a_2) + b_1{}^*\text{Democratic Date} + b_2{}^*\text{Republican Date.}$$

Unfortunately, it is impossible to make a reliable estimate of this last equation, because of a severe multicollinearity problem. In most states, the Democrats and Republicans hold their primaries or caucuses on the same day, with the result that the Democratic date variable and the Republican date variable are very highly correlated.[5]

Given this problem, we have chosen to estimate a somewhat different model, which (staying with the highly simplified model outlined earlier) is

$$\text{Total Coverage} = a_1 + b_1{}^*\text{Average Date,}$$

where Average Date is a weighted average of the Democratic and Republican dates. That is,

$$\text{Average Date} = w_1{}^*\text{Democratic Date} + w_2{}^*\text{Republican Date.}$$

The key question then becomes, How do we determine the values of the weights, w_1 and w_2? Though it is easy to imagine a number of quite elaborate ways of calculating these weights, in table 3-5 we assume that the weights are a simple function of the total amounts of press coverage each party received throughout the nomination cycle. In 1988, for example, the Center for Media and Public Affairs, which was also responsible for our measure of total state media coverage, determined that during the entire nomination season, there were a total of 635 network television stories on the Democratic race and 459 stories on the Republican contest. Hence the Democratic weight in 1988 is .58 (635/1,094), and the Republican weight is .42 (459/1,094).[6] In a similar fashion, the 1980 weights are .50 for Democrats and .50 for Republicans.[7] In 1992 the weights are .64 for Democrats and .36 for Republicans.[8]

With that as background, the independent variables in table 3-5 are as follows:

—*Date of primary or caucus:* As indicated above, the date variable is simply a weighted average of the date of the Democratic primary or caucus and the date of its Republican counterpart. Where the date of a Republican caucus could not be precisely identified, we again coded it as missing data and excluded that state from the equation.

—*Number of convention delegates:* To give the proper emphasis to each party, two weights are actually necessary here. First, it is necessary to weight each party so that they have approximately equal numbers of delegates, so that one delegate has approximately the same significance in both parties. In all of the years analyzed here, the Democratic national convention had almost twice as many delegates as its Republican counterpart. Because what matters in determining media coverage is the relative size of a state's delegation rather than the absolute number of delegates at stake, we have weighted the number of Democratic delegates so that the Democratic total equals the Republican total.[9] We then computed a weighted average of the number of Republican delegates and the (already weighted) number of Democratic delegates.

—*Selection system used:* In most states, the Democrats and Republicans employ the same type of delegate selection system (that is, either both use primaries or both use caucuses), and there is consequently no problem in creating a dummy variable that distinguishes between primary states and caucus states. We have also, however, created a second dummy variable for the small number of states (on average, about six in each election) in which one party used a primary while the other selected its delegates through a caucus-convention system. If primaries receive more press coverage than caucuses, as seems to be the case, then we assume that states that employ a mixed system will fall somewhere in between full primary and full caucus states, gaining some coverage from the fact that one party holds a primary but not gaining as much as it might if both parties held primaries. In all of the fully specified equations in table 3-5, this is, in fact, exactly what happens.

—*Iowa and New Hampshire:* Again, separate dummy variables were created for each state.

—*Number of other events on the same day:* This variable is a simple count of the total number of other states that held a primary or caucus, in either party, on the same day. As with the date and number of delegates variables, we have computed separate values of this variable for the Democrats and Republicans and then calculated a weighted average of the two.

A Note on
Delegate
Counts

Delegate counts are compiled by news organizations as a way of monitoring the progress of a nomination race. As delegates are selected in primaries and at state and district conventions, the delegate counts record which candidate, if any, they are pledged to as well as the number who are uncommitted.

Particularly during the prereform election cycles, the most publicized and reputable delegate counts—in some cases, the only counts available—were those compiled by the Associated Press (AP). The AP counts have, from our perspective, several attractive features. The standard the AP used for classifying delegates seems to have been pretty consistent over time and was also, compared with the criteria employed by other news organizations, a fairly conservative one. In brief, the AP credited a candidate with those delegates who either were legally bound to vote for that candidate by state law; were instructed by majority vote in a state or district convention; or had openly and explicitly indicated that they intended to vote for that candidate.[1] The AP did not count delegates who were merely said to be "leaning" toward a candidate, or "projected delegates" who had not yet been selected but who might, given certain rather questionable assumptions, ultimately support a particular candidate.

There are two principal challenges in using these data for the kind of analysis we undertake in chapter 3. The first is to make sure that the delegate counts are as comparable as possible across elections. It is for this reason that we have tried wherever possible to use AP delegate counts or, where these were not available, counts from other organizations that used a reasonably similar standard for determining delegate commitments. In the years between 1952 and 1968, however, the greatest challenge is not to find comparable data but to find any data at all.[2] The Associated Press, of course, did not actually publish any of its delegate count stories; it simply made them available to subscribing newspapers who might or might not decide to print them, depending, presumably, on how interesting the story seemed and what other stories were competing for limited news space. In some election cycles, the *New York Times* was quite good about providing regular updates on the AP counts; in other years, particularly 1968, the *Times* seems almost to have had a concerted policy not to use them at all.

In a few cases, AP delegate counts from the prereform period do not provide detailed information on the votes received by favorite-son candidates. Precise counts are listed for the major national contenders, but votes for all other candidates are simply lumped together into an "other" category. In these cases, we have used previous delegate tabulations plus contemporary coverage of the favorite-son candidates to estimate the favorite-son vote.

The following notes are intended to help those who are interested in checking our results or in using the delegate count data for other purposes.

1952 Democrats: Delegate count by the Associated Press. End of primary and convention eve figures are taken from, respectively, *New York Times,* June 26, 1952, p. 20; and *New York Times,* July 20, 1952, p. 34.

1952 Republicans: Delegate count by the Associated Press. End of primary and convention eve figures are taken from, respectively, *New York Times,* June 8, 1952, p. 52; and *New York Times,* July 6, 1952, p. 34.

1956 Democrats: Delegate count by the Associated Press. End of primary and convention eve figures are taken from, respectively, *New York Times,* June 10, 1956, sec. IV, p. 5; and *New York Times,* August 13, 1956, p. 13.

1960 Democrats: Delegate count by the Associated Press. End of primary and convention eve figures are taken from, respectively, James W. Davis, *Presidential Primaries: Road to the White House* (Thomas Y. Crowell, 1967), p. 85; and *Washington Post,* July 10, 1960, p. A6.

1964 Republicans: Delegate count by the Associated Press. End of primary and convention eve figures are taken from, respectively, *New York Times,* June 4, 1964, p. 22; and *New York Times,* July 12, 1964, p. 57.

1968 Democrats and Republicans: Perhaps because of uncertainties concerning the roster of likely candidates (for example, Johnson's withdrawal, Humphrey's late entrance, Kennedy's assassination), there are few contemporary articles on delegate counts during the 1968 primary season—and almost no mention of the AP counts. On the weekend before the convention, we have located two detailed counts for each party. One was conducted by the *New York Times* (August 4, 1968, p. 53; and August 25, 1968, p. 72) but is difficult to compare with the AP results because a rather large proportion of the delegates are classified as "leaning" toward one of the major candidates. The other, which is the source we have used for tables 3-6 and 3-9, was compiled by the *Los Angeles Times* (August 4, 1968, p. 22A; and August 25, 1968, p. 6). The *Los Angeles Times* stories unfortunately do not make clear what standard was used for classifying delegates or how its counts compare with those of the Associated Press.

1972 Democrats: Delegate count by the *New York Times*. Unlike the *Times*'s 1968 counts, their 1972 counts do not include "leaning" delegates in the totals for individual candidates. Delegate numbers from just before the convention, it is worth noting, vary a good deal from day to day as a series of last-minute court decisions affected the disposition of several large delegations, particularly California and Illinois. End of primary and convention eve figures are taken from, respectively, *New York Times*, June 22, 1972, p. 1; and *New York Times*, July 7, 1972, p. 10.

1976 Democrats: End of primary figures are based on the delegate count maintained by the *New York Times*, as reported in *New York Times*, June 3, 1976, p. 31; *New York Times*, June 8, 1976, p. 22; and *New York Times*, June 10, 1976, p. 42. Convention eve figures are based on the Associated Press delegate count and are taken from an unpublished AP article of July 9, 1976.[3]

1976 Republicans: Delegate count by the *New York Times*. End of primary and convention eve figures are taken from, respectively, *New York Times*, June 10, 1976, p. 42; and *New York Times*, August 16, 1976, p. 1.

1980 Democrats: Delegate count by the Associated Press. End of primary and convention eve figures are taken from, respectively, unpublished AP articles of June 4, 1980, and August 9, 1980.

1980 Republicans: Delegate count by the Associated Press. End of primary and convention eve figures are taken from, respectively, unpublished AP articles of June 4, 1980, and July 13, 1980.

1984 Democrats: Delegate count by United Press International.[4] End of primary and convention eve figures are taken from, respectively, *Congressional Quarterly Weekly Report,* June 9, 1984, p. 1345; and *Congressional Quarterly Weekly Report,* July 7, 1984, p. 1629.

1988 Democrats: Delegate count by the Associated Press. End of primary figures are reported in *Congressional Quarterly Weekly Report,* June 11, 1988, p. 1582.

1988 Republicans: Delegate count by the Associated Press. End of primary figures are reported in *Congressional Quarterly Weekly Report,* June 11, 1988, p. 1582.

1992 Democrats: Delegate count by the Associated Press. End of primary and convention eve figures are taken from, respectively, unpublished AP articles of June 3, 1992, and July 13, 1992.

1992 Republicans: Delegate count by the Associated Press. End of primary figures are taken from an unpublished AP article on June 3, 1992.

1996 Republicans: Delegate count by the Associated Press. End of primary figures are reported in *Congressional Quarterly Weekly Report,* June 15, 1996, p. 1704.

2000 Democrats: Delegate count by the *New York Times.* End of primary figures are taken from an unpublished *Times* tabulation of June 29, 2000.

2000 Republicans: Delegate count by the *New York Times.* End of primary figures are taken from an unpublished *Times* tabulation of June 29, 2000.

Notes

Chapter One

1. For a sampling of some of the best critiques of the contemporary presidential nomination process, see Anthony King, "How Not to Select Presidential Candidates: A View from Europe," in Austin Ranney, ed., *The American Elections of 1980* (Washington: American Enterprise Institute, 1981), pp. 303–28; James I. Lengle, *Representation and Presidential Primaries: The Democratic Party in the Post-Reform Era* (Westport, Conn.: Greenwood, 1981); James W. Ceaser, *Reforming the Reforms: A Critical Analysis of the Presidential Selection Process* (Cambridge, Mass.: Ballinger, 1982), esp. chap. 4; Nelson W. Polsby, *Consequences of Party Reform* (Oxford University Press, 1983); Scott Keeter and Cliff Zukin, *Uninformed Choice: The Failure of the New Presidential Nominating System* (Praeger, 1983), esp. chap. 8; Thomas E. Mann, "Should the Presidential Nominating System Be Changed (Again)?" in George Grassmuck, ed., *Before Nomination: Our Primary Problems* (Washington: American Enterprise Institute, 1985), pp. 35–46; and James W. Davis, "The Case against the Current Primary-Centered System," in Robert E. DiClerico and James W. Davis, eds., *Choosing Our Choices: Debating the Presidential Nominating System* (Lanham, Md.: Rowman and Littlefield, 2000), pp. 27–50.

2. Reagan's credentials as an extremist have, of course, been rather seriously tarnished by the fact that he was twice elected president, in both cases winning a majority of the popular vote and the electoral votes of at least forty-four states. The characterization in the text does reflect, however, a widespread perception among political analysts and commentators in the middle to late 1970s. See, for example, Norman H. Nie, Sidney Verba, and John R. Petrocik, *The Changing American Voter*, enl. ed. (Harvard University Press, 1979), chap. 17, in which the

authors use Reagan as the exemplar of an extremist candidate for a series of mock elections.

3. Ronald Brownstein, "GOP Leaders Fear That Frantic Pace of Primaries Leaves Voters Out in Cold," *Los Angeles Times,* March 11, 1996, p. A5; Gerald F. Seib, "Primary Issue: If It's Broke, Why Not Fix It?" *Wall Street Journal,* March 20, 1996, p. A16; William Safire, "Primary Reform Now," *New York Times,* March 28, 1996, p. A25; and David S. Broder, "Primary Madness," *Washington Post,* March 3, 1996, p. C7.

4. "Democrats Delinquent," *Washington Post,* May 27, 2000, p. A26; Fred Brown, "And the First May Be the Least," *Denver Post,* February 2, 2000, p. 2D; Ken Foskett, "So Many Primaries, So Little Time . . . ," *Atlanta Constitution,* February 24, 2000, p. 18A; Liz Halloran, "Primaries: Who Ordered This Chaos?" *Hartford Courant,* March 3, 2000, p. A1; "Primary Reforms," *St. Petersburg Times,* March 14, 2000, p. 8A; Noel Rubinton, "Eye on the Media: Speed Cuts Depth in Campaign Coverage," *Newsday,* March 7, 2000, p. A35; Jack W. Germond and Jules Witcover, "Looking Ahead to 2004," *Baltimore Sun,* March 22, 2000, p. 21A; and "Primary Responsibility," *Los Angeles Times,* May 4, 2000, p. B10.

Chapter Two

1. The word *front-loading* was originally used to describe a type of contractual arrangement in business. According to *Webster's Collegiate Dictionary* (10th ed.), to front-load is "to assign costs or benefits to the early stages of (as a contract, project, or time period)." It is not clear who first applied the term to the delegate selection calendar, but it does not seem to have been used in this context until the early 1980s. The first appearance of the term that we have been able to find in a major national media outlet is in Rhodes Cook, "New Democratic Rules Panel: A Careful Approach to Change," *Congressional Quarterly Weekly Report,* December 26, 1981, pp. 2563–67, 2566. In a personal communication to the authors, however, Cook was quite certain that he did not originate the term and that it was already in general usage among political practitioners when his article was published.

2. With a few exceptions to be noted later, the Democratic and Republican primary calendars are in most years all but identical. Hence in tables 2-1, 2-4, and 2-5 we show results for only one party.

3. Byron E. Shafer, *Quiet Revolution: The Struggle for the Democratic Party and the Shaping of Post-Reform Politics* (New York: Russell Sage Foundation, 1983), p. 28.

4. See *Buckley* v. *Valeo,* 424 U.S. 1 (1976), 7.

5. For a more detailed discussion of this trend, see Michael G. Hagen and William G. Mayer, "The Modern Politics of Presidential Selection: How Changing the Rules Really Did Change the Game," in William G. Mayer, ed., *In Pursuit of the White House 2000: How We Choose Our Presidential Nominees* (New York: Chatham House, 2000), pp. 1–55, 9–12.

6. An earlier challenge almost came from Alaska. In May 1971 the Alaska legislature passed a bill that would have established a presidential primary in February, but the governor of Alaska vetoed the bill on the grounds that holding

a later primary would increase voter participation and work to the overall benefit of Alaska's voters. See "February Primary for the Presidency Is Vetoed in Alaska," *New York Times*, June 5, 1971, p. 25. This decision is further testimony to the fact that, as of the early 1970s, many well-informed observers had not yet come to appreciate the fundamental dynamics of the new nomination process and the considerable value of holding an early primary or caucus.

7. "New Hampshire Votes Earlier Primary Date," *New York Times*, July 8, 1971, p. 38.

8. On the jockeying for position between Florida and New Hampshire, see "New Hampshire Measure," *New York Times*, June 5, 1971, p. 25; "Florida Passes Bill," *New York Times*, June 5, 1971, p. 25; "Florida to Hold Primary on March 14," *New York Times*, June 23, 1971, p. 30; "New Hampshire Action Set," *New York Times*, June 23, 1971, p. 30; "New Hampshire Votes Earlier Primary Date"; "New Hampshire Shifts Vote," *New York Times*, July 13, 1971, p. 37; "1972 Presidential Primaries: 17 Set, 27 Possible," *Congressional Quarterly Weekly Report*, April 9, 1971, pp. 819–24, 819; and "Early Primary Bill Passed," *Tampa Tribune*, June 5, 1971, p. 13A.

9. On the attempt to establish a New England regional primary and New Hampshire's reaction to it, see "Regional Primary Urged," *New York Times*, May 30, 1975, p. 11; John Kifner, "Primary: New Hampshire Again Alone," *New York Times*, June 12, 1975, p. 18; "G.O.P. Weighs Challenge," *New York Times*, September 14, 1975, p. 31; "N.H. Legislators Vote to Retain Primary Status," *Boston Globe*, May 29, 1975, p. 33; Michael Kenney, "N.E. Leaders Back Regional Primary Plans," *Boston Globe*, May 30, 1975, p. 41; Michael Kenney, "O'Neill Predicts 'One Big Campaign' as Mass. Votes Primary Bill," *Boston Globe*, September 11, 1975, p. 3; and F. Rhodes Cook, "Delegate Selection: Change Goes On for 1976," *Congressional Quarterly Weekly Report*, August 16, 1975, pp. 1807–17, 1815.

10. One of the thirteen, North Carolina, held its 1972 primary on May 6 but in 1976 moved it to March 23.

11. See, for example, Cook, "Delegate Selection"; Rhodes Cook, "The Caucuses: A Few People and a Lot of Power," *Congressional Quarterly Weekly Report*, December 20, 1975, pp. 2803–10; "Picking a Candidate for '76—Like Nothing U.S. Has Seen Before," *U.S. News and World Report*, September 8, 1975, pp. 21–22; "The Spirit of '76," *Newsweek*, January 12, 1976, pp. 16–28; R. W. Apple Jr., "Election Curtain Up in Iowa Tomorrow," *New York Times*, January 18, 1976, p. 1; and Jules Witcover, *Marathon: The Pursuit of the Presidency, 1972–1976* (Viking, 1977), pp. 19–32, 647–50.

12. The Winograd Commission was actually created in 1975, but it received an expanded mandate from the 1976 Democratic National Convention and did most of its work in 1977–78. The subject of front-loading is mentioned nowhere in the commission's final report. See Commission on Presidential Nomination and Party Structure, *Openness, Participation, and Party Building: Reforms for a Stronger Democratic Party* (Washington: Democratic National Committee, 1978).

13. Cook, "New Democratic Rules Panel," p. 2566. However, David E. Price, the staff director of the Hunt Commission, would later conclude that, in terms of providing actual remedies for the front-loading problem, "the commission was

able to do little more than raise warning flags in its final report." See Price, *Bringing Back the Parties* (Washington: CQ Press, 1984), p. 179.

14. The South Carolina Republican presidential primary was actually held on Saturday, March 8, three days before voters in Alabama, Florida, and Georgia went to the polls.

15. See "Early Primary for Georgia," *New York Times,* July 6, 1979, p. 6; Terence Smith, "Carter Expects to Recoup in South after Kennedy Successes in North," *New York Times,* October 20, 1979, p. 1; and Rhodes Cook, "Presidential Primaries Reach Record Level," *Congressional Quarterly Weekly Report,* August 4, 1979, pp. 1609–16, 1613–14. Supporters of John Connally, hoping to give a boost to his candidacy, similarly tried (though without success) to move the Texas primary to March 11. See Adam Clymer, "Democrats in Texas Seek to Gain Edge by Shift to March Primary," *New York Times,* April 29, 1979, p. 1; William K. Stevens, "12 Austin Senators Still in Hiding, Embarrassing the Texas Rangers," *New York Times,* May 21, 1979, p. A1; and "12 Texas State Senators, Claiming Political Victory, Come Out of Hiding," *New York Times,* May 23, 1979, p. A16.

16. Included in this category are a small number of states that moved their primary date forward or backward by one week or less.

17. Price, *Bringing Back the Parties,* p. 227.

18. Jack W. Germond and Jules Witcover, *Wake Us When It's Over: Presidential Politics of 1984* (New York: Macmillan, 1985), p. 43.

19. The transfer of the Super Tuesday label to the second week in March actually says more about how most observers were handicapping the 1984 campaign than about the reality of the schedule. Though deprived of the moniker, five states, including California, still held their primaries on the first Tuesday in June. Indeed, in both parties, the primaries held on June 5 selected about 30 percent more delegates than the five primaries that took place on "Super Tuesday."

20. The 1984 caucus calendar, shown in table 2-6, suggests that the Mondale campaign may have been somewhat more successful in promoting front-loading among caucus states. In terms of the long-term trend, however, it should be noted that many of the 1984 caucuses were one-shot affairs: cases in which a state that had held a primary in 1980 used a caucus in 1984 and then abandoned it in 1988.

21. Charles D. Hadley and Harold W. Stanley, "The Southern Super Tuesday: Southern Democrats Seeking Relief from Rising Republicanism," in William G. Mayer, ed., *In Pursuit of the White House: How We Choose Our Presidential Nominees* (Chatham, N.J.: Chatham House, 1996), pp. 158–89, 162.

22. See especially Hadley and Stanley, "Southern Super Tuesday"; Barbara Norrander, *Super Tuesday: Regional Politics and Presidential Primaries* (University Press of Kentucky, 1992); and Paul-Henri Gurian, "Less Than Expected: An Analysis of Media Coverage of Super Tuesday 1988," *Social Science Quarterly,* vol. 72 (December 1991), pp. 761–73.

23. According to figures computed by Barbara Norrander, of the seven southern states that held Democratic primaries in both 1984 and 1988, the turnout rate rose substantially in two, declined significantly in one, and exhibited little or no change in the other four. See Norrander, *Super Tuesday,* p. 125.

24. See Richard L. Berke, "California Guarantees Warm Primary Season," *New York Times,* September 23, 1993, p. A16.

25. The 1996 Democratic calendar had somewhat fewer primaries—thirty-four as opposed to forty-one on the Republican side—partly because the Democratic Party's national rules attempted to discourage states from holding primaries before March and partly because, with Clinton running unopposed, some Democratic state parties decided to forgo a primary and select their delegates by caucus.

26. The following discussion draws on William G. Mayer, "The Presidential Nominations," in Gerald M. Pomper, ed., *The Election of 2000: Reports and Interpretations* (New York: Chatham House, 2001), pp. 12–45, 13–16.

27. See "Coming Soon: The Bicoastal Primary," *New York Times,* September 5, 1998, p. A10 (emphasis added).

28. Three advisory Democratic primaries were held between February 1 and March 7, but because they played no role at all in the delegate selection process they were, with one exception, roundly ignored by both the candidates and the media. The exception was Washington state, where Bill Bradley, faced with the prospect of losing all eleven primaries on the first Tuesday in March, made a last-ditch effort to pump some momentum into his campaign, though without any noticeable effect.

29. For most of the time period being examined here, the Republican Party had no provision limiting the time when primaries or caucuses could be held. In 2000, for the first time, the party instituted such a window, which extended from the first Monday in February to the third Tuesday in June.

30. For one of the few detailed discussions of how nonprimary states selected their national convention delegates in the days before McGovern-Fraser, see Paul T. David, Ralph M. Goldman, and Richard C. Bain, *The Politics of National Party Conventions* (Brookings, 1960), chap. 11. For a description of Democratic caucus and committee selection procedures in 1968, see Commission on Party Structure and Delegate Selection, *Mandate for Reform* (Washington: Democratic National Committee, 1970), pp. 56–63.

31. In some states that use presidential primaries, the selection of individual delegates to the national conventions is accomplished at caucuses of each candidate's supporters that are held weeks or months after the primary. But these caucuses have no discretion as to how many delegates are awarded to each candidate: the distribution of delegates to particular candidates is determined entirely by the results of the primary. These caucuses simply determine which particular individuals will go to the convention as Reagan delegates, which as Bush delegates, and so on. In those few cases in which caucuses or conventions pick delegates without regard to the primary vote, those delegates are specifically excluded from all data and calculations reported in tables 2-1 to 2-5.

32. For a comparison of the precinct caucus results and the composition of the national convention delegation in Iowa that emphasizes precisely this point, see Hugo Winebrenner, *The Iowa Precinct Caucuses: The Making of a Media Event* (Iowa State University Press, 1987), pp. 59–62, 82–85.

33. It is still difficult to get precise dates for many Republican caucuses. In many states, the caucuses take place over a period of four to eight weeks.

34. See *Delegate Selection Rules for the 1976 Democratic National Convention* (Washington: Democratic National Committee, 1975), Rule 3A. This rule was based on Guideline C-2 of the McGovern-Fraser Commission.

35. *Delegate Selection Rules for the 1980 Democratic National Convention* (Washington: Democratic National Committee, 1978), Rule 10A. From 1992 through 2000 the Democratic window started on the first Tuesday in March.

36. The only exceptions over the past three election cycles were the Kansas Democratic caucuses in 1996 and 2000, which were held on May 4 and May 6, respectively. In both cases, however, this late date was, in a sense, forced upon the state party. Kansas had been scheduled to hold a presidential primary in both years, only to have the state legislature decide at the last instant not to fund it. Given the lateness of the state legislature's decision, there simply was not time to schedule the caucuses earlier than May.

37. Though no primaries were held during this period, there were a number of caucuses, especially in 1976 (see table 2-6). By and large, however, they did not receive a great deal of publicity or attention from the candidates.

38. The decision by the Rules and Bylaws Committee required approval by the full Democratic National Committee; that approval came in mid-January 2002.

39. Both phrases are quoted from a letter written by Terry McAuliffe, chair of the Democratic National Committee, to the *Wall Street Journal*. See "Democrats Play Catch-Up with GOP," *Wall Street Journal*, February 14, 2002, p. A21.

40. When the new window was approved by the Democratic National Committee, committee chair Terry McAuliffe said that Democrats in South Carolina, Michigan, and Arizona were "almost certain" to hold their primaries on the same date as their Republican counterparts. See David S. Broder, "DNC Moves Up '04 Primary Schedule," *Washington Post,* January 20, 2002, p. A4.

41. As quoted in David S. Broder, "Democrats Push Up Calendar on Presidential Primaries," *Boston Globe,* November 28, 2001, p. A25.

Chapter Three

1. Michael J. Robinson and Margaret A. Sheehan, *Over the Wire and On TV: CBS and UPI in Campaign '80* (New York: Russell Sage Foundation, 1983), pp. 174–80. For similar results in other years, see William C. Adams, "As New Hampshire Goes . . . ," in Gary R. Orren and Nelson W. Polsby, eds., *Media and Momentum: The New Hampshire Primary and Nomination Politics* (Chatham, N.J.: Chatham House, 1987), pp. 42–59; and S. Robert Lichter, Daniel Amundson, and Richard Noyes, *The Video Campaign: Network Coverage of the 1988 Primaries* (Washington: American Enterprise Institute, 1988), pp. 12–14.

2. Michael J. Robinson, "Media Coverage in the Primary Campaign of 1976: Implications for Voters, Candidates, and Parties," in William Crotty, ed., *The Party Symbol: Readings on Political Parties* (San Francisco: W. H. Freeman, 1980), pp. 178–91. As suggested above, the Iowa caucuses had not yet become a major media story in 1976. Iowa accounted for just 7 percent of all newspaper stories and 6 percent of television stories.

3. Lichter, Amundson, and Noyes, *Video Campaign*, p. 14.

4. In the seven election cycles since the establishment of federal matching funds, only four major candidates have declined to accept them: John Connally in 1980, George Bush in 2000, and Steve Forbes in both 1996 and 2000.

5. So far as we can determine, the only source that has attempted to make a complete count of the number of days the major presidential candidates spent campaigning in all fifty states is John H. Aldrich, *Before the Convention: Strategies and Choices in Presidential Nomination Campaigns* (University of Chicago Press, 1980), pp. 68–71, 232–33. Unfortunately, Aldrich's count does not appear to begin until the election year itself and thus excludes much of the time candidates spent in Iowa and New Hampshire.

6. Based on figures presented in Barbara Norrander, *Super Tuesday: Regional Politics and Presidential Primaries* (University Press of Kentucky, 1992), table 3.1, p. 94.

7. For the nomination races shown in table 3-3, just eight days separated Iowa and New Hampshire, so in some cases the nomination preference question was never posed to a national sample in the period between these two events.

8. See Library and Archives of New Hampshire's Political Tradition, *First in the Nation: The New Hampshire Primary: What It Means to the State and the Nation* (Concord, N.H., 2001). As the report notes, $264 million represents only a small fraction of the state's overall economy, about six-tenths of one percent of the gross state product. But the proportionate contribution of the primary to certain industries, such as hotels and restaurants, is undoubtedly far more significant. Moreover, the report's estimate strikes us as quite conservative, particularly in the method it uses to calculate the value of all the publicity New Hampshire receives from the primary.

9. In the fall 1988 American National Election Study survey, only 10 of 1,738 respondents—six-tenths of one percent—named a farming issue of any kind when asked what they thought was the "most important problem facing this country."

10. On the general way that presidents use their control over the executive branch to reward states and constituencies that are important to their reelection, see Kathryn Dunn Tenpas, *Presidents as Candidates: Inside the White House for the Presidential Campaign* (New York: Garland, 1997), pp. 78–83, 89–94.

11. Stephen A. Holmes, "Influx of U.S. Aid before Primary Draws Fire," *New York Times,* January 12, 1992, p. 17.

12. James M. Naughton, "Ford Calls 8 Fit to Run with Him," *New York Times,* January 23, 1976, p. 38.

13. Peter Goldman, "See Jimmy Run—in Place," *Newsweek,* February 18, 1980, pp. 45–46, 45.

14. David E. Rosenbaum, "Kennedy Supporters Sue Carter Aides on Fund Use," *New York Times,* December 29, 1979, p. 37.

15. We focus on these three elections because they represent the time when front-loading was first becoming a significant trend. In addition, in 1991 the Federal Election Commission substantially loosened the state spending restrictions, exempting many types of spending from the state limits and thus making the state totals less reliable as a measure of how much attention each state received from

the candidates. On the latter development, see Anthony Corrado and Heitor Gouvêa, "Financing Presidential Nominations under the BCRA," in William G. Mayer, ed., *The Making of the Presidential Candidates 2004* (Lanham, Md.: Rowman and Littlefield, 2003), pp. 45–82, 47–49.

16. For a similar finding derived from a different model and data, see Tom W. Rice, "The Determinants of Candidate Spending in Presidential Primaries: Advice for the States," *Presidential Studies Quarterly*, vol. 12 (Fall 1982), pp. 590–97. Though the parallel is not exact, Paul-Henri Gurian has written a series of articles showing that campaign spending per state is strongly affected by "momentum," which he operationalizes as the product of sequence (that is, the date on which a primary or caucus takes place) and state media coverage. See, in particular, Gurian, "Resource Allocation Strategies in Presidential Nomination Campaigns," *American Journal of Political Science*, vol. 30 (November 1986), pp. 802–21; and Paul-Henri Gurian and Audrey A. Haynes, "Campaign Strategy in Presidential Primaries, 1976–88," *American Journal of Political Science*, vol. 37 (February 1993), pp. 335–41.

17. Under the 1974 Federal Election Campaign Act, all candidates who accept federal matching funds are required to limit the total amount of money they spend during the nomination phase of the campaign. The limit was set at $10 million in 1974 (plus another 20 percent for fund-raising expenses) but is adjusted for inflation in each election cycle. In 2000 the limit was $33.8 million.

18. Both Ronald Reagan in 1980 and George Bush in 1988 also stuck it out to the end, of course, but in both cases, all of their major opponents had withdrawn from the race before the conclusion of the delegate selection season.

19. The number-of-other-primaries variable is also significant in both the 1980 and 1992 equations but has only a modest effect on the coefficient for the date-of-primary variable, reducing it somewhat in 1980 and increasing it slightly in 1992.

20. For a similar conclusion, see David S. Castle, "Media Coverage of Presidential Primaries," *American Politics Quarterly*, vol. 19 (January 1991), pp. 33–42; and Paul-Henri Gurian, "The Distribution of News Coverage in Presidential Primaries," *Journalism Quarterly*, vol. 70 (Summer 1993), pp. 336–44. William C. Adams as well as Michael J. Robinson and S. Robert Lichter claim to find evidence that, except for Iowa and New Hampshire, early primaries and caucuses do not receive more coverage than later events. In both cases, however, that conclusion is based on an underspecified model. Both sources calculate a simple correlation coefficient between total coverage and a state's position in the campaign calendar (with Iowa and New Hampshire excluded), without controlling for other factors such as the number of delegates in the state. See Adams, "As New Hampshire Goes . . . ," pp. 42–59; and Michael J. Robinson and S. Robert Lichter, "'The More Things Change . . .': Network News Coverage of the 1988 Presidential Nomination Races," in Emmett H. Buell Jr. and Lee Sigelman, eds., *Nominating the President* (University of Tennessee Press, 1991), pp. 196–212.

21. New Hampshire has actually been holding the first presidential primary in the nation since 1920, but through 1948 the state did not have a presidential preference or "beauty contest" line on its ballot. The primary was used only as a mechanism for selecting national convention delegates. It was thus difficult for

the media to interpret the results as a victory or defeat for any particular candidate. The presidential-preference line was added to the ballot by state law in 1949.

22. See especially James R. Beniger, "Winning the Presidential Nomination: National Polls and State Primary Elections, 1936–1972," *Public Opinion Quarterly*, vol. 40 (Spring 1976), pp. 22–38.

23. The belief that the presidential nomination process was dramatically altered by the changes in the delegate selection rules and campaign finance laws adopted in the early 1970s is widely but not universally shared among those political scientists who have studied that process. Howard Reiter, in particular, has written a much-praised and widely cited book arguing that changes in the rules had much less effect than is generally believed and that many important features of the contemporary nomination process had clearly emerged before the new rules were promulgated. See Howard L. Reiter, *Selecting the President: The Nominating Process in Transition* (University of Pennsylvania Press, 1985). Though we take issue with one of Reiter's specific conclusions (see note 28 to this chapter), as a general matter the changes we emphasize in the rest of this chapter are ones that Reiter either concluded *did* come about as a response to the new rules (for example, the proliferation of primaries) or did not analyze at all. In particular, when Reiter wrote his book, in the early to middle 1980s, front-loading had not yet emerged as the central issue in nomination politics that it has since become. As a result, front-loading is simply not mentioned or discussed anywhere in the book.

24. One of the few campaigns from this era that was successful at penetrating state caucuses was that of Barry Goldwater in 1964. See Andrew E. Busch, *Outsiders and Openness in the Presidential Nominating System* (University of Pittsburgh Press, 1997), chap. 3.

25. For a more detailed discussion of the transformation of presidential caucuses, see William G. Mayer, "Caucuses: How They Work, What Difference They Make," in William G. Mayer, ed., *In Pursuit of the White House: How We Choose Our Presidential Nominees* (Chatham, N.J.: Chatham House, 1996), pp. 105–57.

26. In an earlier work, one of us defined a favorite son as any candidate who received at least 50 percent of the convention votes from his or her home state and less than 2 percent of the remaining convention votes. See Michael G. Hagen and William G. Mayer, "The Modern Politics of Presidential Selection: How Changing the Rules Really Did Change the Game," in William G. Mayer, ed., *In Pursuit of the White House 2000: How We Choose Our Presidential Nominees* (New York: Chatham House, 2000), pp. 1–55, 19–21. Here we adopt a somewhat looser definition that includes candidates who received a substantial number of votes from their home state but not necessarily a majority. We also exclude from the favorite-son category those candidates, like Hubert Humphrey in 1960, who entered a number of primaries and clearly tried to mount a national campaign but were unsuccessful in winning many delegates to their cause except in their home state.

27. A number of favorite-son candidates from this period publicly admitted that they had no real chance of winning their party's nomination. See, for example, W. H. Lawrence, "Johnson Defeats Shivers in Texas by a Wide Margin,"

New York Times, May 6, 1956, p. 1; and "Lausche to Allow Bid," *New York Times,* May 29, 1956, p. 14.

28. Reiter contends that the decline in uncommitted delegates began before 1972. See *Selecting the President,* pp. 25–26. His conclusion, however, derives to a large extent from a set of *New York Times* delegate counts from 1968 that are not fully comparable with the data from earlier election cycles. For further discussion, see appendix C.

29. For data on this point, see Hagen and Mayer, "Modern Politics of Presidential Selection," pp. 21–32.

30. See William G. Mayer, *The Divided Democrats: Ideological Unity, Party Reform, and Presidential Elections* (Boulder, Colo.: Westview, 1996), pp. 35–41. Of course, a candidate's fund-raising success is often correlated with his current and likely future support within the electorate. But as the preceding discussion indicates, the correlation is far from perfect. On the one hand, there are candidates like Gephardt and Tsongas who ran quite well in the primaries whenever they had the resources but still found themselves running out of money. On the other side, there are candidates who were prodigious fund-raisers even though they had little appeal to the mainstream electorate. (Prominent examples include John Connally in 1980, Pat Robertson in 1988, and Phil Gramm in 1996.) In general, the correlation between money raised during the invisible primary and support in the national polls just before Iowa is .71. In other words, support among likely voters explains only about half of the variance in fund-raising. In short, fund-raising must be considered an independent influence on the nomination race; and a system that uses money as a proxy for popularity will inevitably amplify the voices of some candidates and, what is worse, deny other candidates an adequate opportunity to make their case to the voters.

31. See Herbert E. Alexander, *Financing the 1972 Election* (Lexington, Mass.: Lexington Books, 1976), pp. 376–77. In all, these forty-one contributors accounted for 25 percent of the money McGovern raised for his presidential bid.

32. Jules Witcover, *Marathon: The Pursuit of the Presidency, 1972–1976* (Viking, 1977), p. 317.

33. James T. Bacchus, in Jonathan Moore, ed., *Campaign for President: The Managers Look at '84* (Dover, Mass.: Auburn House, 1986), pp. 69–70.

34. Robin Toner, "Tsongas Abandons Campaign, Leaving Clinton a Clear Path toward Showdown with Bush," *New York Times,* March 20, 1992, pp. A1, A14.

35. One indication of this is that, over the past two decades, stories about the delegate count have rarely been published on the weekend before the convention—which explains why so many of the entries under this heading in tables 3-6 and 3-9 have been left blank. According to several reporters we spoke with, a number of news organizations still compile these counts all the way up to the final convention balloting, but with the nomination race clearly over, the results almost never make their way into print.

36. Martin Plissner has recently argued that the transformation of New Hampshire from a "marginal political event" to a "unique showcase and proving ground for presidential aspirants" really began in 1964, when the three major television networks first decided to send "over a thousand correspondents, producers, tech-

nicians, and support people" to the state. See Plissner, *The Control Room: How Television Calls the Shots in Presidential Elections* (Free Press, 1999), pp. 7–8.

37. Nelson W. Polsby, "Decision-Making at the National Conventions," *Western Political Quarterly,* vol. 13 (September 1960), pp. 609–19, 616–17 (emphasis added).

38. As one reflection of this point, it is instructive to observe how Daley played his cards in 1976. Instead of delaying his decision until the convention, Daley effectively announced his support for Carter on the morning of the final day of primaries. This move played a major role in establishing Carter as the all-but-certain nominee—and earned Daley considerable credit with the Carter forces. For a good account of the whole episode, see Witcover, *Marathon,* pp. 349–51.

39. As quoted in "Primary Reform," *Boston Globe,* December 8, 1998, p. A26.

40. See Marty Cohen, David Karol, Hans Noel, and John Zaller, "Beating Reform: The Resurgence of Parties in Presidential Nominations, 1980 to 2000," paper presented at the annual meeting of the American Political Science Association, San Francisco, August 30–September 2, 2001, pp. 12–13.

41. We concentrate on the Democrats here for the simple reason that until the 2000 election cycle, the Republicans had nothing in their national rules that even purported to regulate the timing of primaries and caucuses.

42. See Guideline C-4 in Commission on Party Structure and Delegate Selection, *Mandate for Reform* (Washington: Democratic National Committee, 1970), p. 47. For a discussion of the sorts of practices this guideline was designed to prohibit, see pp. 29–30.

43. The principal report of the McGovern-Fraser Commission contains a list of twenty-four states in which some or all of the delegates to the 1968 convention "were selected by a process which began before the calendar year of the Convention." Eighteen of the twenty-four were caucus-convention states. See Commission on Party Structure and Delegate Selection, *Mandate for Reform,* p. 29.

44. *Slate-making* was the practice by which a state party committee or group of party leaders would put together its own, quasi-official list of delegate candidates for the national convention. In the wake of the 1968 convention, the McGovern-Fraser Commission made a major effort to regulate or even prohibit slate-making. See Commission on Party Structure and Delegate Selection, *Mandate for Reform,* Guideline C-6. By 1976, however, the Democrats had adopted a considerably more moderate policy, in which "any individual or group of Democrats [could] sponsor or endorse a slate of candidates for convention delegates" but no slate could receive "preferential treatment or a preferential place on a delegate selection ballot." See *Delegate Selection Rules for the 1976 Democratic National Convention* (Washington: Democratic National Committee, 1975), Rule 14.

45. The 1968 New York presidential primary was held on the third Tuesday in June.

46. Ironically, in 1984 both the Iowa caucuses and the New Hampshire primary were ultimately held in violation of the national Democratic rules (see chapter 6). When Vermont tried to hold a nonbinding primary on the same day as the New Hampshire primary, the Granite State reacted, much as one might have ex-

pected, by moving its primary up a week—to fourteen days before the start of the Democratic window. Iowa then moved its caucuses up a week as well. The important point for now, however, is that although the specific time limits were ignored, the new exemptions policy did have the intended effect of reducing the period between Iowa and New Hampshire to eight days.

47. This is another case in which the Republican Party was clearly affected by rules changes initiated within the Democratic Party. When the Iowa Democratic caucuses were rescheduled, so were that state's Republican caucuses.

48. For contemporary coverage of the new rule, see Rhodes Cook, "New Democratic Rules Panel: A Careful Approach to Change," *Congressional Quarterly Weekly Report*, December 26, 1981, pp. 2563–67; Rhodes Cook, "Democrats' Rules Weaken Representation," *Congressional Quarterly Weekly Report*, April 3, 1982, pp. 749–51; Rhodes Cook, "1984 Democratic Party Rules Seek to Cure Past Problems but Could Create New Ones," *Congressional Quarterly Weekly Report*, August 6, 1983, pp. 1609–14; Adam Clymer, "Larger Democratic Delegation Urged," *New York Times*, November 7, 1981, p. 30; Adam Clymer, "It's Almost 1982! Time to Argue about 1984," *New York Times*, December 27, 1981, sec. IV, p. 5; "Democrats Act to Improve Convention Roles," *New York Times*, January 15, 1982, p. A9; Adam Clymer, "Democrats Reduce Campaign Season," *New York Times*, January 16, 1982, p. 8; Adam Clymer, "Democratic Rules Changes Produce Few Conflicts," *New York Times*, January 17, 1982, p. 30; and Adam Clymer, "Democrats Alter Delegate Rules, Giving Top Officials More Power," *New York Times*, March 27, 1982, p. 1. A good analysis of the Hunt Commission's work has also been provided by David Price, a political scientist who served as its executive director. See David E. Price, *Bringing Back the Parties* (Washington: CQ Press, 1984).

49. Primarily because of concerns over the length of the nomination process, the new exemptions policy was generally well received in nonparty circles. It was, for example, specifically commended in an editorial in the *New York Times*. See "The 1984 Window," *New York Times*, January 18, 1982, p. A18.

50. On the Hunt Commission's abortive attempts to deal with front-loading, see Price, *Bringing Back the Parties*, pp. 181–82.

51. Price cites this as one major reason why the Hunt Commission did not take action against front-loading. Ibid., p. 182.

52. Thomas E. Mann, as quoted in Rhodes Cook, "Many Democrats Cool to Redoing Party Rules," *Congressional Quarterly Weekly Report*, August 24, 1985, pp. 1687–89, 1687.

53. This may sound like a hair-splitting distinction. In fact, the difference between these two motives is enormous and fundamental. Not to recognize the distinction is like saying that the thirty thousand or so people who drive their cars to an NFL football game actually desire a traffic jam. Of course, they desire no such thing. Each simply wants to get to and from the game as quickly, safely, and conveniently as possible; the traffic jam is the unintended, wholly unwanted consequence of all their separate decisions. Similarly, we know of no evidence indicating that states that move up their primaries and caucuses actively hope that lots of other states will also move up their primaries and caucuses and thereby cause a logjam at the head of the calendar. To the contrary, each would almost

certainly prefer to have an early date all to itself, with all the other states coming weeks or months later. But they have no way of bringing this result about on their own, any more than one person can drive to a football game and prohibit everybody else from doing so.

54. The efforts of the Mondale campaign to increase front-loading are accorded particular significance in Cohen et al., "Beating Reform."

55. Twenty-three states and the District of Columbia held binding Democratic presidential primaries in 1984; twenty-seven states used caucuses. But the twenty-four primaries accounted for 54 percent of the convention delegates, whereas just 32 percent were selected by caucus. (The other 14 percent were superdelegates.) The number of states holding Democratic caucuses fell to nineteen in 1988 and then to seventeen in 1992.

56. See Jack W. Germond and Jules Witcover, *Wake Us When It's Over: Presidential Politics of 1984* (New York: Macmillan, 1985), pp. 175, 182–83.

Chapter Four

1. For a recent and particularly thoughtful exposition of this criticism, see Anthony King, *Running Scared: Why America's Politicians Campaign Too Much and Govern Too Little* (Free Press, 1997). However, a number of British scholars made the same complaint well before King. See, in particular, Harold J. Laski, *The American Presidency: An Interpretation* (London: Allen and Unwin, 1940), pp. 73–74; and Richard Rose, "Learning to Govern or Learning to Campaign?" in Alexander Heard and Michael Nelson, eds., *Presidential Selection* (Duke University Press, 1987), pp. 53–73.

2. We use data from these two election cycles because they most completely cover the invisible primary period. In other years, the wording of the question was changed in the middle of the series, or the question was never asked at important points in the campaign, or coverage of the full field of candidates was not as thorough.

3. In the 1992 election cycle, it is worth recalling, the invisible primary was substantially shortened by the events associated with the Gulf war. Indeed, as of early September 1991, Paul Tsongas was the only announced Democratic candidate. Hence polling on the 1992 nomination race did not begin in earnest until October 1991.

4. What makes these figures even more remarkable is that they make no allowance for respondents who pretend to have more knowledge than they really possess or who confuse one of the candidates mentioned with some other public figure (for example, Senator Bob Kerrey of Nebraska with Senator John Kerry of Massachusetts). Though it is difficult to know how many respondents provide these sorts of "erroneous" ratings, evidence from other research suggests that in some circumstances, the number can be quite large. In a famous 1978 experiment, for example, George Bishop and his colleagues found that 33 percent of their sample took a position in favor of or opposed to the 1975 Public Affairs Act—a completely fictitious piece of legislation. See George F. Bishop, Robert W. Oldendick, Alfred J. Tuchfarber, and Stephen E. Bennett, "Pseudo-Opinions on Public Affairs," *Public Opinion Quarterly*, vol. 44 (Summer 1980), pp. 198–209.

5. The low level of public knowledge about the major presidential contenders and the limited amount of learning that takes place during the primary and caucus season is also a major theme in Scott Keeter and Cliff Zukin, *Uninformed Choice: The Failure of the New Presidential Nominating System* (Praeger, 1983).

6. The survey referred to is the Continuous Monitoring component of the 1984 American National Election Study. The study discussed in the next several paragraphs is Henry E. Brady and Richard Johnston, "What's the Primary Message? Horse Race or Issue Journalism?" in Gary R. Orren and Nelson W. Polsby, eds., *Media and Momentum: The New Hampshire Primary and Nomination Politics* (Chatham, N.J.: Chatham House, 1987), pp. 127–86.

7. As Brady and Johnston put it, "The real problem with primaries is not that citizens do not eventually learn about the candidates. Rather, they learn too slowly about every aspect of the candidates except their viability." Ibid., p. 184.

8. On this last point, see Ronald B. Rapoport and Walter J. Stone, Testimony before the RNC Advisory Commission on the Presidential Nominating Process, as reprinted in Advisory Commission on the Presidential Nominating Process, *Nominating Future Presidents: A Review of the Republican Process* (Washington: Republican National Committee, 2000), p. 145.

9. Ken Foskett, "So Many Primaries, So Little Time . . . ," *Atlanta Constitution*, February 24, 2000, p. 18A.

10. As quoted ibid.

11. Noel Rubinton, "Eye on the Media: Speed Cuts Depth in Campaign Coverage," *Newsday*, March 7, 2000, p. A35.

12. As quoted in Rhodes Cook, "Running for President? What's the Rush?" *Congressional Quarterly Weekly Report*, June 16, 1979, pp. 1167–72, 1168.

13. For example, in a book on political reform published in 1996, G. Calvin Mackenzie argued that the contemporary presidential nomination process "has a strong tendency to promote the candidacies of outsiders who have little or no Washington experience and who are often strangers to the leading members of their own party." See Mackenzie, *The Irony of Reform: Roots of American Political Disenchantment* (Boulder, Colo.: Westview, 1996), p. 50.

14. See William G. Mayer, "Forecasting Presidential Nominations," in William G. Mayer, ed., *In Pursuit of the White House: How We Choose Our Presidential Nominees* (Chatham, N.J.: Chatham House, 1996), pp. 44–71, 60–64.

15. As is well known among political junkies, Carter did not actually win the Iowa caucuses—he came in second to the uncommitted vote. But with a remarkable degree of unanimity, the media interpreted it as a win.

16. See Anthony Corrado, "Financing the 1996 Elections," in Gerald M. Pomper, ed., *The Election of 1996: Reports and Interpretations* (Chatham, N.J.: Chatham House, 1997), pp. 135–71, 141–45.

17. The following account draws on Lamar Alexander, "Off with the Limits," *Campaigns and Elections* (October–November 1996), pp. 32–35; Corrado, "Financing the 1996 Elections"; Kevin Sack, "Lamar Alexander: Campaign Funds Slow to Come In," *New York Times*, February 19, 1996, p. A11; and Ruth Marcus, "Difficulty Ahead for Alexander," *Washington Post*, February 21, 1996, p. A14.

18. Alexander, "Off with the Limits," p. 33.

19. For polling data on the 1996 New Hampshire primary, see William G. Mayer, "The Presidential Nominations," in Gerald M. Pomper, ed., *The Election of 1996: Reports and Interpretations* (Chatham, N.J.: Chatham House, 1997), pp. 21–76, 40–42.

20. Alexander, "Off with the Limits," p. 33 (emphasis in original).

21. The figure is cited by two different Alexander campaign officials in Marcus, "Difficulty Ahead for Alexander."

22. Actually, it comes up almost a million dollars short of this figure, since Alexander's estimate of $100,000 a day specifically excluded Sundays.

23. The following account draws on John M. Broder, "His Success in New Hampshire Brings McCain an Overnight Infusion of Cybercash," *New York Times*, February 3, 2000, p. A23; Don Van Natta Jr., "McCain Gets Big Payoff on Web Site," *New York Times*, February 4, 2000, p. A24; John M. Broder, "McCain Finds Support from Odd Corner: Lobbyists," *New York Times*, February 11, 2000, p. A26; Don Van Natta Jr., "Courting Web Cash," *New York Times*, February 13, 2000, sec. IV, p. 4; Don Van Natta Jr. and John M. Broder, "With a Still-Ample Treasury, Bush Builds a Green 'Fire Wall' against McCain," *New York Times*, February 21, 2000, p. A12; Richard L. Berke, "After Stumbling in South Carolina, McCain Is Trying to Regain His Footing," *New York Times*, February 22, 2000, p. A17; Don Van Natta Jr., "A Daunting Edge in Campaign Cash Narrows for Bush," *New York Times*, February 25, 2000, p. A1; John Mintz, "McCain Enjoys a Big Net Advantage," *Washington Post*, February 9, 2000, p. A1; Tom Brazaitis, "Money Just a Mouse-Click Away," *Cleveland Plain Dealer*, February 7, 2000, p. 1A; and Michael Isikoff, "How He's Catching a Cash Wave," *Newsweek*, February 14, 2000, p. 35.

24. Max Fose, as cited in Trevor Potter and Daniel Manatt, "Internet Politics 2000: Overhyped, Then Underhyped, the Revolution Begins," *Election Law Journal*, vol. 1 (2002), pp. 25–33, 29.

25. Both of these points are made in Michael Cornfield and Jonah Seiger, "The Net and the Nomination," in William G. Mayer, ed., *The Making of the Presidential Candidates 2004* (Lanham, Md.: Rowman and Littlefield, 2003), pp. 199–228, 208–10. As the discussion in the text indicates, one could argue that there were actually two "technologies" that aided the McCain fund-raising effort: the Internet and the credit card. In 1999 the Federal Election Commission cleared the way for the McCain campaign by ruling (in response to a query from the Bradley campaign) that credit card contributions were eligible for federal matching funds. See Potter and Manatt, "Internet Politics 2000," pp. 26–27.

26. In the week after the 1988 Iowa caucuses, Gephardt's win was largely overshadowed by what had happened on the Republican side: Pat Robertson had finished second and Bush wound up in third place. In 1992 Tsongas's New Hampshire victory had to share the spotlight with Pat Buchanan's better-than-expected showing in the Granite State. Indeed, in the two weeks immediately after the New Hampshire primary, the Republican nomination race received more coverage than the Democratic race. See the Center for Media and Public Affairs's *Media Monitor*, vol. 6, no. 3 (1992), p. 2. In 1996 the most intriguing story in the early weeks of the delegate selection season was the surging campaign of Pat Buchanan, who came in

second in Iowa and then won in New Hampshire, in both cases finishing ahead of Alexander.

27. Actually, more than fifty-one, if one includes the small number of delegates selected in U.S. territories such as Puerto Rico, Guam, and the Virgin Islands. It appears, however, that most candidates—and the media—pretty much ignore territorial primaries and caucuses.

28. There are many examples to prove this statement, but one of the most compelling is the Maine Democratic caucuses of 1984. Well before the caucuses took place, the Mondale campaign had invested heavily in establishing an extensive network of supporters and party activists throughout the Pine Tree State. They also had the support of almost all of the state's labor unions and Democratic elected officials. Hart, by contrast, had at best a skeleton organization. Yet because the Maine caucuses came four days after the New Hampshire primary, Hart beat Mondale there 50 percent to 45 percent. See Jack W. Germond and Jules Witcover, *Wake Us When It's Over: Presidential Politics of 1984* (New York: Macmillan, 1985), pp. 171–74.

29. The 1996 Rhode Island Republican primary provides a nice test of the effect of ballot access. Because of its early filing deadline, a number of major Republican candidates, including Pat Buchanan and Steve Forbes, did not get on the Rhode Island ballot, which had a substantial effect on the number of votes they received there. In every other primary held on March 5, Buchanan won at least 15 percent of the total vote. In Rhode Island, where he could only get write-ins, Buchanan received just 2.6 percent of the vote. Similarly, Forbes won an average vote of 15.8 percent in the seven states in which he was listed on the ballot, as compared with 0.9 percent in Rhode Island.

30. Though this type of provision invests a party or elected official with a certain amount of discretion in determining who qualifies as a "nationally recognized" candidate, in general it appears that such criteria are interpreted rather liberally and that all plausible nomination candidates are usually included on the ballot. The only recent candidate who seems to have had a major problem in this regard was David Duke in 1992. For understandable reasons (Duke was a former Grand Wizard of the Ku Klux Klan), many state Republican parties did not wish to acknowledge Duke as a member of their party, much less a serious candidate for their party's presidential nomination, and hence kept him off their state ballot.

31. Since 1996 national Democratic Party rules have stipulated that no state may require a candidate to submit more than five thousand signatures or pay a filing fee of more than $2,500 to have his or her name listed on the presidential primary ballot.

32. Both parties' national rules specifically require that all district delegates be residents of the district from which they are elected. See *Delegate Selection Rules for the 2004 Democratic National Convention* (Washington: Democratic National Committee, 2002), Rule 11H; and *The Rules of the Republican Party* (Washington: Republican National Committee, 2000), Rule 15b(5).

33. Jesse Jackson also won one delegate. The count reported here includes all announced commitments and changes up through the final assignment of at-large delegate seats by the Florida Democratic Committee in early May. It is also based only on those delegates selected through the primary—that is, it excludes

superdelegates. See "Six Florida Delegates Are Contested by Hart," *New York Times,* May 6, 1984, p. 26; and "Hart Loses Delegate Dispute," *New York Times,* May 19, 1984, p. 8.

34. The general procedure was as follows: First, we needed to determine the division of the presidential preference vote within each of a state's congressional districts. Though we had these data for Illinois (courtesy of Rhodes Cook), in Florida we had to generate them ourselves, by taking the votes reported in each county, figuring out which counties and parts of counties fit within each congressional district, and then adding the relevant county votes together. This method is particularly problematic in large counties, such as Dade County in Florida, that contain several congressional districts. Fortunately, because Hart had filed complete delegate slates in each of the Dade County districts, it was unnecessary to estimate the preference vote in those cases. For those districts in which Hart had not filed a full slate, we then made the following assumptions: If a candidate won the preference vote in that district by at least 3 percentage points, he would have won all of the district delegates. If a candidate carried the district by less than 3 percent, he would have split the delegates with the second-place finisher.

Based on the results in those districts in which Hart did file a full slate of delegate candidates, these assumptions seem to be generally correct, though in a number of cases a candidate managed to win some or most of the delegates even though he lost the preference vote. That is to say, the vote for pledged delegates is highly correlated with the preference vote but by no means identical to it. Fortunately, the wrong predictions—the cases in which a candidate won more delegates than would have been predicted on the basis of the preference vote—do not seem to favor one particular candidate. So if we have overestimated Hart's delegate take in some districts, we have probably underestimated it in others.

35. The rule for the 2004 Democratic National Convention reads as follows: "A presidential candidate or his/her authorized representative(s) should act in good faith to slate delegate and alternate candidates, however, in any event, if a presidential candidate (including uncommitted status) has qualified to receive delegates and alternates but has failed to slate a sufficient number of delegate and alternate candidates, then additional delegates and alternates for that preference will be selected in a special post-primary procedure." See *Delegate Selection Rules for the 2004 Democratic National Convention,* Rule 12C.

36. According to a poll conducted by ABC News and the *Washington Post,* in the week before the Iowa caucuses Mondale led Hart in New Hampshire, 37 percent to 13 percent. Just eight days after Iowa, when New Hampshire held its primary, Hart garnered 37 percent of the vote to Mondale's 28 percent.

37. William C. Adams, "Media Coverage of Campaign '84: A Preliminary Report," *Public Opinion,* vol. 7 (April–May 1984), pp. 9–13, 11.

38. For a good account of how the March 13 results were reported, see Germond and Witcover, *Wake Us When It's Over,* pp. 195–200.

39. Besides Hart in 1984, the closest any candidate has come to achieving this sort of unstoppable momentum is probably Lamar Alexander in 1996. Had Alexander won just 4 percent more of the vote in New Hampshire—a matter of about seventy-six hundred votes—he, rather than Dole, would have come in second, further tarnishing Dole's front-runner credentials and possibly leading Dole

to withdraw from the race entirely. In either case, the 1996 race might have been defined as a showdown between Alexander and Pat Buchanan—a showdown Alexander almost certainly would have won. One could also argue that with a little more luck and fewer self-inflicted wounds, both Paul Tsongas in 1992 and John McCain in 2000 might have converted their New Hampshire victories into a major-party presidential nomination.

40. See, for example, Ronald D. Elving, "Gramm Launches Campaign Stressing Familiar Themes," *Congressional Quarterly Weekly Report,* February 25, 1995, p. 630; Kristin Brainerd, "With an Eye toward Speakership, Gephardt May Soon Spurn Presidential Bid," *CQ Weekly,* January 23, 1999, pp. 197–98, 197; Eric Pooley, "The Priest at the Party," *Time,* April 27, 1998, pp. 36–38, 36; Jennifer Preston, "Bradley Takes First Step toward Presidential Race," *New York Times,* December 5, 1998, p. A8; B. Drummond Ayres Jr., "Presidency in 2000: $2,893 an Hour," *New York Times,* January 12, 1999, p. A17; and "Quayle Plans a Bid in 2000 for President," *New York Times,* January 22, 1999, p. A17.

41. Stan Huckaby, as quoted in Jackie Calmes, "Campaign 2000: Dole's Exit Reflects Rocketing Costs of Presidential Race," *Wall Street Journal,* October 21, 1999, p. A24.

42. As quoted in Adam Clymer, "Standing on the Sidelines, Analyzing the Reasons Why," *New York Times,* January 18, 2000, p. A21. See also Harold W. Stanley, "The Nominations: The Return of the Party Leaders," in Michael Nelson, ed., *The Elections of 2000* (Washington: CQ Press, 2001), pp. 27–53.

43. The mandate is quoted from the beginning of the commission's report; see Commission on Party Structure and Delegate Selection, *Mandate for Reform* (Washington: Democratic National Committee, 1970), p. 9.

44. The coverage in America's two largest weekly newsmagazines offers a good example. In its March 18 issue (the first published after the March 5 primaries), *Time* called Dole "the presumptive nominee" and said that the previous week marked "the unofficial start of the general election." In its issue of the same date, *Newsweek* did not even bother to talk about what had happened in the March 5 primaries, featuring instead a lengthy story about the upcoming battle between Dole and Clinton. See Nancy Gibbs and Michael Duffy, "See You in November," *Time,* March 18, 1996, pp. 38–44; and Joe Klein, "Saxophone vs. Sacrifice," *Newsweek,* March 18, 1996, pp. 22–25.

45. The turnout data in table 4-8 are calculated using a normal-vote-based estimate of the eligible electorate in each state. In brief, this method uses past election results to compute the proportion of Democratic and Republican voters in each state, which is then multiplied by the voting-age population in the state. For a good explanation and defense of the method, see Barbara Norrander, "Measuring Primary Turnout in Aggregate Analysis," *Political Behavior,* vol. 8, no. 4 (1986), pp. 356–73. In table 4-8 the normal vote is based on an average of the last three presidential elections and the last six congressional elections.

46. As noted in chapter 2, in early 2002 the Democrats decided to move up the start of their delegate selection window from the first Tuesday in March to the first Tuesday in February, in part because they were concerned that "ced[ing] the spotlight to the Republicans for an entire month" put their party at a "competi-

tive disadvantage." See Terry McAuliffe, "Democrats Play Catch-Up with GOP," *Wall Street Journal*, February 14, 2002, p. A21. The data presented in table 4-8 suggest that these concerns may have been justified.

47. A proposal like this was actually advanced by Thomas E. Patterson in *Out of Order* (Vintage, 1993), chap. 6.

48. The project in question was called the Vanishing Voter Project. For a report on its findings, see Thomas E. Patterson, *The Vanishing Voter: Public Involvement in an Age of Uncertainty* (Knopf, 2002), esp. chap. 4.

49. Both figures refer to the amount of money candidates are allowed to spend for campaigning. The campaigns are also allowed to spend additional monies for fund-raising and for legal and accounting purposes.

50. All figures are taken from the reports each campaign filed with the Federal Election Commission on April 20, 1996, which cover all financial activity through March 31.

51. This is the consensus judgment of most reporters and experts who looked into the matter. See, for example, Stephen Labaton, "Limited Cash Likely to Restrict Dole's Campaign Message," *New York Times*, May 16, 1996, p. B11; Phil Kuntz, "Dole's Campaign May Appear Broke, but GOP Can and Will Spare a Dime," *Wall Street Journal*, May 17, 1996, p. A16; and Michael Kranish, "Dole Bemoans Preconvention Spending Limits," *Boston Globe*, July 14, 1996, p. 7.

52. The details in this paragraph are all taken from Anthony Corrado and Heitor Gouvêa, "Financing Presidential Nominations under the BCRA," in William G. Mayer, ed., *The Making of the Presidential Candidates 2004* (Lanham, Md.: Rowman and Littlefield, 2003), pp. 45–82, 65–66.

53. As quoted in Labaton, "Limited Cash Likely to Restrict Dole's Campaign Message."

54. The Republican fund-raising advantage over the Democrats is considerably more decisive in hard money than in soft money. In the 2000 election cycle, the Democrats and Republicans raised almost equal amounts of soft money. As of mid-October, the Democratic National Committee, Democratic Senatorial Campaign Committee, and Democratic Congressional Campaign Committee reported $199 million in soft-money receipts, as compared with $211 million for their Republican counterparts. By contrast, the three Republican national committees raised $295 million in hard money versus $173 million for the Democrats. See Anthony Corrado, "Financing the 2000 Elections," in Gerald M. Pomper, ed., *The Election of 2000: Reports and Interpretations* (New York: Chatham House, 2001), pp. 92–124, 116–20.

55. Rules and Bylaws Committee of the Democratic National Committee, *Beyond 2000: The Scheduling of Future Democratic Presidential Primaries and Caucuses* (Washington: Democratic National Committee, 2000), p. 11.

56. Martin P. Wattenberg, "The Republican Presidential Advantage in the Age of Party Disunity," in Gary W. Cox and Samuel Kernell, eds., *The Politics of Divided Government* (Boulder, Colo.: Westview, 1991), pp. 39–55, 40, 42.

57. See William G. Mayer, *The Divided Democrats: Ideological Unity, Party Reform, and Presidential Elections* (Boulder, Colo.: Westview, 1996), chap. 3. See also Lonna Rae Atkeson, "From the Primaries to the General Election: Does a

Divisive Nomination Race Affect a Candidate's Fortunes in the Fall?" in William G. Mayer, ed., *In Pursuit of the White House 2000: How We Choose Our Presidential Nominees* (New York: Chatham House, 2000), pp. 285–312.

58. Top officials in the Carter administration seem particularly disposed to this viewpoint. See in particular Hamilton Jordan, *Crisis: The Last Year of the Carter Presidency* (G. P. Putnam's Sons, 1982), pp. 306–07, 334–36, 376; and Jimmy Carter, *Keeping the Faith: Memoirs of a President* (Bantam, 1982), pp. 530–32.

59. On Brown's attempts to shorten the 1992 nomination race, see Robin Toner, "Democrats Plan Talks on '92 Race," *New York Times*, May 18, 1991, p. 7; Kevin Sack, "Cuomo to Discuss '92 Role with Democratic Chairman," *New York Times*, October 23, 1991, p. B2; Kevin Sack, "National Party Says It May 'Turn up the Heat' on Cuomo to Decide," *New York Times*, November 14, 1991, p. B7; Larry Agran, "And We Call Ourselves Democrats?" *New York Times*, January 21, 1992, p. A21; and Gwen Ifill, "Brown Is Rebuked by Party Chairman for Harsh Attacks," *New York Times*, March 27, 1992, p. A1.

60. The discussion here is based on the plan Patterson presented in the final chapter of his book *Out of Order*, which was published in 1993. In a more recent book, however, Patterson himself seems to have recognized many of these problems. In *The Vanishing Voter*, published in 2002, he puts forward a quite different proposal for restructuring the presidential nominating process, one that begins with a series of single-state contests spaced a week or two apart. See *Vanishing Voter*, pp. 157–61.

61. Patterson does not explicitly say that he is trying to encourage front-loading. In fact, he criticizes the current system on the grounds that "the weeding-out process occurs too quickly" (*Out of Order*, p. 210) and suggests that while the nomination process should be shortened, it also needs to be slowed down. Yet it is clear that his proposal would considerably increase front-loading—and that most of its purported advantages actually derive from this increase. Condensing the process from eighteen weeks to six or eight inevitably means that more states will be voting in any given week, even if the states distribute themselves evenly throughout the period (as seems most unlikely). Patterson also makes clear that he wants more states to vote on the first Tuesday in the primary season, not just one state, as in the present system. See Patterson, *Out of Order*, chap. 6.

62. Ibid., pp. 223–24.

63. Jonathan Bernstein has recently argued for the importance of a loose network of partisan consultants and campaign activists in the presidential nomination process, but he does not claim that their role has been affected by front-loading, nor is there any obvious reason to think that it would be. See Bernstein, "The New New Presidential Elite," in William G. Mayer, ed., *In Pursuit of the White House 2000: How We Choose Our Presidential Nominees* (New York: Chatham House, 2000), pp. 145–78.

64. See especially Walter J. Stone, Lonna Rae Atkeson, and Ronald B. Rapoport, "Turning On or Turning Off? Mobilization and Demobilization Effects of Participation in Presidential Nomination Campaigns," *American Journal of Political Science*, vol. 36 (August 1992), pp. 665–91; and James A. McCann, "Presidential

Nomination Activists and Political Representation: A View from the Active Minority Studies," in William G. Mayer, ed., *In Pursuit of the White House: How We Choose Our Presidential Nominees* (Chatham, N.J.: Chatham House, 1996), pp. 72–104, 93–98.

Chapter Five

1. In his first annual message to Congress, in 1913, Wilson urged "the prompt enactment of legislation which will provide for primary elections throughout the country at which the voters of the several parties may choose their nominees for the Presidency without the intervention of nominating conventions." See *The Papers of Woodrow Wilson*, edited by Arthur S. Link, vol. 29 (Princeton University Press, 1979), p. 7. The 1912 Progressive Party platform had also endorsed "nation-wide preferential primaries for candidates for the presidency." See *National Party Platforms*, edited by Donald Bruce Johnson, vol. 1, *1840–1956* (University of Illinois Press, 1978), p. 176.

2. For one example of such a plan, see Everett Carll Ladd, "A Better Way to Pick Our Presidents," *Fortune*, May 5, 1980, pp. 132–42.

3. For an interesting attempt to defend the national primary on the grounds of its simplicity and directness, see Michael Nelson, "Two Cheers for the National Primary," in Thomas E. Cronin, ed., *Rethinking the Presidency* (Boston: Little, Brown, 1982), pp. 55–64, 55–56. We would find Nelson's argument more persuasive were it not for his assertion that simplicity and clarity were also virtues much prized by the Framers of the Constitution, a proposition we find impossible to square with the electoral college system they designed.

4. Two comprehensive studies compare turnout in initial and runoff primaries. The first, by Stephen Wright, examined 186 Democratic congressional, senatorial, and gubernatorial runoffs and found that in 77 percent of these contests fewer votes were cast in the runoff than in the initial primary. In the second study, Charles Bullock and Loch Johnson analyzed more than nineteen hundred primaries and concluded that "two-thirds of the time fewer voters participated in the runoff than in the initial primary." See Stephen G. Wright, "Voter Turnout in Runoff Elections," *Journal of Politics*, vol. 51 (May 1989), pp. 385–96; and Charles S. Bullock III and Loch K. Johnson, *Runoff Elections in the United States* (University of North Carolina Press, 1992), chap. 6.

5. On this last point, see James W. Davis, *U.S. Presidential Primaries and the Caucus-Convention System: A Sourcebook* (Westport, Conn.: Greenwood, 1997), pp. 202–03.

6. Outside of Florida and Texas, Dukakis averaged only 14 percent of the vote in the former Confederate states.

7. Our discussion of the Packwood plan draws on the actual bill and Packwood's discussion of it in *Congressional Record*, 92d Congress, 2d sess., 1972, vol. 118, pt. 12, pp. 15231–34, and the analysis of it in Austin Ranney, *The Federalization of Presidential Primaries* (Washington: American Enterprise Institute, 1978), pp. 5–6; "Presidential Primaries: Proposals for a New System," *Congressional Quar-*

terly Weekly Report, July 8, 1972, pp. 1650–54; and Davis, *U.S. Presidential Primaries,* pp. 206–08.

8. There is some disagreement as to whether the Packwood plan would have required all states to hold primaries or would have allowed them to use caucuses if they wished and thereby avoid participating in a regional primary. *Congressional Quarterly* says the former, Ranney the latter. See "Presidential Primaries: Proposals for a New System," p. 1653, and Ranney, *Federalization of Presidential Primaries,* p. 6. The two sources may be referring to different versions of the bill. The text of the 1972 bill, as we read it, is ambiguous on this point.

9. Our description of the NASS plan is based on National Association of Secretaries of State, "Rotating Regional Primary Plan Endorsed by National Association of Secretaries of State," press release of February 16, 1999.

10. One issue that we have not seen addressed in any of the existing time-zone primary proposals is what to do about states that fall into two different time zones. There are actually twelve such states. For table 5-1, we have assigned each state to the time zone in which a majority of its population resides. We also assume, although again we have not seen the issue explicitly addressed, that Alaska and Hawaii would vote along with the Pacific time zone states, even though neither state is actually part of that zone.

11. For a defense of time-zone primaries, see James I. Lengle, "Reforming the Presidential Nominating Process," in Stephen J. Wayne and Clyde Wilcox, eds., *The Quest for National Office: Readings on Elections* (St. Martin's, 1992), pp. 305–11.

12. "Personal Statement of Secretary of State Bill Jones," in Advisory Commission on the Presidential Nominating Process, *Nominating Future Presidents: A Review of the Republican Process* (Washington: Republican National Committee, 2000), pp. 61–62, 62.

13. This advantage is sometimes thought to be equivalent to a favorite-son effect: that is, that candidates will run conspicuously well in their own home region. See, for example, "Personal Statement of Secretary of State Bill Jones," p. 61. But as table 5-2 indicates, many candidates actually run best in a region other than their own. In 1976, for example, Gerald Ford's best region was not his own Midwest but the Northeast. Whether the advantage falls on a favorite son or an outsider, however, is irrelevant: the essential point is that the vote does vary by region and that the order in which regions vote may therefore be important in determining who gets nominated.

14. The kind of analysis conducted in table 5-2 is only meaningful in a race in which approximately the same set of candidates contest a large number of primaries. In those instances in which one of the candidates listed withdrew from the race before the end of the primary season, we include only those primaries that took place before the withdrawal date. In 1996 and 2000 the races came to an end so quickly as to make a regional analysis of questionable value.

15. "Primary Responsibility," *Los Angeles Times,* May 4, 2000, p. B10.

16. These figures exclude the Rhode Island primary, where Forbes was not on the ballot, and the New York primary, where no preference vote was taken.

17. The data in table 5-4 actually understate the extent to which blacks are underrepresented in the first group of states under the Delaware plan. The Dis-

trict of Columbia, which is part of group 1, is 60 percent black; the other twelve states in the group are, on average, just 2.8 percent black.

18. In explicit recognition of this problem, the special Republican commission that endorsed the Delaware plan also recommended that American Samoa, Guam, Puerto Rico, and the Virgin Islands be included in group 1. Because each of these territories has a nonwhite majority, adding them to group 1 would, the commission hoped, "strengthen the voice of minority voters early in the process." See Advisory Commission on the Presidential Nominating Process, *Nominating Future Presidents*, p. 36. Though this is a commendable attempt, we think it unlikely that it would accomplish its intended purpose. The evidence of the past three decades strongly indicates that both the candidates and the media simply do not take territorial primaries and caucuses very seriously.

19. While North and South Dakota are sometimes classified as part of the Midwest, their demographic and political characteristics are clearly very different from those of Illinois, Ohio, Michigan, and Indiana.

20. See Thomas Cronin and Robert Loevy, "The Case for a National Pre-Primary Convention Plan," *Public Opinion*, vol. 5 (December–January 1983), pp. 50–53. For other versions of the plan, see Gerald L. Baliles, "'A Better Way to Pick a President' (Cont.)," *Washington Post*, April 19, 1992, p. C7; and Stephen J. Wayne, "A Proposal to Reform the Presidential Nomination Process," in Advisory Commission on the Presidential Nominating Process, *Nominating Future Presidents: A Review of the Republican Process* (Washington: Republican National Committee, 2000), pp. 129–31.

21. Cronin and Loevy, "Case for a National Pre-Primary Convention Plan," p. 51.

22. Cronin and Loevy apparently disagreed on this point. One wanted the primary limited to the top two finishers on the second ballot, as long as each received a minimum of 30 percent of the votes. The other wanted a lower threshold—25 percent—with the possibility of having three candidates competing in the national primary. In this case, the national primary would use an "approval voting" procedure. See Cronin and Loevy, "Case for a National Pre-Primary Convention Plan," p. 51.

23. Wayne clearly favors this option. See "Proposal to Reform the Presidential Nomination Process," p. 130. Baliles is a bit more ambiguous but seems to favor a convention consisting largely of ex officio delegates.

24. Cronin and Loevy claim that "a candidate need do well in only a handful of states to prove his or her abilities and capture at least some national delegates"; see "Case for a National Pre-Primary Convention Plan," p. 53. But to win the nomination, or even to make it to the second ballot, would plainly require more than success in a handful of states.

25. Ibid.

26. There clearly is a consensus among those who have run presidential campaigns that caucuses are cheaper than primaries. See, for example, the comments of John Deardourff in Jules Witcover, *No Way to Pick a President* (Farrar, Straus and Giroux, 1999), p. 42; and those of Richard Stearns in John Foley, Dennis A. Britton, and Eugene B. Everett Jr., eds., *Nominating a President: The Process and the Press* (Praeger, 1980), p. 43. In chapter 3, it may be recalled, our regression

analysis of candidate spending by state consistently showed that, even after controlling for the number of delegates a state had, candidates spent less money in caucuses than in primaries. See table 3-4.

27. On this point, see the results in table 3-5.

28. The phrase seems to have originated with former senator and presidential candidate Howard Baker. See Jack W. Germond and Jules Witcover, *Blue Smoke and Mirrors: How Reagan Won and Why Carter Lost the Election of 1980* (Viking, 1981), p. 96.

29. The first four figures are taken from the Federal Election Commission reports the candidates filed in mid-March 1996. Since Forbes did not receive federal matching funds, he was not required to break down his spending by state. The $4 million estimate appears in Ernest Tollerson, "Forbes Calls 4th-Place Finish New Hampshire 'Springboard,'" *New York Times*, February 13, 1996, p. A19.

30. Cronin and Loevy, "Case for a National Pre-Primary Convention Plan," p. 53.

31. For detailed data on turnout at the 1988 and 1992 caucuses, see William G. Mayer, "Caucuses: How They Work, What Difference They Make," in William G. Mayer, ed., *In Pursuit of the White House: How We Choose Our Presidential Nominees* (Chatham, N.J.: Chatham House, 1996), pp. 105–57, 126–28.

32. The same is true of the Wayne and Baliles plans: both include provisions that make it possible that the national primary would never take place.

33. For a more detailed analysis of how the Hunt Commission dealt with this issue, see David E. Price, *Bringing Back the Parties* (Washington: CQ Press, 1984), pp. 181–82.

34. For a detailed account of this task force, see Andrew E. Busch, "New Features of the 2000 Presidential Nominating Process: Republican Reforms, Front-Loading's Second Wind, and Early Voting," in William G. Mayer, ed., *In Pursuit of the White House 2000: How We Choose Our Presidential Nominees* (New York: Chatham House, 2000), pp. 57–86.

35. The task force originally recommended bonuses of 10, 15, and 20 percent, but the rules committee of the Republican national convention voted to cut those numbers in half.

36. We define position in the calendar in terms of which particular week in a given month the primary took place. Thus the Massachusetts primary is classified as having the same position in both years because it was held in the first week in March, even though the actual date in 2000 (March 7) was two days later than the 1996 date (March 5).

37. As quoted in Jack W. Germond and Jules Witcover, "Looking Ahead to 2004," *Baltimore Sun*, March 22, 2000, p. 21A.

38. Political action committees (PACs) were allowed to give $5,000; but unlike congressional elections, most PACs are reluctant to get involved in presidential nomination races. Political action committees account for only about 1 percent of the total funds in presidential nomination campaigns. See Anthony Corrado, "The Changing Environment of Presidential Campaign Finance," in William G. Mayer, ed., *In Pursuit of the White House: How We Choose Our Presidential Nominees* (Chatham, N.J.: Chatham House, 1996), pp. 220–53, 226–27.

39. Jules Witcover, *Marathon: The Pursuit of the Presidency, 1972–1976* (Viking, 1977), p. 652.

40. Campaign Finance Study Group to the Committee on Rules and Administration of the United States Senate, *Financing Presidential Campaigns: An Examination of the Ongoing Effects of the Federal Election Campaign Laws upon the Conduct of Presidential Campaigns* (Cambridge, Mass.: Institute of Politics, John F. Kennedy School of Government, Harvard University, January 1982), p. 1. The recommendation is discussed on pp. 4 and I-26–I-27.

41. The assumption is that each of these contributors would give $1,000, the first $250 of which would be eligible for federal matching funds. Of course, no presidential campaign ever funds itself entirely from $1,000 contributions. Our point is that, as the size of the average contribution declines, campaigns must locate an even larger number of contributors.

42. All data in this paragraph on contributor behavior under the BCRA are drawn from Clyde Wilcox, Alexandra Cooper, Peter Francia, John C. Green, Paul S. Herrnson, Michael Munger, Lynda Powell, Jason Reifler, Mark J. Rozell, and Benjamin Webster, "With Limits Raised, Who Will Give More? The Impact of BCRA on Individual Donors," in Michael J. Malbin, ed., *Life after Reform: When the Bipartisan Campaign Reform Act Meets Politics* (Lanham, Md.: Rowman and Littlefield, 2003, forthcoming).

43. Specifically, the candidate must raise at least $5,000 in contributions of $250 or less in at least twenty states. Any candidate who receives federal matching funds is also required to abide by both total and state spending limits and cannot contribute more than $50,000 to his or her own campaign.

44. For specific figures, see Corrado, "Changing Environment," table 7.2, p. 227.

45. See Barbara Norrander, "Is the Nomination Process Broken?" in Advisory Commission on the Presidential Nominating Process, *Nominating Future Presidents: A Review of the Republican Process* (Washington: Republican National Committee, 2000), pp. 133–38.

46. If either change is adopted, it will also be necessary to find additional revenues for the matching-fund program. Under the original legislation, money for public financing was provided by a voluntary tax checkoff on the federal income tax forms. Though the amount of the checkoff was tripled in 1993, the fund has long struggled to pay candidates all the money to which they are entitled.

47. There is a strong parallel between the argument we are making about the role of money in presidential nomination campaigns and the view held by most congressional scholars regarding the role of money in congressional elections. As Gary C. Jacobson in particular has shown, campaign spending by House and Senate incumbents has much less effect on the vote than spending by challengers. Thus to make congressional elections more competitive and reduce the advantages of incumbency, it is much more important to increase the amount of money going to challengers than to reduce or limit spending by incumbents. See Jacobson, *Money in Congressional Elections* (Yale University Press, 1980); and

Jacobson, "The Effects of Campaign Spending in House Elections: New Evidence for Old Arguments," *American Journal of Political Science*, vol. 34 (May 1990), pp. 334–62.

48. How well losing candidates fare under proportional representation depends, in part, on whether or not state law or party rules include a threshold provision. A *threshold* is some minimum percentage of the vote that a candidate must receive to qualify for any delegates. Since 1992 national Democratic Party rules have set a 15 percent threshold for all states: in other words, a candidate who wins only 14 percent of the primary vote will not receive a single delegate. The 2000 Republican advisory commission similarly recommended that a 15 percent threshold be used in future Republican primaries and caucuses.

49. For a more extended discussion of these issues, see William G. Mayer, *The Divided Democrats: Ideological Unity, Party Reform, and Presidential Elections* (Boulder, Colo.: Westview, 1996), pp. 13–33.

50. The 2000 Democratic nomination calendar was less front-loaded than the Republican calendar, but as indicated in chapter 2, the reason for this was not the different allocation rules the parties employed: rather, Democratic Party rules prohibited any state except Iowa and New Hampshire from voting before the first Tuesday in March, whereas Republican Party rules allowed all states to start selecting their delegates on the first Monday in February. In 1992 and 1996 the two parties' calendars were, for all practical purposes, identical.

51. The next two paragraphs draw heavily on the discussion in Mayer, *Divided Democrats*, pp. 21–22.

52. This suggestion was recently renewed by Ronald B. Rapoport and Walter J. Stone, in testimony before the Republican Advisory Commission on the Presidential Nominating Process. See Advisory Commission on the Presidential Nominating Process, *Nominating Future Presidents*, p. 146.

Chapter Six

1. An important exception is Austin Ranney, *Federalization of Presidential Primaries* (Washington: American Enterprise Institute, 1978).

2. For a more detailed look at the data discussed in the next two paragraphs, see William G. Mayer, "Public Attitudes on Campaign Finance," in Gerald C. Lubenow, ed., *A User's Guide to Campaign Finance Reform* (Lanham, Md.: Rowman and Littlefield, 2001), pp. 47–69, 61–66.

3. The locus classicus of this argument is, of course, Philip E. Converse, "The Nature of Belief Systems in Mass Publics," in David E. Apter, ed., *Ideology and Discontent* (Free Press, 1964), pp. 206–61.

4. William Schneider and I. A. Lewis, "Public Opinion and the Nominating Process," in John Foley, Dennis A. Britton, and Eugene B. Everett Jr., eds., *Nominating a President: The Process and the Press* (Praeger, 1980), pp. 141–47, 142, 147.

5. American attitudes toward political parties are well described in Austin Ranney, *Curing the Mischiefs of Faction: Party Reform in America* (University of

California Press, 1975), pp. 48–57; and Jack Dennis, "Trends in Public Support for the American Party System," *British Journal of Political Science,* vol. 5 (April 1975), pp. 187–230.

6. National Association of Secretaries of State, "Rotating Regional Primary Plan Endorsed by National Association of Secretaries of State," press release of February 16, 1999.

7. Ibid. Though the NASS press release suggests that their plan exempted Iowa and New Hampshire out of a concern that presidential candidates have some opportunity to "meet with individual voters and practice retail, rather than media-driven, politics," it also reflects, we suspect, a tacit admission that they had no real way of enforcing their plan on recalcitrant states. Had the NASS tried to include Iowa and New Hampshire in one of the regional groups, both states would have immediately announced their refusal to cooperate.

8. The following discussion draws upon the more detailed analysis presented in Andrew E. Busch, "The Rise and Fall of the 2000 Rocky Mountain Regional Primary," *PS: Political Science and Politics,* vol. 36 (April 2003), pp. 171–74.

9. In the 2000 election cycle, the Democratic Party window began on March 7, so a traditional primary held on March 10 clearly would have complied with the rules. But several of the Rocky Mountain states apparently contemplated using mail-in ballots. In late 1998 the Rules and Bylaws Committee of the Democratic National Committee ruled that in any state using a 100 percent mail ballot system, the ballots could not be mailed out before March 7, thereby effectively precluding a primary in which the ballots would have had to be mailed back by March 10. Interview with Philip A. McNamara, director of party affairs and delegate selection for the Democratic National Committee, April 8, 2003.

10. The best source on the history of federal primary legislation is Joseph B. Gorman, "Federal Presidential Primary Proposals, 1911–1979," Congressional Research Service Report 80-53 GOV, February 20, 1980. Information on the 106th Congress and an updated count on the number of bills submitted are taken from Kevin Coleman, "Presidential Nominating Process: Current Issues and Legislation in the 106th Congress," Congressional Research Service Report for Congress, March 21, 2000, reprinted in Advisory Commission on the Presidential Nominating Process, *Nominating Future Presidents: A Review of the Republican Process* (Washington: Republican National Committee, 2000), pp. 101–06.

11. Gorman does not provide a precise breakdown for all federal primary legislation. Of the 127 bills that sought to establish a direct national primary, 104 were cast in the form of constitutional amendments. See Gorman, "Federal Presidential Primary Proposals," pp. 18–19. It appears, however, that most of the recent primary bills have been ordinary legislation. Indeed, not one of the federal primary bills filed in the past thirty years that we have examined calls for a constitutional amendment.

12. *Burroughs* v. *United States,* 290 U.S. 534 (1934), 545.

13. Ibid., 546. In this passage, the Court was actually quoting its decision in *Ex parte Yarbrough* 110 U.S. 651 (1884).

14. See *Buckley* v. *Valeo* 424 U.S. 1 (1976), 13–14. The question of congressional authority over the presidential selection process was not a major issue in

the *Buckley* decision and was dealt with very briefly. As the Court noted, "The constitutional power of Congress to regulate federal elections is well established and *is not questioned by any of the parties in this case*" (13, emphasis added).

15. *Oregon v. Mitchell*, 400 U.S. 112 (1970), 124.

16. See *United States v. Classic*, 313 U.S. 299 (1941). Black's opinion quotes the *Classic* decision two pages before making the statement quoted in the preceding sentence.

17. There was no opinion of the Court in *Oregon v. Mitchell*; that is to say, there was no line of reasoning that could command the assent of a majority of the justices. A majority did uphold the provision that lowered the voting age in federal elections to eighteen, but four justices (William O. Douglas, William Brennan, Byron White, and Thurgood Marshall) did so on the basis of the equal protection clause of the Fourteenth Amendment, a line of reasoning that does not give any obvious support to national primary legislation. In other words, Black was the only justice convinced by the argument quoted above. Unfortunately, many references to Black's opinion pass over or blur this point. See, for example, Justice Marshall's dissenting opinion in *O'Brien v. Brown*, 409 U.S. 1 (1972), 15; and Committee on Federal Legislation, "The Revision of the Presidential Primary System," *Record of the Association of the Bar of the City of New York*, vol. 33 (May–June 1978), pp. 306–34, 316–17.

18. V. O. Key Jr., *Politics, Parties, and Pressure Groups*, 4th ed. (New York: Thomas Y. Crowell, 1958), p. 411.

19. The best history of the early growth of state regulations respecting political parties is still C. Edward Merriam, *Primary Elections: A Study of the History and Tendencies of Primary Election Legislation* (University of Chicago Press, 1908).

20. Ranney, *Curing the Mischiefs*, p. 81.

21. Blacks were, of course, almost completely excluded from voting in southern general elections during this period, but precisely because of the Fifteenth Amendment, their exclusion was accomplished through means other than outright prohibition, such as literacy tests, poll taxes, and threats of violence.

22. *Smith v. Allwright*, 321 U.S. 649 (1944), 663 (emphasis added).

23. *Rice v. Elmore*, 165 F.2d 387 (1947), 389.

24. See *Terry v. Adams*, 345 U.S. 461 (1953). Justice Felix Frankfurter claimed that the Jaybird primary was state action because county election officials participated in it, even if not in an official capacity. Justice Tom Clark and three other justices claimed that the Jaybird Association operated "as part and parcel of the Democratic Party," though the evidence they cited fell well short of proving this contention. Justice Black, in a rather ambiguous opinion, seemed to argue that it did not matter whether the association was public or private. None of these opinions, we think it fair to say, stands up well to close scrutiny.

25. It can be argued that all of the major cases in which the courts treated party primaries as state action involved race and that the courts were simply attempting to devise some sort of remedy for a set of invidiously discriminatory practices. Yet we think that this point is clearer in retrospect than it was at the time. Certainly there is nothing in the text of *Smith v. Allwright* or *Terry v. Adams* that suggests that parties might enjoy certain rights or freedoms when dealing with non-race-

related issues. Indeed, the notion that a right of association exists under the Constitution was not clearly set forth until *N.A.A.C.P.* v. *Alabama* 357 U.S. 449 (1958).

26. *Cousins* v. *Wigoda*, 419 U.S. 477 (1975), 490 (internal quotation omitted).

27. One of the few exceptions is *Marchioro* v. *Chaney*, 442 U.S. 191 (1979). Yet even here the Court did not so much hold that a state could legitimately limit a party's First Amendment rights as rule that the alleged burden on party freedoms derived not from the law but from the party's own decisions.

28. The cases referred to are, respectively, *Democratic Party of United States* v. *Wisconsin*, 450 U.S. 107 (1981); *Tashjian* v. *Republican Party of Connecticut*, 479 U.S. 208 (1986); *Eu* v. *San Francisco County Democratic Central Committee*, 489 U.S. 214 (1989); and *California Democratic Party* v. *Jones*, 530 U.S. 567 (2000).

29. In various decisions, the Court has undeniably recognized a compelling state interest in such things as "fostering informed and educated expressions of the popular will," limiting the damage caused by "splintered parties and unrestrained factionalism," and "preserving the integrity of its election process." But the Court has then typically denied that these interests were actually and legitimately protected by the various laws and regulations governing political parties.

30. Indeed, even at the state level, there is no case that directly confronts the question of whether a state may require the political parties to select their nominees by primary rather than by some alternative procedure, such as a caucus-convention system. A number of cases explicitly assume that the states do have this power (see, for example, *American Party of Texas* v. *White*, 415 U.S. 767 [1974], 781), but all such comments are obiter dicta. As Justice John Paul Stevens notes in his dissent in *California Democratic Party* v. *Jones*, 530 U.S. 567, 594, "the point [that a state may require parties to use the primary format for selecting their nominees] has never been decided by this Court."

If the courts have never explicitly confronted this question, there are a number of law review articles arguing that the line of reasoning set forth in cases like *Cousins* v. *Wigoda* and *Tashjian* v. *Republican Party of Connecticut* will ultimately compel the Court to grant parties the right to refuse to nominate their candidates by primary. See, for example, Stephen E. Gottlieb, "Rebuilding the Right of Association: The Right to Hold a Convention as a Test Case," *Hofstra Law Review*, vol. 11 (Fall 1982), pp. 191–247; and Karl D. Cooper, "Are State-Imposed Political Party Primaries Constitutional? The Constitutional Ramifications of the 1986 Illinois LaRouche Primary Victories," *Journal of Law and Politics*, vol. 4 (Fall 1987), pp. 343–78.

31. The same point was made by then–law professor Antonin Scalia in his article "The Legal Framework for Reform," *Commonsense*, vol. 4 (1981), pp. 40–49, 45.

32. That count, of course, excludes the first ten amendments, all of which were enacted during the new government's first three years of operation and may reasonably be regarded as a kind of "touch-up job" on the original document.

33. Bill Brock, "Introduction," Advisory Commission on the Presidential Nominating Process, *Nominating Future Presidents: A Review of the Republican Process* (Washington: Republican National Committee, 2000), p. 7.

34. According to Gorman's comprehensive study, of the 272 federal primary bills introduced in either the House or the Senate between 1911 and 1979, only 5 were the subject of floor action. Three were decisively rejected; one was briefly discussed but never voted on. The other bill did pass the Senate in 1976, but it only called for the creation of a commission to study the presidential nomination process. In any event, the provision was deleted from the final bill by a conference committee. See Gorman, "Federal Presidential Primary Proposals," pp. 14–16.

35. See Michael Nelson, "Two Cheers for the National Primary," in Thomas E. Cronin, ed., *Rethinking the Presidency* (Boston: Little, Brown, 1982), pp. 55–64, 62.

36. Nelson W. Polsby has made precisely this argument about the consequences of the McGovern-Fraser reforms. Because the Democratic Party was more ideologically divided than the Republicans, it had a correspondingly greater need for institutional mechanisms and processes to help bind the party together and forge coalitions. By greatly weakening those institutions, Polsby concluded, the new system conferred a significant advantage on the Republicans in presidential elections. See Polsby, *Consequences of Party Reform* (Oxford University Press, 1983), pp. 85–88.

37. Byron E. Shafer, *Quiet Revolution: The Struggle for the Democratic Party and the Shaping of Post-Reform Politics* (New York: Russell Sage Foundation, 1983), p. 28.

38. Ibid., pp. 495–96.

39. The following discussion draws on Shafer, *Quiet Revolution*, especially chaps. 8–18.

40. Ibid., p. 251.

41. William J. Crotty, *Decision for the Democrats* (Johns Hopkins University Press, 1978), p. 257.

42. The most complete account of the struggle between Iowa and New Hampshire and the national Democratic Party is Emmett H. Buell Jr., "First-in-the-Nation: Disputes over the Timing of Early Democratic Presidential Primaries and Caucuses in 1984 and 1988," *Journal of Law and Politics*, vol. 4 (Fall 1987), pp. 311–42. Our account also draws on the coverage in Susan Smith, "New Hampshire Battling to Keep First Primary," *Congressional Quarterly Weekly Report*, January 29, 1983, p. 225; Susan Smith, "Power Shifts South for '84 Democratic Meet," *Congressional Quarterly Weekly Report*, February 12, 1983, pp. 351–52; "Plan for New Hampshire Held to Violate Democratic Rules," *New York Times*, June 18, 1983, sec. I, p. 8; Phil Gailey, "Democrats Seek Compromise with 3 States on Election Dates," *New York Times*, October 15, 1983, sec. I, p. 6; Phil Gailey, "3 States Gain in Defying Democratic Vote Rules," *New York Times*, October 28, 1983, p. A28; Phil Gailey, "Democrats Tell 3 States Rules Will Be Enforced," *New York Times*, October 29, 1983, sec. I, p. 12; "The Showdown Begins," *New York Times*, November 3, 1983, p. B12; "Iowa Democrats Vote to Hold Caucuses Early," *New York Times*, November 20, 1983, p. 27; Phil Gailey, "Dark Horses Like Iowa Caucus Rules," *New York Times*, November 21, 1983, p. A12; Phil Gailey, "Accounts Differ about Democratic Caucus Tangle," *New*

York Times, November 23, 1983, p. A19; Phil Gailey, "Earlier Dates Likely for Iowa Caucus and New Hampshire Primary," *New York Times,* December 22, 1983, p. A17; Phil Gailey, "Manatt's Problem: Not the Game, Just the Rules," *New York Times,* January 6, 1984, p. A12; "Democrats May Not Seat Iowans at Convention," *New York Times,* April 3, 1984, p. B4; and "Iowa and N. Hampshire Get Convention Rooms," *New York Times,* April 6, 1984, p. A23.

43. Gailey, "Democrats Tell 3 States Rules Will Be Enforced." The exception was Reubin Askew.

44. See "Democrats May Not Seat Iowans at Convention." Besides the likelihood that the new elections would be boycotted and thus embarrass the party, there was a second, even larger flaw in the plan. Throughout the lead-up to the nomination race, party leaders in Iowa and New Hampshire had been negotiating with various officers and subcommittees of the Democratic National Committee. But the final say on which set of delegates would be seated at the national convention lay not with the national committee but with the convention itself, and almost all the delegates to that convention were pledged to candidates who, as noted earlier, had declared in writing that they would support the delegations selected through the procedures favored by the state parties.

45. The most detailed account of the battle between Wisconsin and the national Democratic Party over the fate of the open primary is Gary D. Wekkin, *Democrat versus Democrat: The National Party's Campaign to Close the Wisconsin Primary* (University of Missouri Press, 1984). Unfortunately, Wekkin's account ends in 1984 and thus fails to take into account the national party's policy reversal in 1985–86.

46. In 1976 the rule in question read as follows: "State Parties must take all feasible steps to restrict participation in the delegate selection process to Democratic voters only." In 1980 and 1984 the wording was tightened in a way that should have removed any lingering doubts about the status of the open primary: "Participation in the delegate selection process in primaries or caucuses shall be restricted to Democratic voters only who publicly declare their party preference and have that preference publicly recorded."

47. The term *open primary* is sometimes used in a looser sense to include any state primary that does not provide for party registration, and therefore allows any registered voter to vote in either party's primary, but does require the voter to state publicly which party's primary they intend to participate in and then makes a public record of that declaration. Throughout the controversy described here, however, the national Democratic Party always permitted this kind of primary but drew a line against the Wisconsin-style open primary. This decision may have been a further concession to the limits of the national party's powers. As David E. Price has noted, "With 13 states utilizing same-day declaration (8 of which hold presidential primaries), the national party has been reluctant to push its case further." See Price, *Bringing Back the Parties* (Washington: CQ Press, 1984), p. 130.

48. Floyd Ciruli, as quoted in Rhodes Cook, "Harmony Is In, Bickering Out as Democrats Consider Rules," *Congressional Quarterly Weekly Report,* March 1, 1986, pp. 509–10, 509.

49. Thomas E. Mann, as quoted ibid.

50. Gary D. Wekkin, "National-State Party Relations: The Democrats' New Federal Structure," *Political Science Quarterly,* vol. 99 (Spring 1984), pp. 45–72, 53. To what extent this characterization generalizes to the Republican Party is difficult to say: to date, the national Republican Party has made few attempts to impose centrally defined rules upon its state affiliates.

51. Our discussion of the Republican Advisory Commission on the Presidential Nominating Process and of the fate of its recommendations is based principally on David S. Broder, "Panel Seeks Overhaul of Primaries," *Washington Post,* May 3, 2000, p. A8; David S. Broder, "GOP Debates States' Bid to Revamp Primary Schedule," *Washington Post,* July 27, 2000, p. A10; David S. Broder, "Floor Fight Shaping Up over Primary Calendar," *Washington Post,* July 28, 2000, p. A14; David S. Broder, "GOP Scraps Plan to Alter Primary Schedule," *Washington Post,* July 29, 2000, p. A6; Adam Clymer, "G.O.P. Panel Seeks to Alter Schedule of Primary Voting," *New York Times,* May 3, 2000, p. A1; Adam Clymer, "Proposal to Shake Up the Primaries Is Met with Scrutiny and Skepticism," *New York Times,* May 4, 2000, p. A25; Adam Clymer, "New Calendar of Primaries for G.O.P. Clears Hurdle," *New York Times,* July 28, 2000, p. A15; and Adam Clymer, "A G.O.P. Overhaul of Primary Season Is Killed by Bush," *New York Times,* July 29, 2000, p. A1.

52. Charles Black, as quoted in Craig Gilbert, "GOP Won't Change Presidential Primaries," *Milwaukee Journal Sentinel,* July 29, 2000, p. 8A; and Jill Zuckman, "Bush Kills Plan That Would Have Threatened N.H. Primary Status," *Boston Globe,* July 29, 2000, p. A11.

53. By the conclusion of the 1970 midterm elections, twenty-nine of the fifty states had Democratic governors. In the lower house of the state legislature, twenty-seven of forty-eight states had Democratic majorities (two states had nonpartisan elections); Democrats also held a majority in twenty-seven upper legislative houses.

54. Dan Walters, "How Bush Squelched a Primary Fight," *Sacramento Bee,* August 1, 2000, p. B8.

55. In particular, concessions on the party rules are far less costly to the nominee than concessions on the platform. If Dukakis had agreed to accommodate Jackson on an issue such as no first use of nuclear weapons or the runoff primary, that concession might have cost the Democratic ticket a lot of votes in the fall. But few people were likely to change their votes because Jackson prevailed on some arcane rules dispute.

56. On the concessions at the 1988 convention, see Rhodes Cook, "Pressed by Jackson Demands, Dukakis Yields on Party Rules," *Congressional Quarterly Weekly Report,* July 2, 1988, pp. 1799–1801. The Democratic National Committee eventually accepted one of Jackson's demands: that all states be compelled to use proportional representation formulas in allocating delegates. It rescinded another key part of the agreement, however, which would have significantly reduced the number of superdelegates, and further gave itself the power to ratify any future rules changes that were made at the national convention. See Andrew Rosenthal, "Democrats Vote to Rescind Part of Dukakis-Jackson Pact," *New York Times,* September 29, 1989, p. A12; and Rhodes Cook, "Democratic Party Rules Changes Readied for '92 Campaign," *Congressional Quarterly Weekly Report,* March 17, 1990, pp. 847–49.

57. See, in particular, Elaine Ciulla Kamarck, "Structure as Strategy: Presidential Nominating Politics in the Post-Reform Era," Ph.D. diss., University of California, Berkeley, 1986.

58. James I. Lengle, "Democratic Party Reforms: The Past as Prologue to the 1988 Campaign," *Journal of Law and Politics,* vol. 4 (Fall 1987), pp. 233–73, 242–43.

59. Our account of the politics of the Winograd Commission draws on Lengle, "Democratic Party Reforms," pp. 241–45; Price, *Bringing Back the Parties,* pp. 152–55; Rhodes Cook, "Democrats Likely to Keep Primary System," *Congressional Quarterly Weekly Report,* July 2, 1977, pp. 1375–76; Rhodes Cook, "Democratic Changes May Aid Carter in 1980," *Congressional Quarterly Weekly Report,* September 24, 1977, pp. 2041–42; Rhodes Cook, "White House Is a Winner on Rules Changes," *Congressional Quarterly Weekly Report,* January 28, 1978, pp. 199–200; Rhodes Cook, "Democrats to Adopt Final Rules for 1980," *Congressional Quarterly Weekly Report,* June 3, 1978, pp. 1392–96; and Rhodes Cook, "Democrats Adopt New Rules for Picking Nominee in 1980," *Congressional Quarterly Weekly Report,* June 17, 1978, pp. 1571–72.

60. The tighter filing deadline was designed to make life more difficult for late entrants in the race. In 1976 the two candidates who beat Carter most often were Jerry Brown and Frank Church, both of whom had waited until mid-March 1976 before announcing their candidacies. The provision finally included in the 1980 Democratic rules required just four states to change their deadlines.

61. The tightening of the delegate selection window, discussed in chapter 2, was actually among the less substantial and least controversial of these changes. Considerably more important were the relaxation of the proportionality requirement in delegate allocation rules and the granting of automatic delegate status to a sizable number of party leaders and elected officials.

62. The best account of the Hunt Commission's work is Price, *Bringing Back the Parties,* pp. 159–83. See also Lengle, "Democratic Party Reforms," pp. 245–51; Rhodes Cook, "New Democratic Rules Panel: A Careful Approach to Change," *Congressional Quarterly Weekly Report,* December 26, 1981, pp. 2563–67; and Rhodes Cook, "Democrats' Rules Weaken Representation," *Congressional Quarterly Weekly Report,* April 3, 1982, pp. 749–51.

63. For a detailed analysis of the politics of the Fairness Commission, see Lengle, "Democratic Party Reforms," pp. 252–60.

64. Jim Nicholson, as quoted in Andrew E. Busch, "New Features of the 2000 Presidential Nominating Process: Republican Reforms, Front-Loading's Second Wind, and Early Voting," in William G. Mayer, ed., *In Pursuit of the White House 2000: How We Choose Our Presidential Nominees* (New York: Chatham House, 2000), pp. 57–86, 60.

Chapter Seven

1. The recommendation is discussed in Advisory Commission on the Presidential Nominating Process, *Nominating Future Presidents: A Review of the Repub-*

lican Process (Washington: Republican National Committee, 2000), pp. 24, 28–29. The commission also recommended, as a safeguard against the abuse of this power, that a two-thirds vote of both the Republican National Committee (RNC) Rules Committee and the full RNC be required. This seems to us a reasonable condition.

2. Lamar Alexander, "Off with the Limits," *Campaigns and Elections* (October–November 1996), pp. 32–35, 33.

3. For example, one of the most often discussed proposals of this type is to give presidential candidates free television time. Though we think this is generally a good idea, it would plainly be a lot easier to implement in the general election, in which there are usually just two major candidates, than in the nomination phase of the race, in which the two parties together may have ten or more serious candidates.

4. The same concern is shown in the provision in Article I, section 4, that allows Congress to regulate the "times, places, and manner" of congressional elections.

5. The exception was 1992. On the Democratic side, one of the major presidential candidates was Iowa senator Tom Harkin, who was thought to be so popular in his home state that none of the other candidates mounted a serious effort there. Meanwhile, the Iowa Republican Party canceled the straw poll that it traditionally holds among caucus attendees and that is the only way of determining how much support each candidate has at the caucuses. The result was that both parties' caucuses were almost entirely ignored by the media.

6. Niall A. Palmer, *The New Hampshire Primary and the American Electoral Process* (Westport, Conn.: Praeger, 1997), p. 179.

7. Ibid.

8. See especially William G. Mayer, "The New Hampshire Primary: A Historical Overview," in Gary R. Orren and Nelson W. Polsby, eds., *Media and Momentum: The New Hampshire Primary and Nomination Politics* (Chatham, N.J.: Chatham House, 1987), pp. 9–41, 26–29; and Emmett H. Buell Jr., "The Changing Face of the New Hampshire Primary," in William G. Mayer, ed., *In Pursuit of the White House 2000: How We Choose Our Presidential Nominees* (New York: Chatham House, 2000), pp. 87–144, 108–19.

9. For a more extended discussion of this point, see Mayer, "New Hampshire Primary," p. 29.

10. This point is made in, among others, Palmer, *New Hampshire Primary*, p. 178.

11. Ibid., p. 147.

12. The phrase is quoted from DNC (Democratic National Committee) Rules and Bylaws Committee, *Beyond 2000: The Scheduling of Future Democratic Presidential Primaries and Caucuses* (Washington: Democratic National Committee, 2000), p. 14.

13. Everett Carll Ladd, "It Is Not Time for a New Presidential Nominating Process," in Gary L. Rose, ed., *Controversial Issues in Presidential Selection*, 2d ed. (State University of New York Press, 1994), pp. 37–46, 37, 38.

14. As quoted in Palmer, *New Hampshire Primary*, p. 161.

15. As we have shown in chapter 2, signs of front-loading appeared as early as 1976, but it was not until 1988 that the delegate selection calendar took on anything like its present shape.

Appendix A

1. See, for example, Larry J. Sabato, "Presidential Nominations: The Front-Loaded Frenzy of '96," in Larry J. Sabato, ed., *Toward the Millennium: The Elections of 1996* (Boston: Allyn and Bacon, 1997), pp. 37–91, 56–57; John Haskell, "Reforming Presidential Primaries: Three Steps for Improving the Campaign Environment," *Presidential Studies Quarterly,* vol. 26 (Spring 1996), pp. 380–90, 382; and Rhodes Cook, *Race for the Presidency: Winning the 2000 Nomination* (Washington: CQ Press, 2000), pp. 8–9.

2. The two systems are not mutually exclusive: some states have primaries that use the presidential preference vote to bind or allocate the delegates but also elect individual delegates on some other part of the ballot.

3. See Michael G. Hagen and William G. Mayer, "The Modern Politics of Presidential Selection: How Changing the Rules Really Did Change the Game," in William G. Mayer, ed., *In Pursuit of the White House 2000: How We Choose Our Presidential Nominees* (New York: Chatham House, 2000), pp. 1–55, 37–38.

Appendix B

1. Specifically, Federal Election Commission, *FEC Reports on Financial Activity, 1979–1980: Final Report, Presidential Pre-Nomination Campaigns* (Washington: Federal Election Commission, 1981), table A8; Federal Election Commission, *FEC Reports on Financial Activity, 1983–1984: Final Report, Presidential Pre-Nomination Campaigns* (Washington: Federal Election Commission, 1986), table A9; Federal Election Commission, *FEC Reports on Financial Activity, 1987–1988: Final Report, Presidential Pre-Nomination Campaigns* (Washington: Federal Election Commission, 1989), table A9.

2. In all Democratic races, the delegate selection season began with the Iowa caucuses. On the Republican side, in both 1988 and 1992 Hawaii actually held its caucuses several days before Iowa's. There is no evidence that Hawaii got much in the way of candidate attention or press coverage from moving to the head of the calendar, but one can hardly ignore a case simply because it works against one's principal hypothesis. Hence we use the day of the Hawaii caucuses as the start of the Republican calendar in these two races.

3. The complete data are shown in Michael J. Robinson and Margaret A. Sheehan, *Over the Wire and On TV: CBS and UPI in Campaign '80* (New York: Russell Sage Foundation, 1983), p. 176.

4. Data were generously provided by Richard Noyes, political studies director of the Center for Media and Public Affairs.

5. The correlation between the Democratic and Republican dates was .90 in 1980, .85 in 1988, and .79 in 1992. The multicollinearity problem would get

even worse if we were to add to the model two variables representing, respectively, the number of Democratic and Republican convention delegates in each state—a factor that, everyone agrees, is essential to a full specification of such a model. In the three years analyzed in table 3-5, the correlation between these variables never falls below .97.

6. See S. Robert Lichter, Daniel Amundson, and Richard Noyes, *The Video Campaign: Network Coverage of the 1988 Primaries* (Washington: American Enterprise Institute, 1988), p. 10.

7. Robinson and Sheehan do not provide precise figures on how much coverage each party received for the entire 1980 nomination season, but they do conclude that both CBS and UPI "provided equality of access to the two major parties during the course of the early campaign." For the period from January 1 through April 1, the breakdown was 52 percent of the coverage to the Democrats, 48 percent to the Republicans. See Robinson and Sheehan, *Over the Wire*, pp. 71–72.

8. This is our own estimate, based on data reported in the Center for Media and Public Affairs's *Media Monitor*, vol. 6, no. 3 (1992) and vol. 6, no. 7 (1992).

9. In 1988, for example, the Democratic national convention had 4,162 delegates, the Republican convention 2,277. Hence the size of each state's Democratic delegation is multiplied by .55 (2,277 / 4,162).

Appendix C

1. For a detailed contemporary description of the early AP criteria, see Charles Mohr, "Arithmetic of the Republican Contest," *New York Times,* June 28, 1964, sec. IV, p. 10.

2. For some initial leads in locating these delegate counts, we benefited greatly from the research of Howard L. Reiter. See *Selecting the President: The Nominating Process in Transition* (University of Pennsylvania Press, 1985), pp. 25–26.

3. All unpublished Associated Press articles were provided to us through the courtesy of David Goodfriend of the AP Washington bureau.

4. In 1984 the UPI count came to be seen as particularly authoritative. See Jack W. Germond and Jules Witcover, *Wake Us When It's Over: Presidential Politics of 1984* (New York: Macmillan, 1985), pp. 321–22.

Index